A Centenary Celebration: Anscombe, Foot, Midgley, Murdoch

ROYAL INSTITUTE OF PHILOSOPHY SUPPLEMENT: 87

EDITED BY

Anthony O'Hear

PUBLISHED BY THE PRESS SYNDICATE OF THE UNIVERSITY OF CAMBRIDGE
The Pitt Building, Trumpington Street, Cambridge, CB2 1RP,
United Kingdom

CAMBRIDGE UNIVERSITY PRESS
UPH, Shaftesbury Road, Cambridge CB2 8BS, United Kingdom
32 Avenue of the Americas, New York, NY 10013–2473, USA
477 Williamstown Road, Port Melbourne, VIC 3207, Australia
C/Orense, 4, planta 13, 28020 Madrid, Spain
Lower Ground Floor, Nautica Building, The Water Club, Beach Road,
Granger Bay, 8005 Cape Town, South Africa

Printed in Great Britain by Bell & Bain Ltd, Glasgow.
Typeset by Techset Composition Ltd, Salisbury, UK

A catalogue record for this book is available from the British Library

ISBN 9781108928274
ISSN 1358-2461

Contents

Contents

Notes on the Contributors

Benjamin J. Bruxvoort Lipscomb *is Professor of Philosophy at Houghton College. His research for the past decade has centered on Anscombe, Foot, Midgley, and Murdoch and the interconnections in their thought. He has also co-edited a collection with James Krueger,* Kant's Moral Metaphysics *(DeGruyter, 2010) and published on animal ethics.*

John Haldane *is J. Newton Rayzor Sr Distinguished Professor of Philosophy at Baylor University, Texas, and Emeritus Professor of Moral Philosophy at the University of St Andrews. His books include* Faithful Reason, *and* Reasonable Faith, *and he is editor of* The Life and Work of Elizabeth Anscombe *(2019).*

Jennifer A. Frey *is assistant professor of philosophy at the University of South Carolina. Her recent publications include* 'Anscombe on Practical Knowledge and the Good' *(Ergo, 2020) and* Self-Transcendence and Virtue *(Routledge, 2018).*

Rachael Wiseman *is a Lecturer in Philosophy at the University of Liverpool. Her recent publications include the* Routledge Philosophy Guidebook to Anscombe's Intention *(Routledge, 2016).*

Candace Vogler *is the David B. and Clara E. Stern Professor of Philosophy at the University of Chicago. Her recent publications include* 'The Intellectual Animal' *(New Blackfriars, 2019) and, with Jennifer Frey,* Self-Transcendence and Virtue *(Routledge, 2018).*

Nakul Krishna *is lecturer in Philosophy at the University of Cambridge. His* History of Oxford Philosophy, 1900–60, A Terribly Serious Adventure *(Picador, 2021) will be published next year.*

John Hacker-Wright *is Associate Professor of Philosophy at the University of Guelph. He is editor in chief of the* Journal of Value Inquiry *and author of* Philippa Foot's Moral Thought *(Bloomsbury, 2013), along with many articles on neo-Aristotelian ethical naturalism and virtue ethics.*

Clare Mac Cumhaill *is Assistant Professor at Durham University. With Rachael Wiseman she is co-director of* In Parenthesis, *which*

doi:10.1017/S1358246120000041

considers the collective writings of Murdoch, Midgley, Foot and Anscombe (www.womeninparenthesis.co.uk). She is co-editor (with Tom Crowther) of Perceptual Ephemera *(OUP, 2018).*

Julia Driver *is Professor of Philosophy at the University of Texas at Austin. She received her Ph.D. in Philosophy from the Johns Hopkins University. She has written several books and a number of articles on issues in normative ethics and moral psychology, including articles published in* The Journal of Philosophy, The Australasian Journal of Philosophy, *and* Philosophy. *She is currently working on moral sentimentalism, blame, and the moral emotions.*

Sabina Lovibond *is an Emeritus Fellow of Worcester College, Oxford, where she taught philosophy from 1982 to 2011. She is the author of* Realism and Imagination in Ethics *(Blackwell, 1983),* Ethical Formation *(HUP, 2002),* Iris Murdoch, Gender and Philosophy *(Routledge, 2011), and* Essays on Ethics and Feminism *(OUP, 2015).*

Hannah Marije Altorf *is Reader in Philosophy at St. Mary's University, Strawberry Hill. London. She has published widely on Iris Murdoch and on philosophical dialogue practices. Together with Mariëtte Willemsen she translated Murdoch's* The Sovereignty of Good into Dutch *(Over God en het Goede, Boom, 2003).*

Liz McKinnell *is a research assistant at Durham University, working on a project mapping the connections between Anscombe, Foot, Midgley, and Murdoch. She is co-editor of* Science and the Self: Animals, Evolution, and Ethics: Essays in Honour of Mary Midgley *(Routledge, 2015). Her recent publications include* 'The Ethics of Enchantment: The Role of Fairy Tales in the Ethical Imagination' *(Philosophy and Literature, 2019) and* 'Mary Midgley' *in David Cooper and Joy Palmer (eds.)* Key Thinkers on the Environment *(Routledge, 2017).*

Gregory S. McElwain *is Associate Professor and Chair of Philosophy and Religious Studies at The College of Idaho, USA. He is the author of* Mary Midgley: An Introduction *(Bloomsbury Academic Press, 2019) and has research interests in animal and environmental ethics.*

David E. Cooper *is Professor of Philosophy Emeritus at Durham University. He has been a Visiting Professor at universities in the USA, Canada, Germany, Malta, South Africa and Sri Lanka. He is the author of many books including, most recently,* Senses of

Mystery: Engaging with Nature and the Meaning of Life *(Routledge 2017)*, Animals and Misanthropy *(Routledge 2018), and a novel,* Street Dog (*Sarasavi 2018*).

Anthony O'Hear *is Professor of Philosophy at the University of Buckingham. He edited* Philosophy *from 1995–2019 and was director of the Royal Institute of Philosophy from 1994–2019.*

Preface

The fifteen papers in this volume were all part of the Royal Institute of Philosophy's annual lecture series in London, for 2018–9. The focus and indeed the motivation for the series was that 2019 represented the centenary of the birth of three highly distinguished philosophers, with one more coming in 2020. All of these philosophers, who were contemporaries and erstwhile colleagues at Oxford in the 1940s, were women, and not coincidentally.

The four philosophers were Elizabeth Anscombe, Mary Midgley and Iris Murdoch, all born in 1919, and Philippa Foot, who was born in 1920. When the lecture series was being planned, Mary Midgley was still alive, and approaching her 100 th birthday; arrangements had been made to involve her in the series, by video link from her home in Newcastle, arrangements to which she had readily agreed. Sadly she died shortly before the planned event could take place. In its stead was a kind of memorial to her, attended by her three sons and other friends and acquaintances, as well as by the usual lecture audience.

The papers which follow will bring out the range and depth of the thought of our four subjects. However it is worth emphasizing at the start that in the 1940s and on into the 1950s these four women represented a powerful and vociferous opposition to what at the time was the dominant and largely male-dominated form of moral philosophy in Oxford, and indeed in the rest of the world of Anglo-American analytic philosophy. This dominant form has come to be dubbed as 'consequentialism'; that it is no longer regarded as to all intents and purposes as unquestionable is due in no small part to the work and influence of the four women we are here celebrating. Having said that, it is important to emphasise that their individual and collective contributions to philosophy and to intellectual life more generally were not confined to the attack on consequentialism, and this will be amply born out in what follows.

The opening paper in this book and also in the lecture series is an overview by Benjamin Lipscomb of the work of the four philosophers and of their multifarious inter-relationships down the years. For those not familiar with this story, and even to those who are, 'The Women Are Up To Something' will provide an invaluable key, including an explanation both of how these four women came to such prominence in the late 1940s in Oxford, and also of the paper's title.

doi:10.1017/S1358246120000053

Lipscomb is then followed by four papers on the work of Elizabeth Anscombe. The first, 'A Philosopher of singular style and multiple modes' by John Haldane, provides an enlightening survey of Anscombe's philosophy and her manner of doing it, including examining her critical stance towards many of the most popular theses among her contemporaries in the philosophical world and the relationship of her work and style to the writings of Wittgenstein and Aristotle. Haldane also considers the relationship between Anscombe's formal philosophy and some of her reflections on religion, addressed to non-philosophical audiences.

Jennifer A. Frey in 'Revisiting Modern Moral Philosophy' argues that the radical message of Anscombe's classic paper of that title has still not been fully taken on board, even by some of those who see themselves as following its precepts. They have not, as Anscombe urged, stopped playing the game altogether. In conclusion Frey argues strongly in favour of Anscombe's view that all human action is moral (or immoral).

In 'Anscombe on Brute Facts and Human Affairs' Rachel Wiseman argues for the stress in Anscombe's moral philosophy on the social context of human action, and indeed, of morality, against a conception of the moral agent as an isolated individual thinking on his or her own. As with our being as agents, our notions of obligation and the rest work within a sense that we are social beings.

Finally on Anscombe Candace Vogler in 'Aristotelian Necessity' emphasizes the primacy of stopping modals (prohibitions) in Anscombe's moral philosophy before showing how this relates to a conception of the human good. In developing this latter point, Vogler suggests that while some of what might be needed here can be explained in terms of an Aristotelian necessity, what is required for a peaceful life together, in quasi-utilitarian mode. However – and maybe in tension what Wiseman says – for Vogler ultimately what Anscombe is asserting about stopping modals requires a conception of a theological or religious sort.

In 'Volunteers and Conscripts: Philippa Foot and the Amoralist' Nakul Krishna attempts a rehabilitation of Foot's early conception of morality as a system of hypothetical imperatives, one in which moral demands depend on the motivation of particular individuals. Foot later abandoned this position because it seemed to give no answer to someone who was motivated to do despicable actions, but Krishna emphasizes human freedom in such matters, and refers to Bernard Williams and the early Foot herself in wondering whether we actually need any more than a basic sense of human sympathy for morality to work. Maybe for most of us, most of the time, a sense that we are ultimately responsible to each other might suffice.

John Hacker-Wright in 'Virtues as Perfections of Human Powers: On the Metaphysics of Goodness in Aristotelian Naturalism' considers Foot's later thought, as expounded in her *Natural Goodness*. Grounding morality in the demands of our nature is not, he argues, an empirical claim, but one based in a notion of flourishing, what he calls 'natural normativity', in the human case one bound up with our natural powers, which include those pertaining to morality, to virtue and vice. In spelling out this thought Hacker-Wright invokes an Aristotelian finality, and also Thomas Aquinas's sense of us as rational animals subject to natural law and exercising our powers against such a background. In this he sees himself as going beyond commentators sympathetic to Foot's approach, such as McDowell, Michael Thompson and indeed Foot herself.

Finally on Foot, Clare Mac Cumhaill interestingly extends Foot's notion of the flourishing involved in natural goodness to encompass the aesthetic as well as the moral. In doing this she brings in references not just to Foot, but also to Iris Murdoch.

On Iris Murdoch herself, Julia Driver, in 'Love and Unsettling in Iris Murdoch' endeavours in a qualified way to resolve a potential tension between trying to see someone clearly, unselfishly, disinterestedly, and loving them, which Murdoch hopes will go together. A tension might arise if seeing them clearly reveals something unpleasant or worse (as appears to be the case in some of Murdoch's novels). Driver suggests that seeing them really clearly might reveal the true self, which can still be loved, overlooking some flaws, providing that the flaws in question do not impact on the true self.

Sabina Lovibond in 'The Elusiveness of the Ethical: From Murdoch to Diamond' in a comparison of Murdoch with Diamond, and with the aid of some fascinating literary passages, argues against what might be called the imperialism of the ethical. She advocates a form of value pluralism, in which other values, such as the aesthetic, are important as well; valuing is ubiquitous in our consciousness, but not moral valuing, and perhaps rightly not ubiquitous. (Does she thus part company with the Anscombian claim, as reported by Frey, that all actions are moral/immoral?)

Hannah Marije Altorf in 'Iris Murdoch and Common Sense, Or What It Is Like to be a Woman in Philosophy' points out that there is reason to believe that Murdoch was not always taken seriously enough as a philosopher because she was a woman – and this, even though, in her later life she herself resisted being given any sort of consideration because she was a woman. Nevertheless Murdoch would probably not have dissented from the view strongly advanced by Altorf that a diversity of viewpoint, including of course that of women, is desirable in philosophy, contributing to a kind of 'common' sense, philosophy as based in experience and contributing to a shared effort to make sense of our life.

That Mary Midgley would not have dissented from that – indeed the idea of philosophy making sense of our life are her words – is clearly demonstrated by Liz McKinnell in 'Philosophical Plumbing in the Twenty-First Century'. McKinnell uses Midgley's thought to explore the value of a diversity of voices for philosophy and society as a whole. In doing this she makes effective use of the relationship between mother and baby, something of which Midgley would undoubtedly have approved, not only in itself, but because it goes strongly against atomistic individualism.

Atomistic individualism of a Hobbesian or free market variety was something against which Midgley fought vigorously in much of her work, as Gregory McElwain demonstrates clearly in 'Relationality in the Thought of Mary Midgley'. And, as he shows, relationality in Midgley's hands extended to our interconnectedness with animals and the natural world generally. Midgley was an early philosophical defender of the significance of animals philosophically and elsewhere, and may even have influenced Foot on the notion of natural goodness here.

David Cooper in ''Removing the Barriers': Mary Midgley on Concern for Animals' takes up Midgley's sense that our attitude to animals is not just hubristic all too often. Even when apparently favourable to animals it is often over-theoretical. What is needed is not more theorizing, pro or contra, but 'attention to actual engagements with animals and to the moral failings or vices that distort people's relationships with them'.

Finally in 'Evolution as a Religion: Mary Midgley's Hopes and Fears', I myself examine Midgley's crusade not just against Dawkins and the selfish gene, but also against what she calls the 'Omega Men', scientists or science writers who predict unimaginable futures as humanity ascends the evolutionary escalator. I qualify some of what she says about Darwin and Social Darwinism, but end with positive remarks about the holistic, quasi-religious vision she espoused about the world as a whole.

On behalf of the Royal Institute of Philosophy I would like to thank the contributors to the book and to the lecture series. We hope that we have produced something worthy of the four philosophers whose centenary we are here marking. I would also like to thank John Haldane, the Chair of the Royal Institute, for suggesting this theme in the first place, and also those involved in production for their assistance in bringing the volume to fruition.

Anthony O'Hear

'The Women are Up to Something'

BENJAMIN J. BRUXVOORT LIPSCOMB

Abstract

In this essay, I offer an interpretation of the ethical thought of Elizabeth Anscombe, Philippa Foot, Mary Midgley, and Iris Murdoch. The combined effect of their work was to revive a naturalistic account of ethical objectivity that had dominated the pre-modern world. I proceed narratively, explaining how each of the four came to make the contribution she did towards this implicit common project: in particular how these women came to see philosophical possibilities that their male contemporaries mostly did not.

1. Introduction

In this essay, I offer an interpretation of the ethical thought of Elizabeth Anscombe, Philippa Foot, Mary Midgley, and Iris Murdoch: interpreting them as contributing in different ways to a common project. Theirs was a project that emerged over time and couldn't have been fully anticipated in advance; together, they made a naturalistic defense of ethical objectivity credible again, after it had been largely abandoned for several centuries. I proceed narratively, explaining how each of the four came to make the contribution she did toward this implicit common project: in particular how these women came to see philosophical possibilities that their male contemporaries mostly did not.

2. Greats and Gate-Keeping

Anscombe, Foot, Midgley, and Murdoch were born within 18 months of one another as part of the modest baby boom that followed the First World War. All born just after the Great War, these women consequently reached university age just at the verge of the Second World War. All four were accepted at Oxford, which was then the most desirable choice for a talented and ambitious young woman in the far-flung British empire. Oxford, unlike Cambridge, granted degrees to women. At the same time, lingering anxieties about the place of women at the University had led (back in 1927) to a freeze on the number of women who could be admitted each year to

doi:10.1017/S1358246120000016

Oxford's four women's colleges.[1] The upshot was, women from Great Britain and the rest of the empire who sought the distinction of an Oxbridge education *and* a degree were in competition with one another for perhaps 250 places a year.

For all that concentration of talent, women who came to study at Oxford did suffer deficits relative to their male peers. The most distinguished and best-resourced public schools in Britain – Eton, Rugby, Winchester – were male-only. And these schools were particularly strong, and schools open to women comparatively weak, in classical languages. This was the subject area that prepared one for the standard philosophy curriculum at Oxford: Greats, which opened with two years of classical literature and history before turning to pre-modern and modern philosophy.[2]

There is almost a parable here about the subtle ways in which gatekeeping works. People could suppose that they are simply insisting on baseline competence in some relevant subjects: on some good, helpful background. And there's no in-principle reason why any kind of person might not have that background. But in fact, given the way the world is, the effect of insisting on that background is to cut off opportunities for people who might be capable of impressive work, if only there were a path open to them that didn't impose those conditions. Novelist Nina Bawden, who read 'Modern Greats' (that is, Philosophy Politics and Economics) a few years later, found that even in that concentration – explicitly designed for students interested in the kind of broad-based education Greats provided but who had never seriously studied Greek – her philosophy tutor didn't know where to begin with her: 'He had not taught girls before,' she wrote, 'nor any student of either sex from a state grammar school, and could not believe I had never learned Greek. He seemed convinced...that I must be concealing this simple and fundamental skill out of some mysterious modesty'.[3]

Foot, like Bawden, read Modern Greats. Her pre-undergraduate education was typical for an upper-class girl of the time: supplied by a shifting series of governesses and centering on comportment and other minor accomplishments, supplemented with whatever bits of history, mathematics, and the like that a particular governess happened to know and chose to emphasize. Foot only ended up at Oxford because a particularly good governess, near the end of her

1 Pauline Adams, *Somerville for Women* (Oxford: Oxford University Press, 1996), 164.

2 Peter Conradi, *Iris* (New York and London: Norton, 2001), 86.

3 Nina Bawden, *In My Own Time* (New York: Clarion, 1994), 68.

teenage years, saw capacity in her and encouraged her to fill in the gaps in her education with correspondence courses and then apply.[4] Foot told a story about overhearing her mother lament to a friend that her daughter was pursuing something as *common* as a university education. 'Never mind, dear', the friend consoled her mother. 'She doesn't *look* clever'.[5] Greats was out of the question for Foot. But Anscombe, Midgley, and Murdoch – each middle-class, each more comprehensively educated – all read Greats. Anscombe was a special case in this regard, as in many others. Her mother had been a schoolteacher and had started her children on Greek at a young age.[6] So, although Anscombe attended a suburban high school of no great distinction, she was reading Plato in Greek before university. Midgley and Murdoch, by contrast, were required[7] to do remedial language study, and Midgley spent the year before going up cramming.[8] No matter what, they were never going to achieve the easy competence of someone who had been doing translations and verse compositions from age 11.

But they were better prepared in other ways, maybe precisely because they'd been less cloistered in a world of privilege. The time that an elite public-school curriculum might have given to Greek, they'd spent instead on history and literature and politics. In her memoir, Midgley writes about a seminar she and Murdoch attended on Aeschylus's *Agamemnon*. She was assigned to a working group with Murdoch and a male peer. She and Murdoch were struck by 'how much better equipped [he was] about the language, and how much less idea he had of the point of what was being said'.[9]

When the storm clouds that had been looming over Europe finally broke with Hitler's invasion of Czechoslovakia, many of Oxford's young men enlisted straightaway, even before conscription began in 1939. Until several years into the war, though, women were encouraged to complete their educations so that they could fill white-collar positions in the government and other critical sectors that were being vacated by men.

[4] Alex Voorhoeve, 'The Grammar of Goodness: An Interview with Philippa Foot', *The Harvard Review of Philosophy* XI (2003), 33.

[5] Peter Conradi and Gavin Lawrence, 'Professor Philippa Foot', *The Independent*, 19 October 2010.

[6] Mary Geach, conversation with author.

[7] G.E.M. Anscombe, 'Introduction', *Metaphysics and the Philosophy of Mind* (Minneapolis: University of Minnesota Press, 1981), vii.

[8] Op. cit. note 2, 610, n. 17.

[9] Mary Midgley, *The Owl of Minerva* (London and New York: Routledge, 2005), 98.

In the meantime, they filled another kind of vacated position: as the preferred protégés of their remaining professors. No one should wish for a war, but the effect of the depopulation of the university on the kind of attention given to women students was profound. Midgley recalls, 'the effect was to make it a great deal easier for a woman to be heard in discussion than it is in normal times. Sheer loudness of voice has a lot to do with the difficulty, but there is also a temperamental difference about confidence: about the amount of work that one thinks is needed to make one's opinion worth hearing'.[10] Anscombe again, was an outlier. The most intimidatingly brilliant of the four, she had been bound for a career in philosophy from well before she went up. As a high schooler, she had been puzzling already about problems in the metaphysics of causation that would occupy her throughout her life. Again, she suffered no deficit of preparation in classical languages and was held back only a little in Greats because she couldn't be bothered to invest much effort in any aspect of the curriculum that wasn't at the center of her concerns.[11]

3. Ayer, MacKinnon and Hare

For the other three, though, mentoring made all the difference. Not just any mentor would have sufficed. It wasn't only that, as women, they didn't fit the preconceived image of a philosopher in the minds of some potential mentors, perhaps even in their own: someone with a deeper, more carrying voice, someone whose style in discussion was more stereotypically masculine, someone with flawless Greek. It was also that the kind of philosophy in fashion at that moment was apt to repel capable students who didn't already think of themselves as philosophers and whose interests ran – like those of many young people in those unsettled times – towards ethics and politics. It took a mentor accustomed to thinking untimely and unconventional thoughts to recognize and encourage their potential and to offer them a model of philosophizing different from the prevailing one.

What was the prevailing model? It was the logical positivism particularly associated with the group of Viennese intellectuals calling themselves 'the Vienna Circle', and popularized in Britain by a brash, attention-seeking young don, A.J. Ayer.

[10] Op. cit. note 9., 123.

[11] Jenny Teichman, 'Gertrude Elizabeth Margaret Anscombe: 1919–2001', *Proceedings of the British Academy* 115 (2001), 38.

In 1935, Ayer published an improbable book, a philosophical best-seller: *Language Truth and Logic*. The book was a sensation, drawing praise and denunciation in the academic and popular press alike. It was an attack on virtually all philosophy that had ever been written.

The opening sentence lays down the challenge: 'The traditional disputes of philosophers are, for the most part, as unwarranted as they are unfruitful'.[12] The reason, Ayer said, is that philosophers have not policed their language, have not made sure that their utterances – in particular, their declarative utterances, their *statements* – are meaningful. And what kinds of statements are meaningful? Just two: statements about the world that can be confirmed or disconfirmed by observation, and statements about the governing principles of our language, its syntax and semantics. There are statements of fact, open in principle to verification or falsification by experience. There are statements defining words or laying out other conventions for their use. There are some derivative cases, like interrogatives. All else is sound and fury.

There are many problems with this view, some of which Ayer came to recognize. For one: do Ayer's own programmatic statements about what sorts of statements are meaningful pass the test that they apply to other statements? But it is the legacy of Ayer's view that is relevant here: particularly its legacy in ethics. The conclusion Ayer drew about ethical discourse was that it is largely meaningless. It merely expresses the approval or disapproval of the speaker. As Ayer wrote, 'If...I...say, "Stealing money is wrong", I produce a sentence which has no factual meaning – that is, expresses no proposition which can be either true or false. It is as if I had written "Stealing money!!" – where the shape and thickness of the exclamation marks show, by a suitable convention, that a special sort of moral disapproval is...being expressed'.[13]

Ayer thus helped codify a dichotomy that had been emerging since the early-modern period: a dichotomy between 'facts' and 'values'. According to this dichotomy, values are human projections onto a value-free reality. So we can't conform our evaluative attitudes and judgments to an independent reality. 'Fact', the term contrasted with 'value' in the fact-value dichotomy, is equally expressive of this conception. Isn't reality just the sum total of the facts? And what is left, after one has accounted for all the facts? Nothing real. Only various subjective attitudes that one might take up toward the facts, with no possibility that one could get these *wrong*.

12 A.J. Ayer, *Language, Truth and Logic* (New York: Dover, 1952), 33.
13 Op. cit. note 12., 107.

Ayer self-consciously embraced this view, drew out its implications, and gave it powerful articulation. He more than anyone set the context in which Anscombe, Foot, Midgley, and Murdoch began reflecting philosophically about ethics; he set them their task. He rendered suspect or invisible virtually all pre-modern ethical reflection, which didn't distinguish fact and value in his way.

For an extended period, before and after the war, philosophers developed their theories in response to Ayer. There was no avoiding the challenge. In a letter to Foot, shortly after their graduation, Murdoch wrote that she was looking ahead and contemplating the significance of life, but added glibly that of course such expressions were meaningless.[14] Ayer was in the air.

As Murdoch's letter illustrates, the effect of Ayer's work was destructive. It didn't help people think about questions like what to do with their lives: questions they were bound to think about, regardless. It *undercut* such thinking. As Murdoch would later come to recognize, Ayer's work *did* imply an ideal: it glamorized a kind of disillusioned toughness that faced up to a world in which words like 'good' have no meaning. But that was not the life-wisdom that Murdoch and her friends sought.

Philosophy was salvaged for Foot, Midgley, and Murdoch when they were assigned theologian-philosopher Donald MacKinnon as their philosophy tutor. More famous now in theological circles, MacKinnon was a philosopher before he was a theologian, and was evidently one of the most impressive intellects of his generation. On joining the philosophy sub-faculty in the mid-30s, the hulking Scotsman was promptly invited to join 'the Brethren', a small coterie convened by the top young philosophers at Oxford, including Ayer, Isaiah Berlin, and J.L. Austin.[15]

MacKinnon was interested in the whole history of philosophy. He taught his students to engage seriously with the kinds of figures Ayer was encouraging readers to dismiss. But as shown by his involvement with the Brethren, he also kept current on contemporary philosophy, and took seriously Ayer's charge that his own areas of concern – ethics and theology – were groundless speculation, even meaningless.

When MacKinnon is not remembered for these things – his brilliance, his preoccupation with the special challenges to ethics and theology in late modernity – he is remembered as a tormented eccentric:

[14] Avril Horner and Anne Rowe, eds., *Living on Paper: Letters from Iris Murdoch 1934–1995* (London: Chatto & Windus, 2015), 25.

[15] Michael Ignatieff, *Isaiah Berlin: A Life* (New York: Henry Holt, 1998), 85.

a man who chewed pencils to splinters or gnawed lumps of coal as his students read out their essays. Midgley writes:

> 'MacKinnon often made strange unpredictable movements and, in particular, strange grimaces, which...seemed to express profound anguish. A lot of the stories about him are true enough. He did wave pokers and other things about in an alarming way.... He did lie on the floor or beat the wall violently.... He was prone to long silences, sometimes not seeming to hear at all what was said to him'.[16]

If MacKinnon suffered from a condition like Tourette's, as Midgley speculates, it may have been exacerbated in those days, when – disqualified from military service – he threw himself into teaching as if to justify his existence, taking on as many students as would ordinarily be divided among three or more tutors.

MacKinnon could be intimidating on first acquaintance. But he also inspired devotion: by his intelligence and insight, by the generosity of attention he lavished on students, by the depth of his engagement with both the material he taught and the crises of the time. The effects of his teaching were transformative: by the end of their undergraduate years, Foot, Midgley, and Murdoch were all considering philosophy as a path. Foot later described MacKinnon as 'holy' and as having 'created' her.[17] This from a committed atheist. For her part, in 1945, Murdoch wrote about MacKinnon, 'after meeting him one really understands...how those people at Galilee got up & followed without any hesitation'.[18]

Under MacKinnon's mentorship, Foot, Midgley, and Murdoch were becoming the kind of philosophers who would turn to out-of-fashion figures in the history of philosophy for light, and whose aim in philosophy was to reflect on what Ayer would have regarded as the meaningless question of the best life for human beings. Once more, on both points, Anscombe was ahead of her friends. She had converted to Catholicism as a teenager, defying her parents. Her parents believed in nothing in particular (her mother was a nominal Anglican), but were determined that if their daughter was going to become religious, she should at least do so in a conventional, respectable way: Church of England. They called in a priest to sort her out. Anscombe promptly buttonholed the poor man: 'Do you think the

[16] Op. cit. note 8, 116.

[17] Op. cit. note 2, 127.

[18] Iris Murdoch, *A Writer at War: Letters and Diaries 1938–1946*, ed. Peter Conradi (London: Short Books, 2010), 256.

bread *is* the body of Christ?' The priest hemmed and hawed, said it was a difficult question and shrouded in mystery. Anscombe was unimpressed: 'well, I do'.[19] She was not only a born philosopher, but a born contrarian. And her Catholicism prompted her to take seriously questions about the best life for humans, and to look for instruction to figures like Thomas Aquinas. The presence of Anscombe in Foot, Midgley, and Murdoch's life – and the awe with which they regarded her – further bolstered their sense that there was another way besides Ayer's.

When did they first set themselves against Ayer's vision? It is hard to know. Late in life, Foot gave a number of interviews in which she identified the day on which she first thought that she had to do ethics in a way that defied Ayer's strictures. She was at the cinema for the newsreels, the day they showed the liberation of the Belsen and Buchenwald camps: the piles of bodies, the emaciated survivors pressing against the fence. Like many of her contemporaries, Foot emerged from the cinema catatonic with shock. From the moment she saw those images, she said, she was committed to the idea that Ayer was mistaken. How, she didn't know yet. But he was; he had to be. 'There was something absolutely wicked about the Holocaust', she said to one interviewer. 'There is something objective here'.[20]

We must note, though: there was another way to react to the war, a way that revised but did not repudiate Ayer's view. And it wasn't the reaction of people who hadn't faced real horror.

R.M. Hare would become the principal professional antagonist to the women I've been discussing. Ayer's views on ethics were crude. But more sophisticated versions of these views were developed over the ensuing decade that addressed the problems with Ayer's views from within Ayer's basic world-picture. Hare was the greatest of the improvers. Cantankerous and profoundly earnest, he stood for everything philosophically that Foot and her friends came to reject. He too was born in 1919, and so went up to Balliol a couple of years before the war. In 1938, when it had become clear that war was coming, Hare gave himself 24 hours to sort out whether he was a pacifist. After a hard night of reflection, he enlisted. He was sent to east Asia, where he spent a happy year teaching Punjabi soldiers to operate British military equipment before Singapore fell and he was captured, plunging his life into darkness. After a couple of years in a prison camp, he was sent off to work on the Burma railway. Between a quarter and a half of his fellow prisoners died

19 Roger Teichmann, conversation with author.
20 Interview with Jonathan Ree, BBC Radio 3, 19 September, 2000.

from day after day of hauling dirt on starvation rations. Hare did not die. He kept himself alive and sane in part by doing philosophy. He stole an accounting ledger from a guard shack and kept it hidden for three years, writing out his life philosophy with any stylus he could manufacture and any time he could scrounge: for instance, when he was judged unfit for work due to dysentery. When Hare was released after the war, he judged that his book was no good, a judgment he seems to have formed under the influence of Ayer's positivism.[21]

The main lessons Hare took away from the war and brought with him into the rest of his career were these: first, there is no reasoning with some people. There was no arguing with his taskmasters on the Burma railway. Past a certain point, reasoning about how to live is futile: not only because people can always refuse to listen, but because, past a certain point, there is nothing more to be said. A person chooses a way of life, explicitly or implicitly, and that is that. Second, and relatedly, if there is any rational necessity in ethics, it is just this necessity of choosing a way of life: a set of principles, as Hare thought of it. Some people do this with more inner strength and clarity of vision, some merely fall into a way of life that they never articulate clearly to themselves. But we all live out some principles, whether we recognize them and own up to them or not, and (here is the link to Ayer) there are no facts that dictate which principles we ought to adopt. We must each simply decide what to live for. Hare was generalizing from his own experience: he had enlisted by an act of reflective self-commitment, and he had kept himself alive and integrated by a further act of commitment. Anyone familiar with the existentialism of Jean-Paul Sartre will recognize the affinities between his ideas and Hare's that Murdoch would later stress.

At the end of the war, Hare like many others returned to university. Thanks to the influx of ex-servicemen – the slow-clearing backlog of people pursuing educations they'd had to postpone – and then another baby boom, an era opened in which there were jobs for most would-be dons. In the second half of the 40s, Anscombe and Foot both secured research fellowships and some teaching at Somerville College. Murdoch was a train ride away at Cambridge doing graduate work, and then landed a position at St. Anne's. Midgley too did some graduate work, at Oxford, which she then abandoned in favor of a job at Reading. Notwithstanding various entrenched, half-conscious prejudices – reflected in small things,

[21] A.W. Price, 'Richard Mervyn Hare: 1919–2002', *Proceedings of the British Academy* 124 (2004), 119.

like a discussion group for rising young philosophers calling itself 'the Brethren' – all four were on their way to being professionally established by the end of the 40s.

Up to this point, I have been talking about how Anscombe, Foot, Midgley, and Murdoch became interested in philosophy and were prepared for the contributions they would later make. Now I am going to sketch the implicit common project I see in their work, one with ongoing relevance to the current philosophical scene and to late-modern Western culture generally. I will continue to give my remarks narrative form, because the project I am highlighting was an unfolding one, not something these women devised one afternoon in the late 40s in a tea shop. This shouldn't surprise us, because what they eventually accomplished involved an imaginative leap outside the strictures endorsed by their contemporaries and predecessors. Perhaps some imaginative leaps come all at once, fully formed. More commonly, though, as Thomas Kuhn describes, people first raise new questions about some dominant framing, freeing people to consider that the dominant framing could be wrong; later, people begin to try out possible alternatives: or perhaps just elements of alternatives. Only then does it become possible to develop these.[22] The leap outside the fact-value dichotomy was this latter kind of leap.

Surely it helped, though, that the people who pursued it were insider-outsiders, and had each been mentored by an insider-outsider (in Anscombe's case, Wittgenstein). They had learned to engage current scholarship. But they had also learned to engage old-fashioned thoughts and topics that no late-modern person was supposed to take seriously.

4. Murdoch's Diagnosis

Murdoch was in some ways the furthest 'outside' of the four, though it depends what kind of externality one has in mind. In any case, she made a contribution that none of her friends could: diagnosing the several theories of ethics they were concerned to reject. When I say Murdoch 'diagnosed' these theories, I mean she identified them as symptoms of something deeper: an underlying cultural condition or outlook. She identified the unexpressed and peculiarly late-modern ideals behind a set of theories that were standardly presented as timeless, value-neutral analyses of moral thought and discourse.

[22] Thomas Kuhn, *The Structure of Scientific Revolutions* (Chicago: University of Chicago, 1962).

This was crucial, I think, if she and her friends were to think sufficiently radically about what to put in place of such theories. If you don't perceive what is motivating an outlook – especially if you carry that motive within yourself, like latent malaria – you're apt to keep collapsing into the same outlook.

Murdoch aspired already in her 20s to be a novelist as well as a philosopher, and to be part of the international community of writers and public intellectuals. She had always had a facility for languages, and kept acquiring them throughout her life. What Murdoch discerned, thanks to her voracious and diverse reading, was the kinship between French existentialism on the one hand and the thought of British philosophers like Ayer and Hare on the other. If neither group was reading the other but they were coming to very similar conclusions, however masked by different vocabularies, Murdoch saw that as suggestive of an underlying intellectual or spiritual condition. I mentioned in passing the kinship between the thought of Sartre and that of Hare. No one had noticed this before Murdoch, and thus no one could go further and ask what lay behind it. Murdoch both noticed and asked.

At one level, the answer is plain: Ayer and Sartre and Hare all adhere to the late-modern world-picture I described above: there are facts and there are values, and values aren't facts; they are subjective attitudes people take up *toward* facts. If one regards this as uncontestable, then one might think there is little more to say: two mostly unconnected groups of scholars converged on the same truth. But if one is troubled by the limitations of this picture – what it doesn't allow one to say about the Nazis – and wonders what could take its place, then it is worth retaining one's curiosity and digging deeper. First, it is helpful to recognize it as late-modern: as culturally and historically local. One can then ask whether there are credible alternatives available from other times and places. Second, it is helpful to recognize that the picture, at least in the way in which it is usually presented and motivated, is not fully self-consistent. It – or its advocates – make the picture much more appealing than it would otherwise be by connecting it with an ideal, the objective validity of which they overtly disavow. According to the picture, ideals are just projections: none more objectively valid than another. But invariably, the picture is motivated in significant part, even given an atmosphere of spiritual grandeur, by the tacit, unscrutinized invocation of tropes of nineteenth-century Romanticism, specifically the Romantic sublime: the exhilaration of staring into the abyss, into the icy valuelessness of it all. To summon the courage and honesty to stare down the cold truth: like

Hector's defiance of his fate in *The Iliad*, this is noble. On the premises of the view in question, such talk of nobility (or, in British authors like Hare, of facing life like an adult[23]) should count as but one more arbitrary projection. But with all the cultural force of deeply internalized Romanticism behind it, it is presented as if it were what the view explicitly disallows: an objectively valid ideal. The seeming gloom of the existentialist is superficial, Murdoch writes. It 'conceals elation'.[24] For one places oneself among the elect who are man enough to face the truth. To recognize these attitudes and outlooks as cultural peculiarities – to be given permission even to smile at their pretension – is to be in a much stronger a position to begin thinking about alternatives. This was Murdoch's contribution, beginning with the pair of radio addresses at the turn of the 1950s that grew into her first book: the first study of Sartre in English.[25]

Murdoch left her position at St. Anne's by the early 60s, ostensibly to focus on her fiction, but also because she had concluded that what she did wasn't really philosophy. If she alone could have offered her diagnosis, offering it nevertheless served to marginalize her further from the academic community to which she belonged. For in Oxford, under the influence of J.L. Austin, an inspiring but also narrow conception of philosophical method had by the early 50s come to dominate.

Austin's method had roots both in the patient textual scholarship he practiced as a classics tutor and in his wartime experiences sifting military intelligence. Working collaboratively with his (male) junior colleagues (whom he convened each Saturday morning during term-time), he tried to get as clear as possible about subtle differences among clusters of topically related words: 'hounding down the minutiae', as he put it.[26] Austin was determined to make *progress* in philosophy, and surveying the wreckage of philosophical history – all the grand systems constructed, then abandoned – he renounced system-building. Or, at any rate, he determined that the only way to build was extremely slowly, piece by piece, scrutinizing our words

[23] R.M. Hare, *The Language of Morals* (Oxford: Clarendon Press, 1952), 196.

[24] Iris Murdoch, 'On God and Good', *The Sovereignty of Good* (London and New York: Routledge, 1970), 50.

[25] Iris Murdoch, *Sartre: Romantic Rationalist* (Cambridge: Bowes, 1953).

[26] J.L. Austin, 'A Plea for Excuses', in J.O. Urmson and G.J. Warnock (eds.), *Philosophical Papers* (Oxford: Oxford University Press, 1961), 123.

and through them our concepts. Under his influence, a whole generation of Oxford philosophers came to share his impatience with generalization and synthesis, his intellectual aesthetic of clarity and cleanliness. 'Words are our tools', he wrote, 'and ... we should use clean tools'.[27]

It is not difficult to see the attractions of Austin's approach: the painstaking carefulness, the submission to the ideal of getting something right, even if it is nothing grand. But in a context obsessed with that ideal, Murdoch's eclectic, allusive essays, concerned with big, competing visions of the world and the human condition, were bound to appear merely sloppy. Murdoch inspired those close to her with her insight and breadth of exposure, but her philosophical writing was less and less appreciated in Oxford as the 50s wore on. People regarded her as a helpful expert on a minor subject, contemporary French thought. Hare's remarks on French existentialism are telling: 'the thing wrong with the Existentialists and the other Continental philosophers is that they haven't had their noses rubbed in the necessity of saying exactly what they mean'.[28]

Murdoch's work didn't register, in her milieu, as being properly disciplined, properly *philosophical*. Isaiah Berlin, who adulated Austin, quipped about Murdoch that she was 'a lady not known for the clarity of her views'.[29] There is something terribly sad about that remark, as Berlin himself was filled with self-doubt on account of the similarly allusive and visionary qualities of his own best work. He didn't think what he did was real philosophy either, because real philosophy, in that time and place, meant 'what Austin did'. One has to wonder whether Murdoch's increasing detachment from philosophy, and perhaps even her curious but vigorous insistence that there is little connection between her novels and her philosophical writings, reflects a similar internalization of a communal judgment that what she did, even if it went under the banner of philosophy, didn't merit the name.

Murdoch was inspiring to her friends – she and Foot were by the mid-50s co-teaching a graduate course on the ancient ethical vocabulary of virtue and vice – but she was marginalized within the philosophical community. What then did it take to get the attention of that community, to get it to begin reconsidering its predominant ways of thinking about ethics? A frontal assault.

[27] Op. cit. note 26, 129.

[28] Ved Mehta, *Fly and the Fly-Bottle* (Boston and Toronto: Little, Brown and Company, 1962), 51.

[29] Op. cit. note 2, 302.

5. Anscombe and Foot

As I've noted, Anscombe was acknowledged by her circle of friends as the most brilliant of the four. This compensated for the fact that she was, socially, even more an outsider than Murdoch. Murdoch was personally magnetic, someone who always had more devoted friends and admirers than she had time to give. By contrast, Anscombe was at once pugnacious and shy, physically awkward, famously dismissive of proprieties of dress and speech. If she hadn't awed everyone around her intellectually, life in Oxford might have been intolerable for her.

From the mid-40s, she and Foot were both (somewhat tenuously) hired on at Somerville, which really had work for only one philosophy tutor but kept finding fellowships for them both (particularly for Anscombe) so as to postpone the day when it had to choose and let one of them go. Despite a workload to rival MacKinnon's from the early 40s, Foot made time daily to, in effect, apprentice herself to Anscombe. Anscombe herself evidently regarded their regular afternoon discussions as important enough to go on making time for them. We should note that Anscombe had more than enough to do herself, even setting aside her work translating Wittgenstein's *Philosophical Investigations*. From the mid-40s through the early 60s, she always had small children at home. Her husband Peter Geach lived and taught several hours away in Birmingham. For Anscombe to take time daily for Foot in this context is impressive. Foot for her part had found an object of intellectual devotion such as she had had before in MacKinnon. She describes their conversations memorably: 'It was like in those old children's comics where a steamroller runs over a character who becomes flattened – an outline on the ground – but is there all right in the next episode'.[30]

The key to Anscombe's character, I think, is not combativeness as such, for she was not always combative. She once characterized herself as 'torn by a *saeva indignatio*'.[31] The reference to Jonathan Swift, from whose epitaph the expression is taken, is apt: like Swift, Anscombe felt herself frequently, painfully out of step with the world around her. Like Swift, the things that made Anscombe feel this way were the world's cozy accommodations with what she regarded as terrible evils. Being shy, she mostly avoided public controversy through the early 50s. Until that is the spring of 1956,

[30] Op. cit. note 4, 34–35.

[31] G.E.M. Anscombe, 'Introduction', *Ethics, Religion, and Politics* (Minneapolis: University of Minnesota Press, 1981), vii.

when she undertook to oppose the nomination of former US President Harry Truman for an honorary degree from Oxford.

As an undergraduate, Anscombe had co-authored a short pamphlet on the traditional doctrine of just war: a piece notable for its prediction that the Allies would descend eventually to direct attacks on civilians.[32] This, she said, could not be squared with the traditional criteria of *jus in bello*, which require that only just means be used to prosecute a war. Direct attacks on civilians, she noted, are not a just means. Direct attacks on civilians are direct attacks on the innocent, i.e., murder. It was the same objection she would press against Mr. Truman's degree, a decade and a half later.

Anscombe's protest, in late spring 1956, became a minor international news item.[33] It was unsuccessful. Anscombe rose to speak in Congregation, the potentially enormous but usually sparsely attended assembly of faculty and alumni with the authority to grant or withhold such degrees and denounced the nomination (one quote has survived from reports of her speech: 'if you do this', she asked, 'what Nero, what Ghengis Khan, what Hitler or what Stalin will not be honoured in the future?').[34] But the University administration, fearing institutional embarrassment, solicited members to show up and vote for the honor. 'The women are up to something' some were told. 'We have to go and vote them down'.[35]

What infuriated Anscombe most were the justifications her colleagues offered, showing either that they believed it all right to attack civilians or that they cared more about losing face than about murder. Anscombe had not until 1956 published anything on ethics, aside from the undergraduate pamphlet. She had some second-hand awareness of recent developments in ethical theory from her daily discussions with Foot. But her energies had been mostly absorbed, for half a decade, in her work as one of Wittgenstein's literary executors. Recall too: from her undergraduate days, she had been selectively attentive to what people thought she should study. As it happened, though, at the same time the University was preparing to honor Truman, and Anscombe was asking herself why 'so many Oxford people should be willing to

32 G.E.M. Anscombe, 'The Justice of the Present War Examined', *Ethics, Religion, and Politics* (Minneapolis: University of Minnesota Press, 1981), 72–81.

33 It was reported for instance in *The New York Times* of 19 June, 1956.

34 *Oxford Mail*, 1 May 1956.

35 G.E.M. Anscombe, 'Mr Truman's Degree', *Ethics, Religion, and Politics* (Minneapolis: University of Minnesota Press, 1981), 65.

flatter such a man',[36] Foot went on leave. Anscombe took up some of her colleague's usual responsibilities, including tutorials in ethics.[37] These two experiences – the Truman protest and the new reading she was doing in preparation for tutorials – converged in Anscombe's mind. 'I get some small light', she wrote in her pamphlet, 'when I consider the productions of Oxford moral philosophy since the First World War, which I have lately had occasion to read'.[38] None of the prevailing theories, she found, categorically excluded the killing of the innocent: that is, murder. None of them indeed categorically excluded anything. None of them then had room for Anscombe's own deepest ethical conviction: that 'we have to fear God and keep his commandments, and calculate what is for the best only within the limits of that obedience'.[39]

She included a paragraph about this at the end of her pamphlet. The result was that a month later, a short note arrived from the BBC Talks Department, asking if Anscombe might 'develop the theme of the relevance of Oxford philosophy to situations such as the one which inspired your pamphlet'.[40] Alight with Swiftian *indignatio*, she agreed. So on a windy evening in late January 1957, Anscombe arrived at Broadcasting House to record, in her famously soft, sweet voice, a work of biting irony, titled 'Oxford Moral Philosophy: Does it "corrupt the youth"?'[41] The gist of the address is as follows: to make the charge stick that Hare and others corrupt the youth, you'd have to show that the youth would have turned out better without their influence. But the youth had been raised in a culture that had no objection to massacring Japanese civilians. So how could one maintain that Hare's philosophy corrupts anyone, just because it offers no resources for critiquing such atrocities?

The irony was subtle enough that her producer first mistook the script for 'a vigorous defence of Oxford morals and moralists'[42] and urged that she quote people who thought Oxford moral philosophy

[36] Op. cit. note 32, 70.

[37] Mary Geach, 'Introduction' in Anscombe, G.E.M., *Human Life, Action and Ethics* (Exeter and Charlottesville: Imprint Academic, 2005), xvii.

[38] Op. cit. note 37.

[39] G.E.M. Anscombe, 'War and Murder', *Ethics, Religion, and Politics* (Minneapolis: University of Minnesota Press, 1981), 61.

[40] BBC Written Archives Centre, RCONT3 – G.E.M. Anscombe, A.E. Harvey to G.E.M. Anscombe, 18 July, 1956.

[41] Subsequently reprinted in *The Listener* 57 (14 February, 1957).

[42] G.E.M. Anscombe, Letter to the Editor, *The Listener* 57 (14 March, 1957).

was corrupting.[43] But when the piece broadcast in early February and subsequently appeared in *The Listener*, its targets understood it well enough. Two of them, Hare and P.H. Nowell-Smith, had letters to the editor in the next issue, filling a column each. Anscombe, who loved a fight, replied: 'I was glad to read [Mr. Hare's] letter and Mr. Nowell-Smith's. They show that what I want to go for is really there'.[44] The correspondence lasted into April, generating more heat than light.

Meanwhile, delighted with the tempest she had stirred, Anscombe drafted a follow-up talk, to be titled 'Principles' and was outraged when it was rejected as being 'too personal'. Denied this outlet, she wrote perhaps the most famous article of her career: 'Modern Moral Philosophy'.[45] It is an odd piece, as anyone who has read it can attest, full of delicious or maddening hit-and-run remarks about a variety of historical and contemporary figures. It reads somewhat like a broadcast talk, in parts.

What did Anscombe say? She offers a Murdochian diagnosis of the ethical theories of her contemporaries and their predecessors and recommends that the whole project of moral philosophy as it has been conceived since the early modern period be abandoned in favor of an attempt to reappropriate the premodern approach of Aristotle and Aquinas. Anscombe herself, having unburdened herself on the subject in this article and in her short but similarly influential book, *Intention*, returned to her preferred scholarly projects, like a commentary on Wittgenstein's *Tractatus*. But with the appearance of her article, a path forward in ethics began to come clear, particularly for Foot and Midgley.

Foot went first. Her contribution was to domesticate Anscombe's radical critique, turning it into a standard-model philosophical research program. Foot took Anscombe's suggestion – that philosophers return to the premodern conceptual vocabulary of virtue and vice – and extracted it from Anscombe's caustic and enigmatic presentation, casting it instead in the form of a series of measured, witty, highly professionalized journal articles, first pointing out some

[43] BBC Written Archives Centre, RCONT3 – G.E.M. Anscombe, T.S. Gregory to G.E.M. Anscombe, 5 December, 1956. In the ensuing controversy, Gregory insisted to Anscombe that he had recognized the irony immediately.

[44] G.E.M. Anscombe, Letter to the Editor, *The Listener* 57 (28 February, 1957).

[45] G.E.M. Anscombe, 'Modern Moral Philosophy', *Philosophy* 33 (1958), 1–19.

difficulties with Hare's theory (taken simply as linguistic analysis), then elaborating the premodern alternative she and her friends had been discussing for a number of years and that Anscombe had finally made unignorable. In so doing, Foot made it possible for other philosophers – including more conventional ones – to join in the work. Putting it in Kuhn's terms, Foot turned the 'revolutionary science' of Murdoch and Anscombe into 'normal science'.

Philosophers tend to associate Anscombe and Foot's ethical outlook with Aristotle more than with any other figure. But Aquinas was arguably more important in framing their contributions. Anscombe knew the writings of Aquinas, Aristotle's leading medieval interpreter, as well as any Aquinas scholar of her time. Perhaps her most important substantive contribution to Foot's work was her suggestion to Foot, during that fateful sabbatical, that she read Aquinas. As Foot took everything Anscombe said deadly seriously, she began reading: in particular the Secunda Secundae of the *Summa Theologiae*, where Aquinas discusses particular virtues and vices in detail. The revelation in these works, to Foot, was of how ethics could be objective: the result she had been seeking since 1945. Each virtue is praised by Aquinas for how it assists humans in the performance of their characteristic activities. Each vice is condemned (one of her favorite examples from Aquinas was 'loquaciousness') because of how it inhibits humans in the performance of their characteristic activities. Reading this, she knew at last what she wanted to say: not just to Hare, but to a kind of Nietzschean skeptic that she had always worried about and addressed in every piece of moral philosophy she wrote from then on. One could summarize her developed position thus: Hare's theory does not enable one to reply effectively to Nietzsche, whereas a Thomistic theory does. As she concluded a broadcast talk in 1957: 'We should be able to turn to the...moral philosopher for an account of the basis of the different kinds of virtues and vices, for their necessary connexion with human harm and good. This is just the sort of work that he should be able to do: but usually we are fobbed off with talk about the favorable attitude which anyone who calls anything a virtue must take up – as if this were enough'.[46]

With this broadcast, with a paper ('Ought and Is') at the Oxford Philosophical Society, and with two other widely discussed papers that came out of these preparatory exercises,[47] Foot came into her

[46] 'Immoralism', BBC Third Programme, 22 September, 1957.

[47] 'Moral Arguments' and 'Moral Beliefs', published in 1958 and 1959, respectively, in *Mind* and *Proceedings of the Aristotelian Society*.

reputation as Hare's foremost opponent. For the next decade, students (who love to see their teachers argue) would attend the lectures and seminars of each and try out the objections of the other.

Foot's reputation was well-deserved. But she achieved something at once vitally important and gently ironic. In her attack on Oxford moral philosophers, she became: an Oxford moral philosopher. It was Foot whom Hare approached in 1958, with the idea of teaching a course together. Foot had become, in certain respects, very like Austin. There was more than a passing resemblance between Austin's work and her criticism of Hare: that moral language was richer and more complex than Hare's theory allowed. As Foot said in the broadcast talk mentioned above: 'Those who accuse the present-day philosophers of fiddling their time away may be surprised at the suggestion that what we need is therefore more detail, and more attention to the meaning of moral terms. But this may well be the case'.[48] Foot's criticism was more effective than Anscombe's in opening up conversation because she was so respectable, so *au courant* even in rebellion.

If any of these women was an insider, it was Foot. This was of course a role to which she had been raised. If she was in lifelong flight from the class-consciousness with which she had grown up, she was also profoundly shaped by it. Her thoroughgoing and instinctive respectability enabled her to achieve things that her friends could not, even as it burdened her.

Trivially, often amusingly, her philosophical writings feature lots of examples and expressions drawn from etiquette and riding to hounds. More seriously and uncomfortably: Foot reflexively classed and ranked philosophers, including her friends. Anscombe was first, she was next, followed by Murdoch and Midgley. She dedicated her book *Virtues and Vices* to Murdoch, who was her dearest friend. But Murdoch does not appear in the index. About Midgley, Foot later remarked, 'Her mind doesn't quite work like most straight Oxford analytic philosophers.... I think she found her forte being witty and sane on television'.[49] And when she went to UCLA in the mid-1970s, she began to gather around her a group of colleagues and students whom she regarded, and sometimes spoke of, as 'the right sort'.[50]

Foot was in flight from this class-consciousness her whole adult life. There is a telling moment in a late interview, when she refers

[48] Op. cit. note 46.

[49] Andrew Brown, 'Mary, Mary, quite contrary', *The Guardian*, 13 January 2001.

[50] Rosalind Hursthouse, conversation with author.

to 'Lady Mary Murray' and then comments, 'If you're called "Lady Mary" somebody, you've got to be terribly grand, much grander than being called "Lady Murray".... I hated it, this sort of knowledge: I can't help it, I know this'.[51] It remained with her, not only as something she couldn't help knowing and introduced for comic effect in her writings. It remained too in her oft-noted elegance of bearing and speech, which left her effortlessly at ease in Oxford society.

This brings us to one final effect of Foot's insider status. That is, she did a vital if unremarked service simply in being Anscombe's friend. Apart from being in a minority as a woman, no one could have fitted into Oxford society more easily than Foot. Foot alone was eventually invited to Austin's Saturday mornings.[52] Without Foot as her friend and champion, it is easy to imagine someone like Anscombe – with her duffel coat and trousers, her cigars and her walleye, her sometimes coarse language and her seven kids helping raise one another under the disapproving stares of some of the St. John's Street neighbors – it is easy to imagine her being completely isolated in Oxford, notwithstanding her brilliance. But Foot venerated her, and everyone loved Foot.

6. Midgley

I turn finally to Midgley. A principal interest of mine in this essay has been in the ways that *outsiders* were especially well-positioned to make key contributions to a transformation in our thinking about ethics. Midgley was as much an outsider as Murdoch or Anscombe.

She is often overlooked even by scholars who note the biographical connections and synergies of thought between Anscombe, Foot, and Murdoch. A number of factors have converged to keep Midgley's work from being discussed alongside that of her friends. There is, first, the unusual shape of her career. Anscombe, Foot, and Murdoch had all taken posts at Oxford by the end of 1948. Midgley was briefly at Reading before marrying and resigning that post. She did not begin lecturing at Newcastle until the mid-1960s, pausing first to raise her three boys. Or again, consider their publication histories: by the mid-1960s, Anscombe had brought out most of the works for which she is famous, Foot had established herself as Hare's leading critic, and Murdoch was turning away from

[51] Interview with Martin Gornall, Somerville College Special Collections, SC/LY/SP/PF/10.

[52] W. David Solomon, conversation with author.

philosophy toward fiction. Meanwhile, the first of Midgley's more than a dozen books was still over a decade off, to be published when she was 59. It has been easy to overlook the generational tie between Midgley and her university friends.

The character of Midgley's work has likewise kept it from being discussed alongside theirs. As eclectic in her interests as Murdoch, and liberated from any professional pressure to concentrate her reading in one discipline, she began in her thirties to read extensively in the emerging field of ethology, as well as literary criticism, intellectual history, politics, and more. She became convinced that moral philosophers must *relate* various bodies of knowledge to one another if they are to achieve an adequate understanding of human life, human motivation, and (thereby) human success or failure. There was distinguished precedent for this kind of work, and Midgley knew it. For this is how Aristotle approaches ethics: as a biologist studying an animal of especially absorbing interest, exploring not only how this animal behaves and why, but also what challenges are set to it by its nature. This had become extremely uncommon, though, in the professionalized – even scholastic – environment of mid-twentieth-century philosophy.

A few years after joining the department at Newcastle, one of Midgley's colleagues urged her to offer an evening course on animal behavior and ethics through the university's adult-education program. It was the pivot-point of her career. In teaching these students, of varying ages and backgrounds, all of whom were enrolled simply because they were interested, Midgley began to work out a biologically grounded framework for talking about human nature and human motivation, a framework she had sought since at least 1951. Writing to her BBC producer that year, she had identified her great theme: 'the many-sidedness of human nature, and the inadequacy of *all* current official ways of regarding it'.[53] Now, in the space of a few years, she brought out her first scholarly articles, culminating in 'The Concept of Beastliness' in 1973.[54] That piece caught the attention of Max Black at Cornell and led to an invitation, first, to come to the States as a visiting scholar, and then, to expand her reflections on ethology and ethics into her first and most important book, *Beast and Man*.

The book begins with an appeal to think more carefully about the likenesses and unlikenesses between humans and other animals, and

[53] BBC Written Archives Centre, RCONT1 – Mary Scrutton – Talks File 1 – 1942–1962, 7 October 1951.

[54] Mary Midgley, 'The Concept of Beastliness: Philosophy, Ethics, and Animal Behaviour', *Philosophy* 48 (1973), 111–135.

to scrutinize the language in which we express these. The Western tradition has often been fearful or disgusted at our animality. But given that 'We are not just rather like animals; we *are* animals',[55] this is apt to leave us with a misleading sense of ourselves. To think about our lives is to think about our nature, and this cannot be understood in isolation from biology.

By Midgley's own testimony, the heart of the book is its eleventh chapter. In that chapter, 'On Being Animal as well as Rational', Midgley offers an account, inspired by Darwin and contemporary ethologists, of the place of reason in human life. The details are complex, but the overall point is straightforward. Our evolutionary history has bequeathed to us a generous assortment of motives. It has moreover bequeathed to us conceptual and imaginative capacities that ramify the conflicts that would occur anyway between such diverse motives. We are distinctive in our ability to anticipate and fret over our conflicting motives, and even to think or imagine our way into new conflicts.

Any animal with a nature this complex and conflictual requires some means of organizing and directing its behavior: that is, of prioritizing and harmonizing its motives. For many animals, this is achieved by the operation of relatively simple, highly specified instincts. In her later book, *Wickedness*, Midgley offers the example of geese who hatch one group of young after another all summer long, then fly away, leaving their last brood to perish, when something – the temperature, the angle of the light – triggers their migratory instinct. For humans, by contrast, the same faculty that aggravates internal conflicts by allowing us to anticipate or even generate them also enables us to deal with them: to conceive, try out, and criticize approaches to living as whole and integrated beings. Midgley's ethics is an ethics of self-integration.

Anscombe, Foot, and Murdoch had all recommended a retrieval of a biologically grounded way of thinking and talking about ethics. We need a return, they argued, to the conceptual vocabulary of virtue and vice, grounded in an account of what enables humans to flourish in the performance of characteristically human activities. But all this work was essentially promissory. Midgley – writing from the margins of the discipline, and unappreciated by any of her friends, save Murdoch – was the first to present a serious proposal for a naturalistic ethics of the kind recommended but not developed by the others. Indeed, she was the only one who could, as she was the

[55] Mary Midgley,, *Beast and Man*, rev. ed. (London and New York: Routledge, 1995), xxxiii.

only one who knew enough biology and enough moral philosophy to try to relate the two fields. Whatever one judges about the details of her view, it clearly represents what it would mean to bring to completion the transformation initiated by Murdoch, Anscombe, and Foot.

7. Conclusion

Every part of this essay could be elaborated. It is a sketch, which I am elsewhere working on filling in. Just one more remark, in closing: it seems to me that contemporary philosophers – and contemporary Westerners in general – remain very much in the grip of the ideas Murdoch, Anscombe, Foot, and Midgley worked to transcend. I could cite as examples the theories of some of the most important moral philosophers writing today: Christine Korsgaard, for instance. But let me give a homelier example of the cultural infusion of these ideas: each of my children in turn has come home from primary school with a language-arts worksheet that's really a lesson in positivist value theory: an exercise in distinguishing 'facts' from 'opinions'. Never mind that one might have opinions about factual matters. The examples make plain enough that it is the fact-value dichotomy at work: the examples of 'opinions' are all judgments of good and bad, better and worse. To think that one design or policy or person or artifact is superior to another is to have an 'opinion'. And that's to be sharply distinguished from any 'fact'. In a linguistic and cultural context in which 'fact' is a loose synonym for 'reality', this is a little exercise for the children in moral subjectivism. Think again of what Foot wanted to find the words – and concepts – to say: that the Nazis were wrong. Well, my children were given to understand, that may be her *opinion*, but it can't be a *fact*.

But Foot and Anscombe and Murdoch and Midgley were right, and the curriculum authors are wrong. It is possible to reframe our thinking about these matters and to articulate how it could be a fact that the Nazis were wrong, that racialized disparities in criminal sentencing are wrong, that the sexual molestation of children is wrong, and a hundred other things. Anscombe's mentor Wittgenstein wrote, 'a picture held us captive'.[56] The picture of the fact-value dichotomy still holds us captive. The ongoing significance of the

[56] Ludwig Wittgenstein, *Philosophical Investigations*, trans. G.E.M. Anscombe, 3rd ed. (Oxford: Blackwell, 1958), s. 115.

four insider-outsiders I have discussed lies in how they refused to accept that picture and in its place drew another.

Houghton College
Benjamin.Lipscomb@houghton.edu

A Philosopher of singular style and multiple modes

JOHN HALDANE

Abstract
Elizabeth Anscombe was one of the most gifted and productive philosophers of the decades following the Second World War. Her writings present challenges to readers: some of them are very difficult to comprehend while others seem philosophically-minded yet situated outside of philosophy as such. There are also the issues of whether she had a philosophical method and of the influence of Wittgenstein on the manner of her approach. A summary and estimate of Anscombe's enduring contributions is presented before exploring the style and aims of her philosophical work. Then two of her writings on religion are examined and their implications for her attitude to philosophy considered.

1. Introduction

Elizabeth Anscombe was without question one of the most gifted, creative, wide-ranging and productive Anglophone philosophers of the post-war period. Her approach was quite distinctive as was her style. It is common to say that her work is difficult to read and comprehend, and certainly that is true of much of it. But other writings of hers are relatively clear. What accounts for this difference is in part a matter of intended audience or readership, but also the circumstances that had occasioned a piece, the nature of the task in which she was engaged, and the tractability or otherwise of the material with which she was dealing. One of her gifts was to expose the complexity of matters that had hitherto been taken to be simple so she often presented readers, who might otherwise have expected a straight and smooth path, with a twisting, turning and unpaved route. Certainly, she never wrote anything trite or facile, however humble the context, such as an address on the topic of morality to an unphilosophical lay audience [1] but nor did she indulge herself in gratuitous displays of philosophical sophistication. Indeed, I would suggest as a rule of thumb the principle if Anscombe makes *it* (the issue) seem difficult that is because *it* is difficult.

[1] See 'Morality' the text of a talk given in 1982 published in C. Marneau ed. *Pro Ecclesia et Pontifice* (London, 1982) and reprinted in M. Geach & L. Gormally eds *Faith in a Hard Ground: Essays on Religion, Philosophy and Ethics by GEM Anscombe* (Exeter: ImprintAcademic, 2008).

doi:10.1017/S135824612000003X

Like most philosophy students or academics, the writings of Anscombe that I first encountered were her most famous essay 'Modern Moral Philosophy'[2], her monograph *Intention*,[3] her Cambridge Inaugural lecture 'Causality and Determination',[4] and her Wolfson College lecture 'The First Person'.[5] Unlike most, however, I also read, at more or less the same time, 'Contraception and Chastity'[6] and 'Transubstantiation'[7], both originally published as pamphlets intended for a non-philosophical readership. It was evident in each of these six writings that the writer was quite distinctive, authorially 'present' in the texts, and of strong mind and opinion. Most commentary about Anscombe has focused on 'Modern Moral Philosophy' and *Intention*, and the last two items ('Contraception' and 'Transubstantiation') are among those writings which, if philosophers are aware of them at all, are treated as eccentric, both in the sense of lying away from the centre of her philosophical work and in being idiosyncratic. I think this is obviously wrong so far as the first is concerned for it is of a piece with her professional philosophical writing about action and ethics. 'Transubstantiation', however, is different but one may learn things from it about her philosophical attitude. I will return to this point later discussing it and another largely ignored essay 'Faith'.[8]

2. Anscombe's anticipations

As a philosopher Anscombe was perceptive, insightful, imaginative, bold, rigorous in argument, independently-minded often given to attacking prevailing orthodoxies as in the four overtly philosophical pieces cited above. She was also creative, turning insights into ideas

[2] 'Modern Moral Philosophy' *Philosophy*, 33 (124) 1958, reprinted in M. Geach & L. Gormally eds *Human Life, Action and Ethics: Essays by G.E.M. Anscombe* (Exeter: ImprintAcademic, 2006).

[3] *Intention* (Oxford: Blackwell, 1957)

[4] *Causality and Determination. An Inaugural Lecture* (Cambridge: University Press, 1971) reprinted in *Metaphysics and the Philosophy of Mind: Collected Philosophical Papers of GEM Anscombe* Vol. II (Oxford: Blackwell, 1981).

[5] 'The First Person' in *Metaphysics and the Philosophy of Mind* op.cit.

[6] *Contraception and Chastity* (London: Catholic Truth Society, 1975) reprinted in M. Geach & L. Gormally eds *Human Life, Action and Ethics* op. cit.

[7] *Transubstantiation* (London: Catholic Truth Society, 1974) reprinted in M. Geach & L. Gormally eds *Faith in a Hard Ground* op. cit.

[8] 'Faith' in *Faith in a Hard Ground* op. cit.

that have become part of common philosophical thinking as in the following examples:

1. That facts are more or less brute.[9]
2. That causes need not necessitate their effects.[10]
3. That actions are intentional under a description.[11]
4. That agents knowledge of their own intentional actions is non-observational.[12]
5. That moral theory requires moral psychology.[13]
6. That moral theories that do not distinguish morally between the intended and the foreseen, and between action and omission, are alike in being consequentialist.[14]
7. That many descriptive concepts, most relevantly those relating to natural functions, include or imply normative aspects.[15]

Her short 1986 statement of 'Twenty Opinions Common among Modern Anglo-American Philosophers'[16] which, as in an ecclesiastical anathema declaration, she states views which she thinks are to be *denied*, allows one to infer a number of other theses which she regarded as important, and which were at odds with modern philosophical orthodoxies. These concern philosophical anthropology and philosophy of mind, ethics and action, metaphysics and natural theology. I group them as follows blending Anscombe's own words with my gloss and occasional expansion upon them.

First, human beings are a species of animal belonging to a natural kind whose essence is human nature. There is no 'self' distinct from a living human individual and nor is human personhood a status involving characteristics that some human beings may fail to acquire or may come to lose. A human corpse is not a human being.

Second, ethical considerations may vary according to the biological nature of the rational beings involved; in particular human ethics, i.e. ethics relating to human conduct, is not independent of facts of human life, including physiological ones. In view of this, imaginary examples

9 'On Brute Facts' *Analysis*, 18 (3) 1958, pp. 69–72.

10 *Causality and Determination.*

11 *Intention* and 'Under a Description' *Noûs*, 13 (2) 1979), pp. 219–233.

12 *Intention.*

13 'Modern Moral Philosophy'.

14 'Modern Moral Philosophy'.

15 'Modern Moral Philosophy'.

16 'Twenty Opinions Common Among Modern Anglo-American Philosophers', in *Persona, veritá e morale. Atti del Congresso Internazionale di Teologia Morale* (Rome: Città Nuova Editrice, 1987) pp. 49–50, reprinted in M. Geach & L. Gormally eds. *Faith in a Hard Ground* op. cit.

involving physical impossibilities for human beings are not relevant to considering moral obligation. With regard to the latter there are absolute and exceptionless prohibitions. At the same time, not all sound practical moral reasoning implies as a conclusion the necessity of taking some course of action; and nor is it always necessary to act for the best; it may be enough that some good was chosen (including the good of avoiding a prohibited kind of action). The difference between action and omission is sometimes morally significant. Properly speaking statements of moral requirement relate to persons not states of affairs, thus we should say 'X ought to A' rather than 'it ought to be the case that X is doing A'. Again, on the personal subject of action, ethics includes virtue and vice which are objectively good and bad kinds of characteristics for a human being to have.

Third, freedom of the will is not compatible with causal determinism, but in any case causation does not entail determinism. Additionally, past and present are asymmetric in so far as the latter is wholly causally closed but the former is not (at least in part, since some effects may be necessitated in their causes, so that if there is no interference in the operation of these causes the future will include these). Laws of nature do not completely explain all that happens. God is not given to emotions, or otherwise subject to change, nor are God's actions based on opinions formed on evidence. Finally, God need not create the best of all possible worlds.

In considering these claims and the seven I listed initially, there are several differences, apart from the previously mentioned fact that the latter have become part of common philosophical thinking. First, the initial 'insights', as that term suggests, involve a penetrative vision discerning features or relationships that had gone unnoticed among her peers and preceding generations. By contrast her counters to views prevailing among her analytic contemporaries belong to the self-same category, namely that of theses, positions, and theories, and are recognizable as pre-existing alternative views – be they minority ones. Second, the insights are broad and have extensive implications, some within fields, notably ethical theory, others across philosophy as a whole. For example, the brute relativity of facts, and the non-necessitating character of efficient causality, may be invoked in epistemology, metaphysics, philosophy of mind and action, and logic. Whereas, the opinions tend to be subject-specific.

Let me illustrate this briefly with regard to the case of the notion of *brute facts* and more generally of *levels of description*. This pair of ideas was introduced in two publications in 1958: 'On Brute Facts' and 'Modern Moral Philosophy' though the former is largely an extract from the latter. Anscombe puts it to use in showing that, contrary to Hume, one may infer statements of requirement from statements of fact. Her example is that of it being true that 1) *she owes her grocer money* (requirement) because 2) *she asked for potatoes and he delivered them and sent her a bill* (facts). Her claim is that her owing the grocer money is itself a fact consisting of her request, his delivery and his submission of a bill, all in a given context, that of certain institutions (of exchange). The request, delivery and submission are brute facts relative to the fact that she owes him payment, and his carting 'a quarter' (28 lbs) of potatoes to her house is itself brute relative to the fact described by saying 'he supplied her with potatoes'.

Subsequently this idea got taken up by John Searle who coined the term 'institutional facts' in his 1964 paper 'How to derive "ought" from "is"'.[17] The extent of his indebtedness to Anscombe is apparent in the main argument of his essay but not in his brief passing reference to her in a footnote to the following sentence: 'We might characterize such facts as institutional facts, and contrast them with non-institutional, or brute, facts: that a man has a bit of paper with green ink on it is a brute fact, that he has five dollars is an institutional fact'. Because of the Searle paper, and because of Anscombe's prior use of the distinction in connection with a partial refutation of Hume's contention that 'ought' cannot be derived from 'is' (partial because she thought he was right in respect of what she termed the strongly deontological 'moral ought'), the idea of brute facts and brute relativity tends to be thought of simply in connection with the logic of requirement. I believe, however, that it has broader application, and like the qualifier 'under a description' is related to Aristotelian ideas. The first (relative bruteness) to that of hylomorphic constitution, the second (under a description) to the 'inasmuch as' or 'qua' construction or to what is predicated with qualification '*secundum quid*' which are variant forms of redulplicative propositions. Consider, then, what Anscombe says about brute facts. She writes:

> In relation to many descriptions of events or states of affairs which are asserted to hold, we can ask what the 'brute facts' were; and this will mean the facts which held, and in virtue of which, in a proper context, such and such a description is true or false, and which are more 'brute' than the alleged fact answering to that description.[18]

[17] John Searle, 'How to derive "ought" from "is"' *Philosophical Review* 73 (1) 1964, pp. 43–58. The reference runs as follows: 'For a discussion of this distinction see G. E. M. Anscombe, "Brute Facts", *Analysis* (1958).'.

[18] 'On Brute Facts' op. cit., 71.

Now compare this with what Aristotle says in the *Physics* about matter and form as causes:

> Since nature is twofold, form and also matter, we should get a theoretical grasp on it … so that we should get a theoretical grasp on natural things neither without their matter nor with regard to their matter [alone] … matter is relative to something, since there is one sort of matter for one form, and another for another … Something is said to be a cause if it is: [1] The component from which a thing comes to be – for example, the bronze of a statue or the silver of a bowl, and also the kinds of these. [2] The form or paradigm, that is, the account of the essence, and kinds. [19]

Anscombe makes no reference to Aristotle in speaking of 'brute relativity', though she does in relation to what may be termed 'description relativity', as represented by the phrase 'under a description'.[20] Yet I think her familiarity with the idea of material and formal causes and of hylomorphic constitution influenced the former. For one way of putting the point about brute facts and brute relativity is to say that the content of a fact-description D1 is brute relative to another D2, if D1 serves as the 'matter' for D2 re-formed by a structural context. So, for example being a quantity of bronze of such and such a shape is, in the context of representational conventions, being a statue, or put linguistically 'A is a piece of bronze of such and such a shape' is brute relative to 'A is a statue'. So here, as in the case of actions and debts, we get insight into a kind of internal relationship between levels which for Hume could only be contingent and forged not by anything on the side of reality but by psychological associations.

The third difference between the particular insights (1–7 above) and the general views ('twenty opinions') is that the first are hard worn discoveries arising in the course of sustained periods of intense thinking about particular problems and perplexities, while the opinions are more assemblages of the fruits of general reflection.

3. Anscombe's methods

This raises a question of whether there is also a contrast in the *methods* by which Anscombe arrived at the insights on the one hand and the contrary theses on the other. I think that in broad terms there is a difference in the *ways* that led her to the two, but that in itself does not

[19] Aristotle, *Physics* II, 2 & 3 translated C.D.C. Reeve (Indianapolis: Hackett, 2018) 23–4.

[20] 'Under a Description', op. cit. note 11, 219.

speak to the matter of *methods* in the sense of procedures or techniques. The difference would be this: the theses were arrived at through processes of reading and listening to philosophers, great ones from the past and significant ones from her own period, and discussing and debating, and synthesizing arguments and conclusions so as to come to more or less settled views. The insights, by contrast, came to her in the course of investigations prompted by questions of the form: 'how is it possible that such and such?'.

This last phrase will immediately suggest a Kantian approach, seeking sufficient and/or necessary conditions of some phenomenon or type of thought or experience; but I have something broader and more varied in mind. One kind of example of the questions that gave rise to her investigations would be 'how is it possible that people could think that it is permissible intentionally to kill the innocent?', a second is 'how is it possible that saying 'I promise' creates an obligation', a third, 'how is it possible that one can resign from a club and so be free of its rules and authority but not resign from being governed by the state?', fourth, 'how is it possible that someone could think that one can only know what is necessary?', fifth, 'how is it possible that we know we see objects rather than just surfaces, or just appearances of objects or surfaces?', a sixth, 'how is it possible to know what to do or not to do without having some kind of ethical theory be it an implicit one?', a seventh 'how is it possible that some philosophers have been convinced that they are immaterial beings while doubting that there is a world of material objects?', an eighth 'how is it possible that some philosophers have been convinced that thought is a brain process while also thinking about non-material realities' and an ninth 'how is it possible that some philosophers can say there is no such thing as language or think that there are no such things as thoughts?'

In the *Theaetetus* Plato has Socrates say 'the feeling of wonder shows that you are a philosopher, since wonder is the only beginning of philosophy'.[21] The wonder in question is related to astonishment but also to puzzlement or else no enquiry would ensue. Characteristically Aristotle is clearer if more prosaic when he writes in the *Metaphysics*, no doubt with the *Theaetetus* passage in mind, that 'It is through wonder that men now begin and originally began to philosophize; wondering in the first place at obvious perplexities, and then by gradual progression raising questions about the greater matters too'.[22]

21 155d.
22 982b12.

Anscombe may well have been struck in reading these passages while studying Greats (Classics and Philosophy) at Oxford for she recalls that while still at school she struggled to justify some 'principle of causality' and 'went around asking people *why*, if something happened, they would be sure it had a cause', and of the period of her early university studies she recounts 'For years I would spend time, in cafes, for example, staring at objects saying to myself: 'I see a packet [of cigarettes]. But what do I really see? How can I say that I see here anything more than a yellow expanse?'.[23] This capacity to be struck by questions and to persist in trying to understand what gave rise to them and how they might be answered, thinking hard and in an undistracted way about these things remained with her and is evident in all her writing.

It also explains her seriousness and with that her preference to engage with great philosophers of the past who were similarly struck by simply stated but profound questions, rather than to engage, as most philosophers now do, with research agendas set by their contemporary peers and pursued in increasing numbers of monographs and articles. At the time when Anscombe began publishing in 1950s it was more common to have few if any footnotes, but by the time she stopped publishing in the 1990s the situation had been completely transformed yet she continued to refer mainly to ancient, medieval and modern writers (generally in her own translations were these were required) making few references to her contemporaries and then for the most part only to leading ones such as Davidson, Kripke, and Quine.

4. Philosophical demeanour

Mary Geach, who is herself a philosopher and Anscombe's literary executor, recalls her mother defining philosophy for the purpose of a Cambridge undergraduate prospectus as 'thinking about the most difficult and ultimate questions'. She then goes on to say 'Some people might want to qualify the word "thinking" as it occurs in this definition, but Anscombe did not go in for a special, different kind of thinking'.[24] This suggests that Anscombe did not believe in or at any rate did not herself make use of a philosophical

[23] Introduction to G.E.M. Anscombe, *Metaphysics and the Philosophy of Mind* p. vii.

[24] Introduction to M. Geach & L. Gormally eds. *Human Life, Action and Ethics* p. xiii.

methodology, but while that may be true in a narrow sense of methodology there is no doubt that her philosophical writings differ from those intended for a general audience in ways that encourage the question are the differences just ones of subject matter or degree of rigour, or is there also something different in *method*?

As it happens there has been some recent discussion of Anscombe's philosophical style, not in the sense of literary manner, though she certainly has one, but of what the authors of these discussions themselves term her 'method': first, by a distinguished former student Cora Diamond in 'Reading the *Tractatus* with GEM Anscombe', part 3 of which is titled 'Anscombe and Philosophical Method'[25], and second, by Ulf Hlobil and Katharina Nieswandt in 'On Anscombe's Philosophical Method'.[26] According to Diamond, in Anscombe's examination of the *Tractatus*

> She lays out, makes open to view, a way of using words, ... she is attempting to put before the reader with the 'extreme intelligibility' with which the account can (she thinks) be presented, what it is to say that something is so [in the case of the *Tractatus*] on analogy with using a picture to say that *this* is so, a picture capable of being used also to say that *this* isn't so. ... She herself is presenting a use of language, the picture-proposition use, which will not make it look like a queer sort of fact that every proposition is either true or false.[27]

According to Hlobil and Nieswandt, meanwhile, a commonly found method when writing on her own account follows a four-stage path:

> First, asking what is x? or 'what does 'X' mean? and with that setting out some answer or answers which purports to be non-circular.
>
> Second, showing that there can be no straightforward answer in the form of a translation or analysis or definition answering the question what x is or what does 'x' mean? but offering something nonetheless explanatory, or explicatory.
>
> Third, identifying practices, typically linguistic' ones in which x features critically,.

[25] Cora Diamond 'Reading the *Tractatus* with GEM Anscombe' in Diamond, *Reading Wittgenstein with Anscombe, Going On to Ethics* (Cambridge, MA.: 2019) Ch. 3.

[26] In J. Haldane ed. *The Philosophy of Elizabeth Anscombe* (Exeter: Imprint Academic, 2019).

[27] Op. cit p. 116.

Fourth, showing how the foregoing description makes sense of x by showing its role in relation to it.

There is something recognizable in both of these accounts though that may be because of their familiarity as philosophical methods more generally. One might think, especially with regard to what Hlobil and Nieswandt write, that the first and second stages are basically Socratic, and the first certainly so in the sense in which analytic philosophy in its heyday saw itself as engaged 'Socratic' definition, and the second then contra-analytic in the manner of Quine in 'Two Dogmas of Empiricism'. Meanwhile, the third and fourth are recognizably late Wittgensteinian. Given Anscombe's education and later formation as a student of Wittgenstein's this is hardly surprising. But I want to introduce two further features the first of which may serve to explain what is surely obvious about much of her writing, namely its great difficulty and which is related to another feature, which I think is important, which I will call her philosophical *demeanour*.

Rush Rhees, who together with Anscombe and Von Wright served as Wittgenstein's first literary executors, gave a report of the master's advice: 'Wittgenstein used to say to me, "Go the bloody *hard* way"'. adding 'I remember this more often, perhaps, than any other single remark of his.'[28] Of course going the bloody hard way oneself is compatible with clearing and preparing the way so that it is signposted and made even, thereby becoming an easier route for those who follow. But Wittgenstein and Anscombe do not do that. Sometimes it is only when we have been led to a dead end and a new start is begun that we realise we were being led along the wrong track. This is not true of 'Modern Moral Philosophy' but that is indicative of its atypicality in her *oeuvre* (a fact rarely referred to) because in it she was setting out for a mixed faculty and student audience, views borne of recent concentrated reading of modern moral philosophy (from Kant to Sidgwick) for the purposes of tutoring undergraduates in it at her college (Somerville). Those views represented her assessment of where the subject had gone wrong and of what cultural shift might lie behind that. The latter aspect incidentally touches on a significant interest on her part in cultural mindsets – *weltanschauungen* (to which she also refers in 'Causality and Determination').[29]

[28] Rush Rhees, 'The Study of Philosophy' in *Without Answers* (London: Routledge, 1969) 169.

[29] She writes 'The truth of this conception [that causation is some kine of necessary connection] is hardly debated. It is, indeed, a bit of *Weltanschauung*: it helps to form a cast of mind which is characteristic of our whole culture'. Op. cit. note 4, 2.

Certainly, misdirection is also a Socratic or Platonic method and she not only read dialogues of Plato, Anselm, Berkeley and Hume with appreciation, she also wrote some of her own. *Intention* itself is hard to read in part because it is neither linear nor paved nor punctuated with clear views back or forward, We remain in rough and often obscure terrain. One explanation might be the desire to show the workings, another is that this is just a reflection of her own mode of thought. Both could be true but I think there is also something else in that, like Wittgenstein, she wants the reader to know the way is hard or at the least not to conceal the fact; and for them, which is to say for *us*, to go that way too. This is why, as in the later Wittgenstein, there is an element of many voicednesss in the text. *Intention* is markedly Wittgensteinean in method and to a degree in its format and mannerisms which explains why its mode may have seemed familiar to her, unfamiliar to most of her contemporaries, and simply perplexing to later readers. Commentators have observed the similarity in style of some of Anscombe's writings to those of Wittgenstein as represented by the *Philosophical Investigations* or *On Certainty*, but those who say this are invariable referring to the English editions, perhaps forgetting that Anscombe produced those translations. I am not suggesting that she substituted her voice for that of Wittgenstein but only that as translators are generally aware the expressive rendering of works tends to involve author and translator as co-producers of the resulting text.

Anscombe was not unwitting in matters of style. She can be very creative in formulating examples or introducing imagery. Also, there is a typescript of an earlier version of material for *Intention* with accompanying comments by Philippa Foot where Anscombe's text is more linear, plain and easily followed perhaps because she had still to recognize difficulties. More likely, however, is that having smoothed things out to her own partial satisfaction she then thought it better to reintroduce or re-expose the bumps, blocks and fissures. There is also perhaps a kind of vanity or pride in being an immediate disciple of one whom she believed (rightly) to be a misunderstood genius, whose profundity of method contrasted with (as she saw it) the superficial facility of theoretical lexicographers such as J.L. Austin whom she hated with a vengeance.

In further though brief characterisation of her demeanour, and in contrast to the preceding, I want to mention a feature that I have not seen discussed though something of the sort has been noted in relation to Wittgenstein, which is a similarity of vision, both in the *way* of seeing things and in the *what* of it, to that of G.K. Chesterton. As with Aurel Kolnai another moral philosopher-convert to Catholicism, with whom she shared many substantive moral opinions, Anscombe's embrace of Catholicism was influenced in part by reading Chesterton. For reasons of space I will not quote a series of parallel passages, and I only pick out the idea that nothing is really hidden, that the facts lie before our eyes but that either because they are so familiar or because we are in the grip of an idea or a spirit that distorts our sight. Here then is Chesterton followed by Wittgenstein's reflections on, or expressions of that idea from *Philosophical Investigations* (129).

> In order to strike, in the only sane or possible sense, the note of impartiality, it is necessary to touch the nerve of novelty. That I may remark in passing is why children have very little difficulty about the dogmas of the Church. I mean that we see things fairly when we them first. ... when its fundamentals are doubted, as at present, we must try to recover the candour and wonder of the child; the unspoilt realism and objectivity of innocence. Or if we cannot do that, we must try at least to shake off the cloud of mere custom and see the thing as new, if only by seeing it as unnatural. Things that may well be familiar so long as familiarity breeds affection had much better become unfamiliar when familiarity breeds contempt. For in connection with things so great as are here considered, whatever our view of them, contempt must be a mistake.[30]

> 126. Philosophy simply puts everything before us, and neither explains nor deduces anything.—Since everything lies open to view there is nothing to explain. For what is hidden, for example, is of no interest to us. One might also give the name "philosophy" to what is possible before all new discoveries and inventions.
>
> ...
>
> 129. The aspects of things that are most important for us are hidden because of their simplicity and familiarity. (One is unable to notice something—because it is always before one's eyes.) The real foundations of his enquiry do not strike a man at all. Unless that fact has at some time struck him.— And this means: we fail to be struck by what, once seen, is most striking and most powerful.[31]

[30] G.K. Chesterton, *The Everlasting Man* in *Collected Works of G.K. Chesterton* Vol. II (San Francisco: Ignatius Press, 1986) 147–8.

[31] Wittgenstein, *Philosophical Investigations* trans. GEM Anscombe (Oxford: Blackwell, 2001).

5. Knowledge and faith

So much for the matter of philosophical method considered in the abstract. I want next to consider two examples of Anscombe's approach: the first relating to the treatment of a familiar philosophical issue: the nature of knowledge, the second to religious or theological ones: faith and transubstantiation. The first cites and then extends her investigation of when it is appropriate to speak of knowledge and of what in the context and background may make sense of this, not from the point of view of traditional 'epistemology' given that the latter is usually associated with a general study of the status of perceptual and doxastic items with regard to conditions of veridicality and justification. Of course, Anscombe was concerned with whether certain beliefs are true and whether they are justified, and with the more specific issue of what the objects of perception may be and the kind of knowledge it may deliver, but it is important to be clear at the outset that as an heir to, and ongoing participant in the Wittgensteinian revolution against Cartesianism in metaphysics and philosophical psychology, she was not concerned with any general task of defining or justifying knowledge, be it perceptual or conceptual.

One reason for the eschewal of definition is that what is called 'knowledge' may be quite different, not just as between knowing *how* and knowing *that* and knowing *of*, but even within uses of these expressions. Famously for example the issue of knowledge without observation discussed in *Intention* requires us to distinguish between what would normally be involved in me knowing that *I* moved my hand when that was intentional on my part, and me knowing that *you* moved my hand, to which we can add as another kind of knowledge, me knowing that you moved *your* hand or indeed my hand *intentionally*.

Here there is a difference between non-observational and observational knowledge, but also between first-person and second-person knowledge of intentional action, as distinguished say from knowledge of another's heartbeat inferred from taking their pulse. So non-inferential knowledge of intentional action isn't the same as non-observational knowledge of such action, though the latter is an instance of it. We might also note differences that seem to cut across the knowing *how*, knowing *that*, knowing *of* distinction as in knowing *where* one is and, what is something different again, knowing *when* one is. The former issue is touched on by Anscombe in an examination, published posthumously, of

'Grounds of Belief'.[32] I do not know whether she discussed the latter though she does have investigations of temporal relations, and of the reality of the past, and of knowledge of it by memory and by testimony, and the last source (testimony) which is relevant to what she says about cases of knowing *where* one is, may also be applied to instances of knowing *when* one is, where the knowledge is not that expressed, if any is so expressed, exclusively by token reflexives such as 'here' and 'now' or 'not there' and 'not then'.

Consider the following exchange:

A. 'Do you know where you are?'

B. 'Yes',

A. 'Where are you then?'

B. 'Here'

A. 'Do you know where here is?

B. 'No'.

There is a difference between knowing what time it is and knowing what century it is, or what era it is, or if it is an era, and again between knowing that one is standing in a building and knowing that one is standing in Bloomsbury or in London or in Europe. It is not just that there is a difference in *expectation* with regard to someone's knowledge of when and where they are, it is that there are differences in what explain these differences. Not knowing the time is common enough, not knowing the century, where this is not because one has oddly forgotten, or is mentally confused, or lives in a culture where that measure doesn't occur, should strike us as odd. Consider another exchange:

A. 'What century is it?'

B. 'I don't know'

A. 'Have you forgotten?'

B. 'No. I have never known'.

One might direct someone ignorant of when it is, to look at the clock but what would one refer them to as evidence of what century it is. There are documents and perhaps 'devices' that report this but it is

[32] 'Grounds of Belief' in M. Geach & L. Gormally eds. *Logic, Truth and Meaning: Writings by G.E.M. Anscombe* (Exeter: ImprintAcdemic, 2015).

not ordinarily by reference to consulting these that one knows the present century as it is by looking at watches and clocks and mobile phones that one knows the time, the day and the date. Also, while someone might be proud of their ability to tell what time it is just by looking at the sky no-one could boast of a comparable skill for telling the day of the week, the date or the century.

No doubt hour, date, century, and era are conventional metrics but there are also significant differences between them. Era is related to time but also to the presence of a physical (in a broad sense) or cultural characteristic enduring through a temporal period, and this seems different from century which again seems different from hour. Of these, century looks to be more independent from a non-temporal feature than does era but some uses relax the temporal boundaries to encompass characteristics, as in 'the long nineteenth century' (1789–1914) or 'a century of progress'. And while in determining temporal location one might look for evidence in each case: hour, century, era, it does not look like *experience* is involved in the usual understanding of this which does apply in the case of knowing that one is in a building. I can see that in a way that even with a watch I do not see the time. On the other hand knowing that I am in Bloomsbury does not seem just to be a matter of observation, even less knowing I am in Europe or in the Western hemisphere.

Certainly, if at a given time I know I am in a particular named street then given collateral knowledge I also know I am in Bloomsbury, and thereby I currently know I am in London, but any of these could alter without me changing spatial location and without immediately observable consequences, for example, the street name could be changed without me knowing so, and what was designated 'Bloomsbury' might be renamed 'East Tottenham' and London restyled 'Central Capital Territory'. Of course, I might infer these facts *from* observation of other things but where they are not inferred nor would I say they are observed. Rather they are matters of common framework knowledge relying on testimony usually communicated implicitly. Thinking back to the earlier issue, if Anscombe is right then I know non-observationally through exercising my agency that I have a body but my knowledge that I am a human being does not, pace Michael Thompson, seem to be non-observational in that sense,[33] but nor does it seem to be observational either. Consider a third exchange:

[33] See Michael Thompson 'Apprehending Human Form' in A. O'Hear ed. *Modern Moral Philosophy* (Cambridge: Cambridge University Press, 2010).

A. 'How do you know you are human?'

B. 'One day I looked and saw that I was'

A. What was it that you saw?'.

B. 'Maybe it wasn't something I *saw*, I think it just a feeling I had'.

6. Traditional epistemology

I embarked on this short reflection having said that one reason Anscombe was not interested in traditional epistemology is that she did not subscribe to the idea that there might be an essence or definition of knowledge in general, and the examples I have given illustrate the diversity of things called knowledge which are different not just in the way of instances of the same phenomenon, but are themselves different sorts of things. Practical competence, propositional knowledge, and acquaintance (where knowing *a* is not equivalent to knowing *that a is f*) are not just defined over different classes of objects or by reference to different kinds of warrant.

Additionally, there is an issue in seeing how even propositional knowledge could be defined in terms of *true belief + warrant*, or *cause*, since belief is a term indicating a quasi- disposition while knowledge is an ability. I say 'quasi-disposition' because as Anscombe points out while 'belief' is a grammatically dispositional concept it is not a real disposition. Her understanding of the latter notion is related to her metaphysics. She writes:

> What I call a real disposition ... is a property D such that to say an object has D is to say that it is such as to do such-and-such under such and such conditions. The only saving clause we have to put in here is 'saving external interference'. By this criterion neither 'knowledge' nor 'belief' signify real dispositions[34]

Certainly, someone who believes something or someone need not tend to a specifiable end as in the manner of a disposition. One may believe that p without ever saying it or anything you take to be implied by it, or even thinking it or as Anscombe puts it 'without the thought [that p] ever coming into one's consciousness'.[35] At the same time the *criteria*, by which I mean something logically different

[34] 'Belief and Thought' in *Logic, Truth and Meaning*, op. cit., 151.
[35] Op. cit.

from evidence, for ascribing belief is connected to sincerely thinking or saying. If we use the more general notion of *doing something* which will cover thinking and saying and exercising non-cognitive capacities then the same is true of ascriptions of knowledge. But that does not show that knowledge is the same kind of thing as belief for as I said, someone who has knowledge has a recognitional capacity for identification or an effective power to do or to make something. As one might say, he or she has an ability to achieve or attain something factive, active or practive. Belief may have truth as its goal but that does not show that someone who has a belief that p tends to the truth that p, or that if p is true and he believes it that this is an achievement or attainment.

As well as not being interested in the *definition* of knowledge, on account of holding a view akin to the Aristotelian dictum that existence is said to be in many ways, she is not interested in the question of the general *foundations* of knowledge because there aren't any, certainly not in the sense that other philosophers have tried to build knowledge out of sense-experience, or on the basis of principles of reason, or innate ideas. As she puts it in one place, 'asked what was given, a present-day English speaking philosopher would be likely to say 'the lot'. We start mediis in rebus; our philosophical activity is one of describing and clarifying this milieu to ourselves'.[36] With regard to the question of the nature of mental reference Anscombe is similarly pluralistic and anti-essentialist. She could not have been forgetful of the question posed by Wittgenstein in the *Investigations* when he asks 'What makes my thought of him my thought of him?' but also mindful that his other simple question 'what is left over if I subtract the fact that my arm goes up from the fact that I raise my arm?' it is both pointing to an issue and looking toward mistaken assumptions about the nature of thought and action. Philosophers, including Aristotle, Augustine, Aquinas, Descartes, Locke and the Wittgenstein of the *Tractatus* have taken these questions seriously in a way that the later Wittgenstein and Anscombe believe is misguided and troublesome. To put it briefly the former group have looked for something like a mechanism, or a causal structure or a metaphysical process that would establish isomorphism, or noetic outreach or causal dependency that could explain intentionality but it does not need and cannot have an explanation from outwith or below. Each of these candidates runs into trouble as regressive or open to counter example or illusory in the sense of a magic trick giving an appearance of something happening because for example

[36] 'Necessity and Truth' in in *From Parmenides to Wittgenstein: Collected Philosophical Papers* Vol I (Oxford: Blackwell. 1981), 84.

we confuse the absence of presence with the presence of absence, such as not observing an agent doing or saying things on an occasion when we might attribute a thought to him and concluding that thought is an essentially private phenomenon of a kind quite unlike saying or doing.

7. Religion and philosophy

Next I turn to the second and contrasting example of Anscombe's approach. As well as being a broadly analytic academic philosopher in the mold of Wittgenstein, Anscombe was also an intellectually committed Roman Catholic, knowledgeable about Hebrew and New Testament Scripture and the major writings of Augustine, Anselm and Aquinas. She wrote on matters of faith, doctrines and morals from a markedly traditional and orthodox perspective and in opposition to what she regarded as the modernist, revisionist, and accomodationist tendencies of twentieth century figures about which, and whom, she could be scornful.

Given the depth and extent of her religious commitments, her great gifts for philosophy which allowed her to make significant and lasting contributions in metaphysics, moral philosophy, philosophy of mind and action, and the history of philosophy, and the pervasive atheism and agnosticism among her Oxford and Cambridge colleagues, it may seem surprising that she did not publicly advance or defend the cause of theism with any of them.[37] Similarly, there is no mention in any of her writings of William Alston, John Hick, Basil Mitchell, Dewi Phillips, Alvin Plantinga, William Rowe, Richard Swinburne or any other philosopher of religion writing during the period of her professional career. This is not to say, however, that philosophical discussion of religion is entirely absent from the writings published during her lifetime, but significantly nor is there much of it, and what there is hardly conforms to the sort of thing usually referred to as 'philosophy of religion'. I will say why I think this is so but first consider what she actually gathered under that heading.

[37] She did engage with the question of the rationality of religious belief and the case for theism privately with Anthony Kenny and Philippa Foot but failed to persuade either of the truth of theism or a fortiori of that of Catholic Christianity. Anthony Kenny recalls that 'From time to time Elizabeth would lament to me that she felt quite unable to offer Philippa a proof of the existence of God'; see Kenny, 'Anscombe in Oxford' in Haldane ed. *The Life and Philosophy of Elizabeth Anscombe* (Imprint), 2019.

The third volume of her *Collected Philosophical Papers*, selected by Anscombe and published in 1981 while she still held the Chair of Philosophy at Cambridge, is *Ethics, Religion and Politics*. It is divided into three parts headed *Ethics*, *Philosophy of Religion* and *Political Philosophy*, the part first containing ten papers and the second and third two each. In the Introduction to the book Anscombe writes as follows:

> Some of the papers in this volume … were written for the general public, for ordinary philosophical meetings or for philosophical journals. Others … were composed to express an explicitly Catholic view; indeed they were mostly written for meetings of Catholics or were addressed to a Catholic readership.
>
> [then later she explains]
>
> In general my interest in moral philosophy has been more in particular moral questions than in what is now called 'meta ethics' (The analogous thing is *unrestrictedly* true about philosophy of religion, as may be seen from papers 11 and 12 in this collection) [*my emphasis*].[38]

The two papers in question are 'On Transubstantiation' and 'Faith'. The first was written as a London *Catholic Truth Society* pamphlet intended for a general, non-academic readership and appears barely philosophical at all, certainly not a philosophical paper. It begins 'It is easiest to tell what transubstantiation is by saying this: little children should be taught about it as early as possible. Not of course using the word 'transubstantiation', because it is not a little child's word'. Note that specifying the 'what' is set within the context of acting; it is a partly ostensive and partly pragmatic definition. She then continues by talking about the Mass and the consecration of the bread and wine, and proceeds in an advisory tone as if to parents or perhaps infant school teachers suggesting how they might explain the idea of religious sacrifice. Much of what follows is expository but now addressed to adults directly, expounding religious understandings of the nature and purpose of Christ's sacrifice.

The only part of the essay that tilts in the direction of familiar academic philosophy is a short discussion of whether the very idea that the bread and wine become the body and blood of Christ is unintelligible or incoherent. This begins:

[38] *Ethics, Religion and Politics: Collected Philosophical Papers* Vol III (Oxford: Blackwell, 1981) 'Introduction' vii-viii.

> But the thing is impossible, contradictory: it cannot be believed! It has to only a figure of speech!". Well, indeed it cannot really be understood how it is possible. But if it is claimed it is impossible, then a definite contradiction must be pointed to, and if you believe in it, you will believe that each claim to disprove it is as contradictory can be answered. [39]

She then considers a putative line of refutation: how can a man be wholly in the small space defined by a host? Agreeing he cannot be present *dimensively* she suggests there are other ways for a body to be in a place writing of this very and perhaps uniquely special case 'when we consider *That* which the bread has become, the place where we are looking has become (though not dimensively) the place where *it* is: a place in heaven'. A little later she writes

> … we can reflect that [the Eucharist] is his [the Lord's] way of being present with us in his physical reality until the end of this age; until he comes again to be dimensively and visibly present [and in a footnote she adds]
>
> Theologians have not been accustomed to say that our Lord is 'physically' present in the Eucharist. I think this is because to them 'physically' means 'naturally' as the word comes to be from the Greek for nature [*physis*] and of course our Lord is not present in a natural manner! But to a modern man to deny that he is physically present is to deny the doctrine of the Catholic Church.[40]

I suppose that by 'physically' she means in a real and substantial way, in contrast on the one hand to being 'symbolically present' and on the other to being 'immaterially present', whatever either of these might mean. In other contexts one would expect Anscombe to bite hard into these terms and distinctions to test which might be real and which illusory or otherwise confused. That she does not do so here and barely clarifies things is a further indication that this is not a philosophical essay or at least not as would generally be recognized. The brevity, conversational style and instructional intent of her discussion contrasts markedly with writings on the same topic by Michael Dummett, another Roman Catholic and Oxford philosopher also influenced by reading Wittgenstein and by studying with and becoming a professional colleague of Anscombe herself.

[39] *Collected Papers III* 108; *Faith in a Hard Ground* 86.
[40] *Collected Papers III* 109; *Faith in a Hard Ground* 87.

Dummett's writings on religion, like Anscombe's, are generally on particular religious questions and addressed to a religious readership rather than philosophical ones prompted by religious concepts and claims. In the case of transubstantiation, however, he wrote two long and in large part philosophical essays. The first is titled 'Transubstantiation' and remains unpublished[41]; the second 'The intelligibility of Eucharistic Doctrine' appeared in 1987 in a festschrift for Basil Mitchell who had retired from the Oxford *Nolluth Chair in the Philosophy of the Christian Religion* three years previously to be succeeded by Richard Swinburne.[42] In neither paper does Dummett refer to Anscombe's essay. This may seem surprising given that he must have known of it but I suspect he regarded it as catechetical rather than investigative and having nothing to offer in resolving the theoretical problems that he was concerned with. Indeed any philosopher learning that Anscombe had written on the subject and that she had gathered that writing in a volume of *Collected Philosophical Papers* in a section head 'Philosophy of Religion' is likely to be disappointed qua philosopher.

Second, although her essay is not a philosophical one it does show the influence of two figures who deeply influenced her approach to philosophy and to religious subjects: Aquinas and again Wittgenstein. Note to begin with the resemblance of her response to the claim that the doctrine of the real presence is impossible and contradictory, viz. that while the doctrine cannot be understood it can be defended by showing there is no contradiction, and what Aquinas writes in Question 1, article 8 of the *Summa Theologiae* 'Whether Sacred Doctrine is a matter of Argument':

> ...If our opponent believes nothing of divine revelation, there is no longer any means of proving the articles of faith by reasoning, but only of answering his objections – if he has any – against faith. Since faith rests upon infallible truth, and since the contrary of a truth can never be demonstrated, it is clear that the arguments

[41] I am completing the editing of a volume of essays by Dummett (many previously unpublished) titled *Society, Ethics and Religion*, 'Transubstantiation' will be included in that.

[42] Michael Dummett, 'The Intelligibility of Eucharistic Doctrine', in William J. Abraham and Steven W. Holzer eds *The Rationality of Religious Belief: Essays in Honour of Basil Mitchell* (Oxford: Clarendon Press, 1987).

> brought against faith cannot be demonstrations, but are difficulties that can be answered.[43]

Next, note the resemblance between what she has to say in seeking to defuse the charge of contradiction and what Aquinas writes in the *Summa Theologiae* discussing 'Whether the body of Christ be in this sacrament in very truth, or merely as in a figure or sign?'

> First, Anscombe: [How can a body be wholly in this small space] Well, indeed not by the coincidence of his dimensions with the hole in space defined by the dimensions of the remaining appearance of bread: let us call this the 'dimensive' way of being in a place. ... [We believe that something is true of *That* which is there, which contradicts it being there dimensively. And certainly the division and separation from one another of all these places where *That* is, does not mean a separation of *it* from itself].[44]

> Second, Aquinas: Christ's body is not in this sacrament in the same way as a body is in a place, which by its dimensions is commensurate with the place; but in a special manner which is proper to this sacrament. Hence we say that Christ's body is upon many altars, not as in different places, but 'sacramentally'[45]

As regards the Wittgensteinian influence, this appears at the very outset. In the passage from the opening part of the *Philosophical Investigations* which I pair here with the opening of Anscombe's essay, Wittgenstein is describing a more primitive stage of inducting a child into a language game but the logic is the same as that which Anscombe employs. Remember also that the translation of Wittgenstein is Anscombe's.

> Anscombe: It is easiest to tell what transubstantiation is by saying this: little children should be taught about it as early as possible ... the thing can be taught and it is best taught at mass at the consecration ... Such a child can be taught then by whispering to it such things as: 'Look! Look what the priest is doing ... He is saying the words that change the bread into Jesus's body ... If the person who takes a young child to mass always does this

43 *Summa Theologiae, Second and Revised Edition* [hereafter *ST*] translated by Fathers of the English Dominican Province ((London: Burns, Oates, and Washbourne,1920) Ia, q1. a8, response.

44 *Collected Papers III* 108–9; *Faith in a Hard Ground* 86.

45 *ST* III, q75, a1, ad 3.

> (not otherwise troubling it) the child thereby learns a great deal'.[46]

> Wittgenstein: An important part of the training will consist in the teacher's pointing to the objects, directing the child's attention to them, and at the same time uttering a word … But if this is the effect of the ostensive teaching, am I to say that it effects an understanding of the word? … No doubt it was the ostensive teaching that helped to bring this about; but only together with a particular kind of instruction. With different instruction the same ostensive teaching of these words would have effected a quite different understanding … I shall also call the whole, consisting of language and the activities into which it is woven, a 'language-game'.[47]

8. On Faith

The second of the collected papers: 'On Faith' was given as an annual lecture at St Mary's College Oscott which then as now was a seminary for the training of Catholic priests, and her audience would have been seminarians, plus the Rector, Vice Rector, Spiritual Director and other teaching staff. Again, therefore, she was addressing co-religionists but ones who could be presumed to have a greater or lesser degree of academic formation in philosophy and theology. The Second Vatican Council had ended a decade before, but already there had been a move away from the kind of neo-scholastic training that had become dominant in the wake of Leo XIII's encyclical *Aeterni Patris* 'On the Restoration of Christian Philosophy' which commended scholastic philosophy and especially that of Aquinas. The manual form in which this had been presented was more dogmatic and purportedly deductive than discursive and some of those present would have recognised if not appreciated the target of some of her criticisms. Having rejected certain tendencies associated with the phrase 'We used to believe' Anscombe continues

> Now there was a 'We used to believe …' which I think could have been said with some truth and where the implied rejection wasn't a disaster. There was in the preceding time a professed enthusiasm for rationality, perhaps inspired by the teachings of

[46] *Collected Papers III* 107; *Faith in a Hard Ground* 86.
[47] L. Wittgenstein, *Philosophical Investigations* I, 5–7.

> Vatican I against fideism, certainly carried along by the promotion of neo-thomist studies. To the educated laity and the clergy trained in those days, the word was that the Catholic Christian faith was *rational*, and a problem, to those able to feel it as a problem, was how it was *gratuitous* – a special gift of grace. Why would one essentially need the promptings of grace to follow a chain of reasoning? … … But there was a greater problem. What about the 'faith of the simple'? They could not know all these things. Did they then have some inferior brand of faith? Surely not! And anyway, did those who studied really think they knew all these things? No: but the implication was that the knowledge was there somehow … In the belief that this was so, one was being rational in having faith[48]

What follows is an interesting exploration of the idea of faith not as propositional belief but as *believing someone*, and of this faith in him or her as having as logical presuppositions certain assumptions or convictions. Divine faith, at least in the Judaeo-Christian conception with which she is concerned, is believing God which is made possible by the transmission of faith and of what it presupposes by way of beliefs about God. Faith is not on this account created by transmission, it is a gift not from previous generations but from God, but it may be transmitted via them (and though she does not say so that may be the normal, and 'appointed' means of receiving this divine gift.) This involves the recipient assuming authority on the part of some others, for believing *someone* in the relevant sense is not just to believe what he says, or even to believe it in consequence of his saying it, but to believe it because he says it, taking his saying it to be an assurance of its truth. She continues:

> And now we come to the difficulty. In all the other [non-religious] cases we have been considering, it can be made clear what it is for someone to believe someone but what can it mean 'to believe God'? Could a learned clever man inform me on the authority of his learning, that the evidence is that God has spoken? No. The only possible use of a learned man is as a *causa removens prohibens*. There are gross obstacles in the received opinion of my time and in its characteristic ways of thinking, and someone learned and clever may be able to dissolve these.[49]

48 *Collected Papers III* 113; *Faith in a Hard Ground* 11.
49 'Faith' p.

Anscombe's conclusion is that Divine faith – believing God – is believing that something '– it may be a voice, it may be something he has been taught – comes as a word from God. Faith is then the belief he accords that word'.[50] Again a few comments are in order. First, one can see again, now in the scholastic phrase *causa removens prohibens* – removing an obstacle that impedes the cause of an action or process – the idea that the role of philosophy in relation to religious claims, and specifically those of Christian doctrine, may not be to establish their natural intelligibility let alone to prove them, but only to remove seeming intellectual blocks to the reception of those teachings. On this account philosophy's role is as handmaiden to sacred doctrine, as again Aquinas states:

> The reasons which are brought forward in support of the authority of faith, are not demonstrations which can bring intellectual vision to the human intellect, wherefore they [the objects of faith] do not cease to be unseen. But they remove obstacles to faith, by showing that what faith proposes is not impossible.[51]

In both 'Transubstantiation' and 'Faith' we can see very clearly the influence of Aquinas and Wittgenstein. What is taken from each is rather different in kind, however. First, Anscombe more or less quotes Thomas (and the point about not seeking to prove a point of doctrine but only to counter allegations of contradiction is also a recurrent theme in Peter Geach's writings on religion whose indebtedness to Aquinas he oft acknowledged). What she takes from Thomas in the case of transubstantiation is something she repeats as part of her own answer. Here then I think we might say that his influence is that of a teacher of substance. In the case of Wittgenstein it is different. What she derives is first a conception of the task of philosophy in general, as conceptual clarification. Elsewhere she writes:

> we want to get clear about the concepts we habitually use before we trust ourselves as philosophers to use them for purposes beyond our immediate ken. So we accept common views or remain in views not arrived at by philosophy while we work at concepts ... the logical features of concepts which we want to describe are such as to make us need tools of philosophical description not always unlike those used by a medieval philosopher.[52]

50 Op. cit.
51 *ST* II, IIae, q2, a10, ad 2.
52 'Necessity and Truth' in *From Parmenides to Wittgenstein: Collected Philosophical Papers* 84.

The example she was concerned with is distinguishing necessity *de re* and *de dicto*, but there is something of deeper and more extensive significance which she almost always refers to Wittgenstein, which is studying the 'grammar of concepts' and which is related to the Aristotelian classification and logic of categorical predications, and that in turn to the logic of specifications of natures and of what belong to them. The latter crops up in various places, as for example in 'Modern Moral Philosophy' when she writes

> Just a man has so many teeth, which is certainly not the average number of teeth men have, but is the number of teeth for the species, so perhaps the species *man* regarded not just biologically but from the point of view of the activity of thought and choice in regard to the various departments of life – powers, and faculties and use of things needed – 'has' such and such virtues and this man with the complete set of virtues is the 'norm' as 'man' with, e.g. a complete set of teeth is a norm.[53]

Again in her essay 'Human Essence' she writes:

> All men not too young and not incapacitated have the blessing of language ... That a new-born baby is speechless is the same sort of fact as a new-born kitten being blind. Earthworms are not blind, it does not belong to their nature to be sighted ... Here we are encountering the concept of a nature or essence. Consideration shews [sic] that, as Wittgenstein observes in the *Philosophical Investigations* (*PI* I 371) 'Essence is expressed in grammar'. Consideration of what? Well, for example, the following absurd sentences: 'Where does this pencil's uncle live?', 'What is the shape of dust?', 'What is a rainbow made of?, 'How many legs has a tree?', 'What does a chair feel?'. 'Do bacteria think?'.[54]

Although the manner of its presentation is very different from anything in Aquinas or other medieval Aristotelians, the issues that Anscombe, following Wittgenstein, is on to are those of certain logical and, though he would not say it, metaphysical distinctions, specifically those between essence, proprium, and accidental accidents. Anscombe never wrote about the parallels but it is this commonality that provides a bridge between her Aristotelianism and her Wittgensteinianism. Neither, however, is much developed in

53 'Modern Moral Philosophy' in *Human Life, Action and Ethics* 188.
54 'Human Essence' in *Human Life, Action and Ethics*, 27. op. cit.

the cause of what we now think of as constructive philosophy of religion or natural theology.

Regarding Wittgenstein she actually thought that the implications of his early philosophical views and later philosophical demeanour were generally troublesome for religion. Writing in the Catholic weekly *The Tablet* in 1954 she remarked:

> I do not think a Catholic could accept Wittgenstein's *Tractatus* if he understood it, because of its teaching on ethics. ('The world is independent of my will' so I cannot be morally responsible for anything that happens; and similarly 'The facts all belong to the task and not to the performance'). This I think is quite closely connected with all the rest. So the whole must be wrong. Of his later work Wittgenstein said 'Its advantage is that if you believe, say, Spinoza or Kant this interferes with what you can believe in religion but if you believe me nothing of the sort' I do not know whether he was right about this.[55]

That latter doubt is worth pondering. Is she really uncertain? or is it dutiful disingenuity or equivocation? On the one hand consider what she wrote in her 1986 'Syllabus of Errors' (Twenty Opinions Common among modern Anglo-American Philosophers'): 'Analytical philosophy is more characterized by styles of argument and investigation than by doctrinal content. It is thus possible or people of widely different beliefs to be practitioners of this sort of philosophy. It ought not to surprise anyone that a seriously believing Catholic Christian should also be an analytical philosopher'.[56] This would support the idea that Wittgenstein's philosophy presents no obstacle if one took her to be thinking of him as an 'analytical philosopher'. But by the same token her uncertainty, if genuine, may warrant a contraposition implying that in her opinion he was not *simply* a philosopher of analytic method but was perhaps an implicit or undercover metaphysician, or perhaps a deflationist, or even a 'Humean' of a kind at odds with religious doctrine. This brings me to 'on the other hand' which is an observation reported by Anthony Kenny who records her as saying 'On the topic of religion Wittgenstein is poison'.[57] Why might she have said this? Here I conjecture two considerations. First, that she had seen people poisoned by his ideas: some perhaps made skeptical about the

[55] Anscombe, 'Misinformation: What Wittgenstein Really Said' *The Tablet* 203, 1954, 13

[56] 'Twenty Opinions' op. cit., 66.

[57] See Kenny, 'Anscombe in Oxford' in Haldane ed. *The Life and Work of Elizabeth Anscombe.*

application of mundane concepts to the idea of a transcendent reality; others believing that he actually provided a means of taking religion seriously but only as a celebration of the human, rather than an acknowledgement of the divine. I am thinking here, as I suspect was she, of the practitioners of 'Wittgensteinian fideism', especially perhaps Rush Rhees and Dewi Phillips the former a fellow student and executor of Wittgenstein, the latter the best known member of the Swansea Wittgenstein school. Anscombe sometimes spoke of 'the Swansea sigh' and in writing about 'The Simplicity of the Tractatus' she reports that Wittgenstein 'once said to his friend Rush Rhees, a sighing man, not to repine and blame himself for something in himself: "that's God's fault not yours"'.[58] The 'Swansea sigh' may refer just to this aspect of Rhees's personal character but given the way in which others picked up both certain skeptical ideas and the manner of this influential figure I think the 'sigh' became a form of Swansea Neo-Wittgensteinian criticism or unarticulated response to what were perceived to be philosophical errors, and the main one with which members of the Swansea school were concerned was 'metaphysics' in a use of the term equivalent to 'crass reification'. But Christian doctrine in an orthodox understanding of it has obvious metaphysical presuppositions, hence hostility to metaphysics would poison serious belief.

Second, there is perhaps a further point which may suggest that she was troubled by the possibility that she herself had been affected by this anti-metaphysical aspect of Wittgenstein's philosophy, for she found it difficult to argue for the idea of an immaterial intellect or a separable immaterial soul, on the grounds that concepts of substance belong to the natural order. This is something she was evidently uncomfortable about and tried not to discuss, for it meant that she could not follows Aquinas in what he argued on philosophical grounds about the persistence of a separated active intellect,[59] and it raised questions about the credibility of Catholic beliefs and practices relating to the souls of the faithful departed. More radically, her failure to

[58] 'The Simplicity of the Tractatus' in M. Geach and L. Gormally eds *From Plato to Wittgenstein: Essays by G.E.M. Anscombe* (Exeter: ImprintAcademic, 2011), 177.

[59] On this see Anscombe, 'The Immortality of the Soul' in *Faith in a Hard Ground*, 'Analytical Philosophy and the Spirituality of Man' in *Human Life, Action and Ethics*, and 'The Existence of the Soul' in R. Varghese ed. *Great Thinkers on Great Questions* (Oxford: Oneworld, 1998); and J. Haldane 'Anscombe and Geach on Mind and Soul' in Haldane ed. *Life and Work of Anscombe*.

persuade Foot and Kenny, the two Oxford philosophers to whom she had been closest, of the case for theism, and the conspicuous absence in her extensive oeuvre of any direct argument for the existence of God, raises the question of whether she doubted the power of philosophy to show the reasonability of theism save in the negative respect already referred to, of defending against arguments intended to show its unreasonability insofar as it advanced or presupposed contradictory claims. There are places in her writings which might seem to suggest a positive disposition towards constructive natural theology, but on closer examination these turn out to be inconclusive speculative explorations, as in her suggestion that Anselm's famous proof is not an ontological argument.[60]

9. Conclusion

Two aspects of Anscombe's work as a philosopher emerge from the foregoing explorations. First, that she used her considerable mental powers to expose and analyse the presuppositions and complexities of important human theoretical and practical thought and action. Second that with regard to the things that mattered most to her, her religious faith and practice, she viewed the role of philosophy rather differently. Here she recognized the limits of constructive reason but also allowed the credibility of revelation as a source of knowledge about *what* human beings are, about *how* they ought to live, and about what they are *for* in the sense of their *telos*. In both endeavours she drew on what she had learned from Wittgenstein and from Aquinas and the fruits of this are a large body of writings that still remain to be comprehended. But where she is clearest is where she was most certain: that morality consists in large part of prohibitions, that these cannot really be made sense of apart from belief in a Divine legislator and that belief in such a providential creative source is philosophically defensible even if it is not philosophically demonstrable. Having previously mentioned Chesterton it is apt to end with a quotation from an essay by Graham Greene which, applied now to Anscombe, in part captures an aspect of the singular style and multiple modes of her thought as shown in her treatment of faith and of transubstantiation. He writes:

[60] See 'Why Anselm's Proof in the *Proslogion* is not an Ontological Argument' and 'Russelm or Anselm?' in M. Geach and L. Gormally eds *From Plato to Wittgenstein: Essays by G.E.M. Anscombe* (Exeter: ImprintAcademic, 2011).

> [Chesterton] succeeded as a religious [writer], for religion is simple, dogma is simple. Much of the difficulty of theology arises from the efforts of men who are not primarily writers to distinguish a quite simple idea with the utmost accuracy.
>
> He restated the original thought with the freshness, simplicity, and excitement of discovery. In fact, it was discovery: he unearthed the defined from beneath the definitions, and the reader wondered why the definitions had ever been thought necessary.[61]

University of St Andrews
jjh1@st-andrews.ac.uk
and
Baylor University
John_Haldane@baylor.edu

61 'GK. Chesterton' in *Graham Greene Collected Essays* (London: Bodley Head, 1969) 136.

Revisiting Modern Moral Philosophy

JENNIFER A. FREY

Abstract
This essay revisits Elizabeth Anscombe's 'Modern Moral Philosophy' with two goals in mind. The first is to recover and reclaim its radical vision, by setting forth a unified account of its three guiding theses. On the interpretation advanced here, Anscombe's three theses are not independently intelligible; their underlying unity is the perceived necessity of absolute prohibitions for any sound account of practical reason. The second goal is to show that Anscombe allows for a thoroughly unmodern sense of 'moral' that applies to human actions; the paper concludes with some reasons to think that this unmodern sense of 'moral' is worthy of further philosophical attention and defense.

1. Introduction

In 1958 the journal *Philosophy* published an essay by Elizabeth Anscombe, who was then a fellow of Somerville College, Oxford, titled, 'Modern Moral Philosophy'.[1] MMP has the distinction of being one of the most widely read and cited essays of Anglo-American analytic philosophy; its publication is often hailed as a watershed event. However, while Anscombe's influence is undeniably wide it has not obviously been deep. Surveying the landscape of contemporary ethical theory, one searches in vain to find a dominant strand of it that is even alive to the central problems she highlights in her essay, let alone explicitly working to resolve them.

Anscombe's essay calls for radical change. She does not ask her readers to rearrange the furniture of moral philosophy more decorously but to burn down the house; notoriously, she asks us to stop doing moral philosophy altogether. But Anscombe's radical vision was either actively resisted, or worse, co-opted in order to advance the very same ends she herself adamantly opposed. For instance, Anscombe's suggestion that we try to

[1] *Philosophy 53* (1958) 1–19 (hereafter, 'MMP'). Reprinted in *Human Life, Action and Ethics: Essays by G.E.M. Anscombe*, eds., Mary Geach and Luke Gormally (Charlottesville, Va: Imprint Academic) 169–194 (hereafter 'HLAE').

doi:10.1017/S1358246119000262

recover the concept of virtue grounded in an account of human flourishing was incorporated into the very same mode of doing moral philosophy that was her principal target, thereby losing its revolutionary character and value.

In this essay, I seek to revisit MMP with two goals in mind. My first task is to try to recover and reclaim its radical vision, and I will attempt to do this by giving a unified account of its three guiding theses. On the interpretation I advance here, Anscombe's three theses are not intelligible independently of each other. There is an underlying concern that unites them: the failure of modern moral philosophy to recognize absolute prohibitions against intrinsically evil acts. As her public opposition to Harry Truman attests,[2] she was all too familiar with our tendency to justify wicked acts such as murder when some great good is at stake. Her complaint against modern moral philosophy in all of its guises is that it has made it either enormously difficult or downright impossible to articulate the thought that murder is intrinsically unjust and must never be done for that reason.

My second task in this essay is to show that Anscombe does allow for an altogether different sense of 'moral' as applied to human actions. Drawing on some of her later essays, I discuss this sense of moral and give some reasons to think it is worthy of further exploration.

2. Anscombe's three theses revisited

Anscombe's essay begins by stating three theses.

(1) It is not profitable for us at present to do moral philosophy; that should be laid aside at any rate until we have an *adequate philosophy of psychology*, in which we are conspicuously lacking.

(2) The concepts of obligation and duty – *moral* obligation and *moral* duty, that is to say – and of what is *morally* right and wrong, and of the *moral* sense of 'ought', ought to be jettisoned if this is psychologically possible; because they are survivals, or derivatives from survivals, from an earlier conception of ethics which no longer generally survives, and are only harmful without it.

[2] For her arguments that President Harry Truman is a mass murderer, see 'Mr. Truman's Degree' in *The Collected Philosophical Papers of Elizabeth Anscombe Volume III: Ethics, Religion and Politics* (Oxford: Basil Blackwell, 1981) 51–71 (hereafter, 'TD')

(3) The differences between well-known English writers on moral philosophy from Sidgwick to the present day are of little importance.[3]

In what follows, I will argue that the third thesis points us to the reasons for adopting the first and second. So, it is the widespread lack of recognition of absolute prohibitions – against, say, murder or the judicial condemnation of the innocent – that explains why she thinks we need to stop doing moral philosophy until we have a sound philosophy of psychology, and also the reason why talk of 'moral' right, 'moral' wrong, and 'moral' obligation is harmful and best jettisoned. More specifically, the harm done by such uses of 'moral' is the explicit recommendation, approval, or even rational command of acts that are intrinsically wicked or unjust. Anscombe holds that such acts must never even be entertained in deliberation, let alone intended and realized in some set of circumstances; such acts are in their essence incompatible with human flourishing.

Anscombe begins her argument by directing our attention to the difference between modern moral philosophizing and the sort of ethical reflection one finds in Aristotle. She notes that Aristotle doesn't foreground the question of what obligation is, and that his use of 'moral' simply marks a contrast within the space of virtue. Moreover, she notes that for Aristotle the concepts of praise and blame do not track the modern use of *moral*, since Aristotle held that simple miscalculation about the means to one's end is blameworthy. Should one read Aristotle with the modern use of 'moral' in mind, one should feel 'like someone whose jaws have somehow got out of alignment'.[4]

Since we cannot look to Aristotle for any understanding of the modern way of speaking of *moral* goodness or obligation, she considers 'all the best-known writers on ethics in modern times' for help: Butler, Mill, Hume, Kant, and Bentham. She raises a host of complaints against these modern moralists, all of which center around the ways that our ability to evaluate particular actions in particular circumstances as *truly* good or bad is made more difficult by some aspect of the moral philosophy of each one of them. It is clear that this bit of argument is not at all intended to be exhaustive; rather, it is a minor preamble to the real problem, which is that 'in present-day philosophy an explanation is required how an unjust man is a bad man, or an unjust action a bad one'.[5] Anscombe

[3] Op. cit. note 1, MMP, 169.
[4] Op. cit. note 1, MMP, 170.
[5] Op. cit. note 1, MMP, 174.

insinuates that the tradition of modern moral philosophy more generally is at least partly to blame for this sorry state of affairs.

Anscombe realizes that the solution to the problem isn't simple or straightforward; it is impossible to return to Aristotle as if we are not all modern now in our language and thought. In order to begin the difficult task of doing moral philosophy in a radically different way, she argues that we would first need to develop a 'sound philosophy of psychology', which we presently lack. We cannot speak of justice as a virtue until we first know what *type of characteristic* a virtue is or how such a characteristic relates to the actions in which it is instanced. But for this, she argues, 'we certainly need an account at least of what a human action is at all, and how its description as "doing-such-and-such" is affected by its motive and by the intention or intentions in it; and for this an account of such concepts is required'.[6] On these matters, Anscombe does not think that Aristotle will be of much use to us, since he 'did not succeed' in making these concepts sufficiently clear.[7]

Given that we lack the requisite philosophical psychology, Anscombe recommends '*banishing ethics totally from our minds*' until we can give an account of concepts such as 'action', 'intention', 'pleasure', and 'wanting'.[8] Getting clear about these concepts, she remarks, is a matter of 'conceptual analysis' or 'the philosophy of psychology' rather than ethical theory. But we cannot even begin to think about virtue, let alone justice, until we have an account of them.

Did readers of MMP take Anscombe's first thesis to heart? It is true that non-ethical attention to these concepts – especially action and intention – flowered in the wake of MMP, but this was largely due to the publication of Anscombe's monograph *Intention*, which has been standardly read and interpreted as if it had no connection with the main claims of MMP.[9] As a result, post *Intention* action theory was

[6] Op. cit. note 1, MMP, 174.

[7] In 'Thought and Action in Aristotle' in *The Collected Philosophical Papers of G.E.M. Anscombe, Volume I: From Parmenides to Wittgenstein* (Oxford: Basil Blackwell, 1981) 71–72, Anscombe argues that Aristotle could not account for cases of deliberate akrasia or malice; for this, she argues, we would need recourse to a concept of intention, which Aristotle lacks.

[8] Op. cit. note 1, MMP, 188, emphasis in original.

[9] *Intention* (Cambridge, Mass.: Harvard University Press, 2000) was originally published one year prior to MMP. For interpretations of *Intention* that pay due attention to its connection with both MMP see Jennifer A. Frey, 'Elizabeth Anscombe on Practical Knowlede and the Good' forthcoming *Ergo*, John Schwenkler, *Anscombe's Intention: A Guide*, Rachael Wiseman, *Routledge Philosophy Guidebook to Anscombe's Intention* (Oxford: Routledge, 2016).

not undertaken by those principally concerned with erecting a proper foundation for an account of justice as a virtue; rather, it was undertaken by those interested in language and mind, or an account of rational agency *tout court*. These philosophers busied themselves with the project of identifying a restricted sense of action – usually by way of appealing to our intuitions about a few examples – into a special class of events, in order to inquire into what intentions are and how they relate to this special class of events. The dominant view within this project – the causal theory – is that intentions are some kind of mental state that causes actions. Not surprisingly, the analytic action-theoretic project doesn't seem to yield anything of foundational importance for moral philosophy generally, let alone our thought about virtue, and one strains to find normative or meta-ethical theorists (including virtue ethicists) seriously engaged in this literature.

Is the current state of affairs in analytic action theory what Anscombe was after when she suggested 'banishing ethics totally from our minds' until we have an account of concepts like 'action' and 'intention'? No. But one crucial element of the story about why things turned out this way is the separation or compartmentalization of Anscombe's first thesis from her second and third. This separation is a mistake, because thesis one is a mere *assertion* shrouded in mystery when considered independent of its relation to thesis two and three. Moreover, shorn of the ethical concerns that animate it, thesis one seems to give its blessing to the current theoretical divorce between action theory and ethics. Although Anscombe is clear that work in the philosophy of psychology and action is not yet ethical theory properly so called, we should not infer from this that she thought these investigations should proceed in isolation from each other. After all, she states rather plainly that one should be theorized as the proper foundation for the other.[10]

So, let us now turn to the second thesis, which is the suggestion that we should jettison use of 'moral' when used adjectivally to qualify ought, obligation, right, and wrong, because in such usage, moral is 'just a word containing no intelligible thought: a word retaining the suggestion of force, and apt to have a strong psychological effect, but which no longer signifies a real concept at all'.[11] The

[10] For an excellent discussion of the divorce between theories of action and ethics since the publication of MMP, see Constantine Sandis, 'Modern Moral Philosophy Before and After Anscombe' Constantine Sandis, forthcoming in *Enrohanar* eds., Sofia Miguens and Dolores Garcia-Arnaldos.

[11] Op. cit. note 1, MMP, 179. For a recent and provocative discussion of this passage, see James Doyle *No Morality, No Self: Anscombe's Radical Skepticism* (Cambridge, Mass.: Harvard University Press, 2018).

concept 'moral', as deployed adjectivally by modern moral philosophers, connotes something like an 'absolute verdict' on one's action. Anscombe argues that the term came to acquire this sense due to the centuries long influence of the Christian divine law account of ethics upon European thought. Although modern moral philosophers no longer ground morality in some explicit conception of divine law, they have retained its central concepts of being bound or obliged and incurring guilt. This modern use of 'moral', Anscombe argues, is a mere survival, something that continues 'outside the framework of thought that made it a really intelligible one'.[12] Since it 'has no reasonable sense', Anscombe recommends that we 'drop it'; once we do this, we might notice that ethics is possible without it (see, for example, Aristotle). She implores her readers to take seriously the thought that:

> 'It would be a great improvement if, instead of 'morally wrong', one always named a genus such as 'untruthful', 'unchaste', 'unjust'. We should no longer ask whether doing something was 'wrong', passing directly from some description of an action to this notion; we should ask ether, e.g., it was unjust; and the answer would sometimes be clear at once.'[13]

Anscombe offers several alternatives to our modern morality talk, including the search for norms in human virtues. Arguments about the norms of virtue would be grounded in the shared knowledge of our own 'species', where this is understood, 'from the *point of view of the activity of thought and choice in regard to the various departments of life*'.[14] To construct such a theory, Anscombe argues, would mark a decisive turn away from 'a law conception of ethics' towards something supposedly quite different – viz. Aristotelian ethical naturalism.[15]

Anscombe's rough sketch of how the ethical naturalist could reason about good and bad human action is as follows:

> 'Since justice is a virtue, and injustice a vice, and virtues and vices are built up by the performances of the action in which they are instanced, an act of injustice will tend to make a man bad; and

[12] Op. cit. note 1, MMP, 177.
[13] Op. cit. note 1, MMP, 180.
[14] Op. cit. note 1, MMP, 188, emphasis in original.
[15] For a discussion of ethical naturalism as a development within the natural law tradition, see Jennifer A. Frey 'Neo-Aristotelian Ethical Naturalism' in *The Cambridge Companion to Natural Law Ethics*, ed., by Tom Angier (Cambridge: Cambridge University Press) 92–108.

> essentially the flourishing of man *qua* man consists in his being good (e.g., in virtues); but for any X to which such terms apply, X *needs* what makes it flourish, so a man *needs*, or *ought* to perform, only virtuous actions; and even if, as it must be admitted may happen, he flourishes less, or not at all, in inessentials, by avoiding injustice, his life is spoiled in essentials by not avoiding injustice – so he still needs to perform only just actions.[16]

Here, Anscombe notes, we find a use of 'ought' and 'needs' that isn't *moral* in the modern sense and relates to ordinary, hum drum uses of 'good' and 'bad'; for example, the good of some piece of machinery depends on oil, so it is true that this machinery needs oil, and so should or ought to be oiled, since running without oil is bad for it, or it will run badly without oil.[17] Again, however, she notes that we cannot return to this *unmodern* way of thinking about human good and bad until we have a sound philosophy of psychology, without which there is no license to avail ourselves of any talk of virtues or human flourishing.

This passage from MMP was one of the principal sources and inspiration for a theoretical movement within normative moral theory we now call 'virtue ethics'. In virtue ethics, there is much talk of the virtues as necessary for the realization of a good human life. But virtue ethics argues in this way independent of any prior investigation into action or intention and virtue ethics is replete with the modern usage of the term moral.[18] For instance, Rosalind Hursthouse, whose influential book, *On Virtue Ethics*, is hailed by Simon Blackburn as 'the defining exposition of the view,' advances the following 'specification' of 'morally' right action:

> An action is right iff it is what a virtuous agent would characteristically do in the circumstances.[19]

[16] Op. cit. note 1, MMP, 193.

[17] Op. cit. note 1, MMP, 174.

[18] It is true that virtue ethics has been concerned to give an account of *moral* psychology, in particular, a search for a proper account of *moral* motivation (as opposed to other kinds, including merely *prudential* considerations). But Anscombe is opposed to the use of moral in this sense, even with respect to motivation. See her discussion in 'Good and Bad Human Action' (Op. cit. note 1, HLAE, 195–201).

[19] Rosalind Hursthouse, *On Virtue Ethics* (Oxford: Oxford University Press, 1999) 28 (hereafter, 'VE'). See back cover for full endorsement by Blackburn.

This account, Hursthouse assures her reader, has a structure that 'closely resembles those of act utilitarianism and many simple forms of deontology'.[20] Hursthouse stresses this because, like its utilitarian and deontic counterparts, she takes virtue ethics to be in the business of giving an account of what it is 'morally' right to do.

It seems important to Hursthouse that virtue ethics be considered 'a genuine rival' to the two dominant strains of contemporary moral philosophy.[21] For this reason, she is anxious to establish that the virtue ethicist is playing the same game as her principal opponents. But MMP does not ask its readers to beat modern moral philosophers at their own game or on their own terms. Anscombe's position is far more radical: she asks us – implores us – to stop playing the game altogether.

One may wonder what, if anything, is really at stake in the choice between radical virtue ethics and its more well established routine counterparts.[22] One consequence of choosing to play the same game (but now with an emphasis on virtue!) is that we end up facing the very problem Anscombe originally laid at the feet of modern moral philosophy: the inability to make the argument that an unjust man is a bad man or an unjust action a bad action.

In order to spell this out more clearly, let us return to Anscombe's concern for the recognition of absolute prohibitions. Human actions such as murder or rape are absolutely ruled out just in virtue of being described as such-and-such actions because they are intrinsically unjust actions; to rape or murder *someone* is to *wrong* them, and this is so regardless of the further intentions with which such acts are carried out by the agent, or any good or bad consequences that might come from their performance in a specific set of circumstances. In order to recognize the force of such prohibitions, we would need a theory of action that provides an account of the intentional descriptions of what one does – that one acts intentionally under such-and-such descriptions – and that can make a principled distinction between the intentions with which one acts and one's further intentions or motives.

[20] Op. cit. note 19, VE, 29.

[21] Op. cit. note 19, VE, 26.

[22] I take the distinction between radical and routine virtue ethics from Solomon, 2003. 'Virtue Ethics: Radical or Routine?' in eds., Linda Zagzebski and Michael DePaul, *Intellectual Virtue: Perspectives from Ethics and Epistemology* (New York City: Oxford University Press, 2003) 57–80.

Hursthouse's own discussion of intrinsically wicked acts falls far short of the mark, and this is due to her inattention to such matters. Her example of an action no virtuous person would ever perform is the sexual abuse of a child for one's own pleasure; the description of the act itself, she writes, 'connotes depravity'.[23]

What's interesting about Hursthouse's discussion is that she does not put forward an instance of what she sets out to discuss: a description of an act of a certain specifiable kind. Rather, she puts forward a description of an act of a specifiable kind *plus* its motive or the further intention with which it is performed (for the sake of pleasure).[24] An act of sexual abuse performed on a child might be done from any number of different motives and for an infinite number of instrumental reasons; it may please the agent or he may find it repugnant. But it is the nature of an *absolute* prohibition that the beautiful (or ugly) motives or further intentions with which they might be carried out are absolutely immaterial to the question of whether the act ought to be entertained or performed. Rather, we know that the act is ruled out just in case it can be described as *such-and-such* an act. If all that is ruled out is raping a child *for the sake of pleasure*, then this leaves open whether raping a child for the sake of saving the human race, appeasing a murderous tyrant, or winning a disastrous and bloody war are still live options for us.[25] For all that Hursthouse

[23] Op. cit. note 19, VE, 87. Other prominent virtue ethicists and put forward theories that seem fairly obviously opposed to the existence of intrinsically wicked acts. This usually comes by way of emphasizing the fundamental importance of motive for the specification of the *morally right* action, or by emphasizing the diversity and holism of the right making properties of action. For the former strategy, see Michael Slote, 'Agent Based Virtue Ethics' in *Moral Concepts: Midwest Studies in Philosophy* 20, eds., Perter A. French, Theordore E. Uehling, Jr., and Howard K. Wettstein (1996) 83–101; for the latter strategy, see Christine Swanton, *Virtue Ethics* (Oxford: Oxford University Press) 242.

[24] The distinctions between motives, the intention with which someone acts, and the further intentions for the sake of which someone acts is central to Anscombe's account of action in *Intention*, and also figures in her analysis of Truman as a mass murderer unworthy of honors in TD.

[25] This problem is noted in Christopher Miles Coope 2006, 'Modern Virtue Ethics' in T. D. J. Chappell (ed.), Values and Virtues: Aristotelianism in Contemporary Ethics. Oxford: Oxford University Press, 51-52. Henceforth 'MVE'. All this is not to deny that motives matter to the goodness or badness of a human action (a particular performance in a particular circumstance). But prohibitions are general, so they attach to human action descriptions or action concepts first and foremost.

has told us, these may be things a virtuous person a virtuous person might do.

Attention to Hursthouse's discussion of intrinsically bad actions shows us the need for the sort of *philosophy of psychology* outlined in MMP. More specifically, we see that we need a principled account of the intentional descriptions under which a person acts, and a principled distinction between the thing one does intentionally (or the intention with which one acts) and the further intentions and motives with which one acts. We are unable to think clearly about absolute prohibitions and sound practical deliberation without these distinctions in hand. Therefore, it is a mistake to take some conception of action for granted, as Hursthouse does in her book, and cast about for a virtue centered approach for picking out *morally* right action. Such an account is a recipe for marginalizing the virtue of justice, because it lets what Anscombe calls 'consequentialism' in through the back door.[26]

To isolate this concern more sharply, we need to turn to the third, final, and central thesis of MMP; Anscombe contends that all the supposedly notable differences amongst British moral theorists since Sidgwick are superficial, since they are all united in one deeply salient respect: each 'has put out a philosophy according to which, e.g., it is not possible to hold that it cannot be right to kill the innocent as a means to any end whatsoever and that someone who thinks otherwise is in error'.[27] The explanation of this unity is their commitment – explicit or merely implicit – to *consequentialism*. Although Anscombe coins the term consequentialism in MMP, her original sense does not track contemporary usage within normative moral theory or meta-ethics. In his encyclopedia article on consequentialism, Walter Sinnot-Armstrong defines consequentialism as a theory that takes normative properties generally (including the moral rightness of acts) as depending on its consequences alone; notably, he does not even mention Anscombe's original discussion of it.[28] Clearly, if we define consequentialism in this way, then Anscombe's insistence that all British moral theorists since Sidgwick are consequentialists is false. But this is not what she meant when she coined the term.

[26] For a discussion of the marginalization of justice in virtue ethics, see MVE.

[27] Op. cit. note 1, MMP, 181.

[28] Walter Sinnot-Armstrong, 'Consequentialism' in *The Stanford Encyclopedia of Philosophy* (Summer 2019 Edition), ed., Edward N. Zalta https://plato.stanford.edu/archives/sum2019/entries/consequentialism.

For Anscombe, consequentialism picks out the denial of any significant distinction between what one does intentionally and what one merely foresees one will bring about by what one does intentionally. She writes that it is 'an ethical thesis' that can be described in the following way: 'it does not make any difference to a man's responsibility for something that he foresaw, that he felt no desire for it, either as an end or as a means to an end'; or, using the language of intention, 'it does not make any difference to a man's responsibility for an effect of his action which he can foresee, that he does not intend it'.[29]

Of course, contemporary consequentialists will be committed to this denial as well, but this denial is not a claim about the status of normative properties generally, nor does it settle questions about the supposed 'moral rightness' of acts. For Anscombe, consequentialism is a claim about the sphere of an agent's personal responsibility. Consequentialism greatly expands this sphere in such a way that it renders the very concept of absolute prohibitions senseless.

An example will suffice to show this. Let us imagine the rule of a wicked tyrant. One day he sends a military officer to a prominent judge with the following order: either condemn an innocent man to life in prison or you will be sent to the newly formed labor camps. The judge clearly foresees that if he is sent to the camps, he will almost certainly die and that, even if he lives, his son will suffer tremendous harms as a result. Now, suppose that he refuses to condemn an innocent man, and great harms befall his child just as he had foreseen. Is he responsible for what happens to his child? Is his action (the deliberative refusal to abuse his office by committing a grave injustice) blameworthy on account of these foreseen harms? In MMP Anscombe clearly wants to say no; she claims that 'a man is responsible for the bad consequences of his bad actions but gets no credit for the good ones; and contrariwise is not responsible for the bad consequences of good actions'.[30]

Let us contrast this unfortunate judge with a man who decides to withdraw support from his child for some reason (suppose, for example, he wants to spend the money on humanitarian aid or he wants to force his ex-wife's hand in a heated custody battle). For the consequentialist as she defines it, there is no essential difference between these two cases of 'withdrawing maintenance for the child,' since the result in either case is the same – viz., that the child is knowingly harmed. The consequentialist believes that, when it comes to

[29] Op. cit. note 1, MMP, 183.
[30] Op. cit. note 1, MMP, 184.

determining the sphere of an agent's responsibility, the foreseen consequences of his action are equivalent to the intended consequences. This greatly expands the sphere of an agent's responsibility – it means that *anything* he foresees will happen as a result of his decision is something for which he is responsible. For Anscombe, this is the critical move that leads one down the royal road to the rejection of absolute prohibitions and the obliteration of justice, since 'the just man is a man who habitually refuses to commit or participate in any unjust actions for fear of any consequences, or to obtain any advantage, for himself or for anyone else'.[31] She wants to rule out any philosophy that forces us to draw the conclusion characteristic of modern moral philosophy: that the 'morally right' thing to do is to commit an act of injustice against another. This conclusion, which presents itself as inevitable, rests on an *unsound philosophical psychology*, a corrupt account of our concepts of 'intention' and 'action.'

Another inevitable result of the embrace of consequentialism is it forces us to focus our attention away from the action itself – what is done, under intentional descriptions, here and now – and towards what happens as a result of its performance. In order to resist this move, we need an account of what falls under the scope of intention proper and what is outside of it; only then can we say that a deliberative refusal to act (which is a kind of intentional action) can have unintended side effects for which the agent is not necessarily responsible. For, without a principled distinction between intention and side effects, we will have to admit that it is always an open question whether one may, for instance, deliberately plan the death of innocent people as a means to achieving a good end.[32] For the whole point of drawing the distinction was to respect two apparent truths at once: (1) there are some actions that are intrinsically unchoiceworthy just in virtue of their description as such-and-such an action; and (2) not everything an agent knowingly causes is part of her sphere of responsibility.[33]

Anscombe sees clearly that if the second is not true then the first is either incoherent or profoundly unstable. For if any general prohibition is defeasible in cases where it brings about a preponderance of

[31] Op. cit. note 1, MMP, 190.

[32] This is exactly what is at stake in her analysis of Truman's decision to drop atomic bombs on civilian targets (see TD).

[33] As Anselm Mueller has pointed out in 'Radical Subjectivity: Morality versus Utilitarianism' *Ratio* 19 (1977) 115–132, these points are also necessary in order to formulate the Socratic maxim that it is better to suffer wrong than to inflict it upon another.

good over evil results, then it is plain that what really matters, in the final analysis, is the results or effects of action rather than the deed itself. And if that is the case, then practical deliberation will inevitably become a matter of weighing up good and bad consequences – the hard cases will prove a decisive point about the nature of practical reason and what it ultimately demands. Now, if practical reason demands that we try to bring about the best results, then 'acting well' isn't about a 'good life', but rather 'good results.' The measure of good action would then be something external to the agent, just as a product is external to its producer. In that case, producing the best results will be what 'morality' demands, or what one 'morally' ought to do, or what is 'morally' right. On such an account of practical reason, there is in principle no limit to what it might demand one do: murder, rape, torture, condemnation of the innocent, treason, and so on.

I conclude that attention to the character and necessity of absolute prohibitions is key to understanding how Anscombe's three theses are fundamentally united; moreover, it helps to isolate the core respect in which her preferred account of virtue is radical by contrast to what is, by the standards of contemporary normative theory, routine.[34]

3. Moral in a resolutely unmodern sense

I have been arguing that Anscombe's central concern in MMP is the need to recognize the centrality of the virtue of justice to a good human life and the importance of absolute prohibitions against intrinsically unjust acts. Her recommendation that we jettison the peculiarly modern usage of the word 'moral' as both senseless and harmful is rooted in this need. But this leaves open the possibility that there is a pre-modern use of 'moral' that Anscombe might not oppose. And if there is such a sense, how would our recovery of

[34] It is clear that Anscombe, like Aquinas and Aristotle, thinks of absolute prohibitions as first principles of practical reason; they tell us the sort of actions we must always avoid because they are evil (taking for granted that practical reason, quite generally, is thought about what goods to pursue and what evils to avoid). There are very few such acts but our knowledge of them as evil is unsophisticated and pre-theoretical. This knowledge structures our sense of what constitutes sound practical deliberation prior to engaging in it; as evil acts, we know that good reasoning will never be in the service of realizing them. If she did not think of absolute prohibitions in this way, then it is very difficult to understand her account of murder.

it depend upon a proper philosophy of psychology? It is to these considerations that I now turn.

Given the centrality of the intention/side effect distinction for an ethics of absolute prohibitions, it is no surprise that when Anscombe's turns her attention to the application of the so-called 'doctrine of double effect' in a later essay, 'Action, Intention, and Double Effect',[35] she begins with an account of what a human action is and how it relates to human action descriptions, or what is the same, general human action concepts. On Anscombe's view, the doctrine of double effect – or what she calls the principle of side effects – is not a guide to what is morally permissible or a principle of sound practical deliberation. Rather, the work it does is to show that some actions that can be truly described as causing death, where the death is not intended but foreseen, does not necessarily incur guilt. What is central to Anscombe's discussion of various cases of unintended but foreseen death is this: the fact that the death is unintentional creates a context in which we might reasonably look for exonerating circumstances.

However, while the principle of side effects demonstrates that the search for excuses is warranted, it tells us nothing about what specific circumstances or needs might excuse an unintended killing or causing of death and carries with it no guarantee that an excuse will be found. Although there is much of interest here, for our purposes what is most salient is the fact that the account of human action and human action descriptions she relies on in her discussion of this principle is characterized as 'moral'. This use of 'moral' raises the question of whether Anscombe is refusing to take her own advice by adopting the very term she told us to abandon, or whether she is using the word in a completely different sense. In order to address this, let us now turn to her account.

Anscombe begins her analysis with an observation about action theory. She notes that the majority of analytic philosophers of action are after a restricted sense of action in their theories, but, following Davidson, they go about this by attempting to isolate a special class of events. She is firmly opposed to this method. When we think about human action, we should not be concerned with the project of sorting out special classes of events by way of identifying their special features or distinguishing properties.[36]

[35] Op. cit. note 1, HLAE, 207–226.

[36] See *Intention*, 28–30; op. cit. note 1, HLAE, 209–210. For discussion of the importance of this point for an understanding of Anscombe's theory of the intentionality of both action and perception, see Christopher Frey and

Anscombe's starting point is different. If we want to restrict our notion of action, then we can simply note that human actions are those '*under the command of reason*', and other acts of a human being – like digesting food, pumping blood, or idly stroking one's head – are merely acts of a human being in so far as they are not under the command of reason.[37] She suggests that we might say that human action is voluntary action, but only insofar as we recognize that it should not include what is voluntary in a merely physiological sense, and should include omissions and sudden impulsive actions. Moreover, we must recognize that what is voluntary includes cases where this is no act of will, no formation of an intention or any deliberative decision. For 'what you were able to do and it was needful you should do, if you omit it in forgetfulness or sloth, falling asleep perhaps and sleeping through the time when you should have been doing it – your omission of it is voluntary'.[38] Anscombe also insists that one demonstrates their consent by 'not taking care when you could have and, in the nature of the case as available to your understanding, you needed to'.[39]

In her discussion of the voluntary character of omissions and negligence, we see a certain restricted sense of possibility and necessity, and these two conditions seem inseparable. So, what is possible for you to do in a set of circumstances conditions what we say it is necessary for you to do; but at the same time, what it is necessary for you to do in a set of circumstances also conditions what we say it is possible for you to do. The sense of necessity is that upon which some good depends, a sense of practical necessity that Anscombe connects with sound practical deliberation about the means to one's intended ends. And the sense of possibility is that which is tied to our practical agency – of what we know how to do and so stand ready to do in the circumstances. There may be cases where we don't know how to do what it is needful that we do. In such cases, Anscombe thinks that we are negligent – we could have and should have possessed such practical knowledge. An example of this might be a parent who never learned basic first aid. Such a parent is truly unable to help her child in a life-threatening emergency, but her lack of this basic parenting skill *does not excuse*. Here the lack of knowledge has a

---

Jennifer A. Frey, 'Anscombe on the Analogical Unity of Intention in Action and Perception' *Analytic Philosophy* 58:3 (2017) 202–247.

[37] Op. cit. note 1, 208.

[38] Op. cit. note 1, 208.

[39] Op. cit. note 1, 209.

voluntary character because it concerns a sphere of life that the agent, *qua* parent, has responsibility for regarding the care of the child, and this is the ground of the necessity for the parent to develop specific practical competencies vis-à-vis the child. The good of the child is what grounds the necessity on the part of the parent.

It is clear from Anscombe's very brief remarks about the voluntary character of omissions and cases of negligence more generally that she thinks of the sort of practical knowledge characteristic of human action and agency generally in normative terms; there can be no account of it that is severed from an agent's general conception of what is good and bad in human life generally.[40]

It follows that we cannot understand human action as being under the command of reason apart from some conception of the good or bad human life. Anscombe makes this clear when she puts forward the following thesis:

> **All human action is moral action. It is either good or bad (it may be both).**[41]

Before she explains her thesis, she notes some of its important implications. First, 'moral' does not pick out a special feature or property that some human actions have that others lack. The search for any such "extra ingredient" that qualifies certain human actions is absolutely ruled out by her thesis, which states that 'human' and 'moral' are equivalent in content – they are two descriptions of one and the same reality. A moral action is a human action, and vice versa. For Anscombe, the importance of this is that nothing is added by saying of something identified as a human action that it is *morally* good or bad, since "the 'moral' goodness of an action is nothing but its specific goodness as a human action. I mean: the goodness with which it is a good action."

But how can she say this? Were we not supposed to put talk of 'moral' on the Index? No, we were only supposed to put talk of *moral obligation, duty, oughts, and rights or wrongs* on the Index. Talk of the sort of specific goodness characteristic of human action – that which is under the command of reason, or what is the same, goodness of actions, passions, and habits of action and feeling – is perfectly licit. It can be given a plain sense, unlike the 'moral' of modern moral philosophy, which cannot.

[40] For a more detailed discussion of the connection between practical knowledge and the good, see Jennifer A. Frey, 'Anscombe on Practical Knowledge and the Good', forthcoming in *Ergo*.

[41] Op. cit. note 1, HLAE, 209, emphasis added.

However, we cannot make sense of Anscombe's thesis unless we have a clear distinction between actions – particular performances by particular agents in particular circumstances – and act types, or what is the same, action concepts or action descriptions. For Anscombe, human actions are always performed *under a description* and thereby characterized as either voluntary or intentional. On the account she gives in *Intention*, action descriptions are those associated with a 'special sense of the question 'Why?''. If an agent acknowledges that the 'Why?' question applies to his performance under a certain description, and gives a sincere response, this response is the agent's reason or intention in acting under that description. What gives the response its reasonableness is its connection to the agent's practical deliberation – i.e, his calculative thought about how what he is presently up to realizes his intention in so acting. Anscombe's theory of the intentionality of action just is an account of action as 'under the command of reason.'

Although the agent's practical knowledge of what he is doing under a description is essential to the specification of an action into a general kind, Anscombe also notes that observers can also see what someone else is doing intentionally. If I walk into the room and see you sitting at the table with a bowl of food and a fork you are raising to your mouth, I am justified in my belief that you are eating. 'Eating' is a human action description or human action concept. I can apply such concepts in my practical thought and deliberation, or I can apply them to what I see others doing in the world.

It is noteworthy that, in *Intention*, Anscombe calls such descriptions 'vital descriptions' and notes that they are not identified by any 'extra property which a philosopher must try to describe' but rather '*a form* of description of events'.[42] Thus, she argues, we can speak of a form of description, human actions, and of the descriptions that can occur under this form. Such a form always looks to the wider context of the life form, or the specific manner of living in which such descriptions typically figure.[43]

Human action concepts or human action descriptions are acquired and deployed within the wider context of human life and its characteristic activities and goods. For this reason, these action concepts are already evaluatively colored: some are positive simply in virtue of being described as *such and such* a human action; some are negative

[42] *Intention*, op. cit. note 9.

[43] For a careful discussion of how many activities are life form dependent, see Michael Thompson, Life and Action (Cambridge, Mass.: Harvard University Press), chapter one.

simply in virtue of being so described; others are neutral or indifferent. But, that you can truthfully say you are performing an action that is intentional or voluntary under a positive human action description, like 'eating' or 'giving alms', does not suffice to determine whether your performance is good or bad *simpliciter*, as a human act. The same is true if you are performing an action that is intentional or voluntary under a negative human action description, like 'amputating.' Although 'amputating a limb' connotes harm, and therefore has a kind of negative moral charge to it, one can act well in 'amputating a limb'. A doctor is 'acting well' – performing a good human action – when he 'amputates a limb' for the sake of the health of his patient, who would die otherwise. It is the fact that the patient would die that renders the amputation *needful* and good. Likewise, a Christian is not acting well if she is 'giving alms' to a woman in distress in order to impress her boss. All that a moral action description does is show that it is good, *unless some aspect of it is bad*, or bad, *unless some aspect of it excuses one from fault, or some justification renders it not wicked or specifically good.*

Anscombe's more controversial claim is that some human action descriptions are not positively or negatively charged just in virtue of being described as such and such an action; these action descriptions are not moral in her sense – relating to goodness or badness of human life generally – but neutral or indifferent. Examples she provides are: 'chucking a pebble into the sea,' 'picking a flower,' or 'walking.' Such action descriptions do not suggest any specific goodness or badness to them.

Anscombe cautions her reader not to infer from this that there are indifferent or neutral human actions. This inference betrays a fundamental misunderstanding of her thesis. The claim that all human action is moral means that every particular human action is always either good or bad *qua* human action. Any specific act of walking done in a certain way, at a certain time, by a certain person, can always either be truthfully described as living well or not.

Anscombe's thesis further allows that in the evaluation of human action, we can recognize respects in which it is good, and still judge that the action is bad. Here we must keep in mind two points. First, that it is good if it is in no way bad. Second, that something can be described as good in some respect and yet still be defective as a human action. What makes an action good *tout court* is whether it can be truthfully described as living well. In order to make sense of this, Anscombe needs to recognize levels of action descriptions. For instance, 'poisoning the inhabitants of the house' can also be described as 'murder' which can also be described as 'unjust.' It is entailed by Anscombe's thesis that all human action can be truthfully characterized, at the highest level of human action description, as 'living well' or as 'not living well.'[44]

Anscombe also discusses cases that are structurally similar to those that figure in the literature on moral luck.[45] In cases where there is not complete exoneration, she argues, we may say his action was bad as needing excuse and therefore pardon. Insofar as there was a minor bit of negligence on the agent's part – a moment of inattention, say – then the action was bad. For if the agent had taken more care, which he could have and should have done, the bad upshot could be avoided. And yet 'the result was not one that, as we say, "was to be expected in the nature of the case"'.[46] And for this reason the action is 'mixed'; it has goodness to it when described intentionally. Moreover, it lacks the defect of being a wicked action, since a bad accidental result does not render it wicked; however, it still has something of badness in it, 'that makes it seem to need pardon'.[47] Here we may avail ourselves of some sort of distinction between exoneration and excuse.

One final point Anscombe makes with regard to her thesis is that sometimes action descriptions are inadequate to the task of evaluation in light of what it means for a human life to be good or bad on the whole. It follows that a true intentional action description, which bears the appearance of neutrality or indifference, such as 'writing his name on a bit of paper,' is not yet a specifying description of what the agent does – e.g., 'signing a contract.' We know from her analysis in *Intention* that there is a specifying description of an action that 'swallows up' the other true intentional descriptions.[48] In her original example, a man intentionally 'moves his arm up and down' 'pumps water into a cistern' and 'replenishes the house water supply', but he performs these actions for the sake of 'poisoning the inhabitants of the house,' whom he is intent on killing. In this example, 'moving his arm up and down' just is the first stage of a 'poisoning'; on its own, 'moving my arm up and down' is an inadequate description of what the man is up to. We need an adequate concept of

[44] For this point, see her essay, 'Practical Truth' in HLAE, op. cit. note 1, 149–158.

[45] For context, see Thomas Nagel, 'Moral Luck' in *Mortal Questions* (New York: Cambridge University Press).

[46] Op. cit. note 1, HLAE, 213.

[47] Op. cit. note 1, HLAE, 207–226.

[48] *Intention*, 46–47.

'intention', one understood as essentially connected to the agent's practical thought and will, in order to make this point clearly.

Another route to the thought that human action descriptions are formally 'vital descriptions' that necessitate a look to the wider context of human life is the contrast between skilled action and human action, and the different senses of praise and blame we use in regard to each. This is a point she underscores in another essay, 'Good and Bad Human Action'.[49]

In this essay Anscombe begins with Kant's notion of a uniquely *moral* motive – acting from duty – as opposed to prudential motives, acting in self-interest. For Kant, she notes, the moral ought is the only proper motive of a rational will. On this view, there is an opposition between moral and prudential motives, or between duty and mere interest. She contrasts Kant's view with what she finds in Aristotle. On Aristotle's view we can say that a human needs to develop good practical judgment – cultivate practical wisdom – and that failure to cultivate this is blameworthy. But there is no thought in Aristotle expressed by the proposition 'there is a moral obligation to have intellectual virtue'. Kant's use of 'moral' doesn't fit into Aristotle's framework. The sense of 'ought' as it figures in the statement, 'human beings ought to have practical wisdom' is this: the human needs practical wisdom in order to live well on the whole – to realize the characteristic goods internal to human life.

Now, for Aristotle it is true that someone may be blameworthy for lacking intellectual virtue, if the lack is voluntary (he had the ability and opportunity to develop it, and the necessity to develop it belongs to him in virtue of being human). But one might also be blameworthy for a mistake in skill rather than virtue, and here the notion of blame seems to be of a different sort. A skilled chef may make a bad pasta – he carelessly forgets a step in the process – and he may be blamed for this. But this seems different than the sort of blame we assign to the father who carelessly forgets the child in the back of the car on a hot summer day, which causes the child's death. So, there seems to be a difference between mistakes of skill and what we might call mistakes in human action. But how do we mark this difference in a principled way? In order to make the case we need to avail ourselves of concepts like 'habit,' 'disposition,' 'practical knowledge' and 'practical reasoning'.

Within the Aristotelian tradition, we could give the following sort of account. A skill involves the possession of a unified body of

[49] Op. cit. note 1, HLAE, 195–206.

practical knowledge. Skill is an intellectual habit, and a habit is a stable disposition or settled state that makes one ready to act in ways that are ordered to the realization of the ends internal to the skill.[50] A skilled cook knows how to attain the end internal to the practice of cooking, and he is disposed to exercise his skill when decision calls for this. The actions of the skilled agent are informed by the rules of the skilled practice. An expert of Italian cuisine knows how to prepare a variety of specific dishes without difficulty. A mistake is blameworthy as a bit of Italian cooking if it is a misapplication of the general rules of Italian cuisine that frustrates the goal of preparing delicious Italian food.

But Anscombe also notes that a skilled person can make mistakes on purpose and this may not be blameworthy in the deeper sense. A skilled cook can purposefully make a mistake in order to teach her students to learn to cook properly: 'don't do this', she says, as she runs the pasta through the machine too many times the wrong way. 'See how it turns out badly?' she asks. In these cases, the bad cooking acts are not blameworthy, because they are performed from the knowledge internal to the skill and for the sake of a good end: transmitting the skill to another person. But what about a skilled cook who intentionally ruins his pasta in order to humiliate his patrons (he wants the food they serve to their guests to taste terrible so they will be humiliated and lose their social standing). He too acts from the knowledge internal to the skill, but he puts this knowledge to use for a bad end. This too is a bad act of cooking but is also a bad human action, and therefore blameworthy in a deeper way.

In order to account for this deeper sense of what is blameworthy, we need to recognize a further dimension of failure: the cook is not simply failing to create a delicious meal but failing to act well simpliciter. The assessment of skilled action is always *qualified* – it is always relative to the ends that define and measure the skill itself. But the chef is not merely a chef who performs skilled acts, but also a human who performs human actions. And every chef act is also a human action. The chef's actions are ordered to ends whose intelligibility goes beyond those specified by his skill; he is also ordered to the ends of human life more generally. The skilled chef can err *qua* chef, but he is also a man, and he can fail *qua* man. Because skillful actions are intentional, they are always subject to this wider context of assessment.

[50] By ready to act, I mean the person is constituted so as to be able to perform the action skillfully and without difficulty.

Therefore, in order to answer Anscombe's question – When is a mistake in skill blameworthy as a human action? – we have to look to the wider context of the life in which the bad act is performed. To do this would be to make the move from a merely technical form of reasoning – habitual deliberation and judgement about how to produce the results internal to skilled practice – to practical reasoning unqualified. The former is more restricted than the latter, but both are ultimately governed by the same end or measure.

If we distinguish between merely technical reasoning and prudence, then we can say that an action is good as a human action even though it is bad as a bit of cooking. And here we have a notion of moral goodness which simply connotes the specific goodness proper to human action as such. Anscombe writes:

> 'What has now become, now, of the notion of the *morally* good or *morally* bad as applied to human actions? They have become equivalent to 'good and bad' as applied to human actions as such. I mean, 'That was a morally good action' is equivalent to 'Qua human action, that was good' or 'That was a good human action', and 'That was a morally bad human action' is equivalent to 'Qua human action, that was bad' or 'That was a bad human action'.'[51]

What is the measure of a bad human action? Or what is the same, what determines the specific goodness that attaches to human actions *qua* human actions? Although I cannot defend it here, the answer that recommends itself is plain: whether the action constitutes or contributes to 'living well' or 'living a good human life'. In order to defend this recommendation, we would need an account of the role of the capacities of reason and will in the determination of both intentional and voluntary action descriptions, and an account of practical deliberation as intrinsically in service of the goal of realizing what is universally good for man. Elsewhere, I have argued that Anscombe gives us such an account in *Intention*.[52] There, she argues that *formal* goal of practical reason is to realize the good, but she does not give a substantive account of what this good consists in. What is truly good, or what belongs essentially to any true conception of a good human life, is a topic for ethical reflection proper. Reflection upon intentional action shows us only that one must operate under some general conception of 'living well' in order to act for reasons at all; the deployment of such a conception in practical thought is part of the account of how human actions come under the

[51] Op cit. note 1, HLAE, 203.
[52] Op cit note 3.

command of practical reason and are thereby *essentially* moral in Anscombe's non-modern sense.

4. Conclusion

In this paper, I have argued that we have failed to take the full measure of Anscombe's radical call to action in MMP, because we have failed to see that her third thesis points us to the reason why she put forward the first and the second. On my view, attention to the character and necessity of absolute prohibitions as the core of the virtue of justice is the key to a unified account of her three guiding theses; it also isolates the core respect in which an account of virtue might be radical rather than routine.

In the second half of this paper I have tried to recover a resolutely *unmodern* sense of 'moral', which figures in an account of human action as *moral* action. On this view, there is a standard internal to human life and action that both defines and measures it as an action. Obviously, the argument is incomplete and stands in need of further detail and defense. But there are good reasons to pursue it further. First, it is a view according to which actions are explained by principles internal to the agents who intentionally bring them into being, and the general account of these principles will provide the formal, defining measure of human action as such. Such an account of action locates the source and the measure of actions in human nature or human psychology, where this is cashed out in terms of the characteristic powers and operations of the human person as they operate for the sake of a single, natural, unifying end: the universal good, or living well, or the good life for a man.

Department of Philosophy, University of South Carolina
frey.jenn@gmail.com

Anscombe on Brute Facts and Human Affairs

RACHAEL WISEMAN

Abstract
In 'Modern Moral Philosophy' Anscombe writes: 'It is not profitable at present for us to do moral philosophy. It should be laid aside at any rate until we have an adequate philosophy of psychology, in which we are conspicuously lacking'. In consideration of this Anscombe appeals to the relation of 'brute-relative-to' which holds between facts and descriptions of human affairs. This paper describes the reorientation in philosophy of action that this relation aims to effect and examines the claim that this reorientation makes possible the sort of philosophy of psychology that can provide a starting point for ethics.

1. Introduction

I am a grocer and I want to supply you with some potatoes. How am I to do this? I consider my circumstances. I observe my surroundings. Well, here are some potatoes. I reason: if I carry these potatoes to your house and leave them there then I will have supplied you with potatoes. So, I pick up the potatoes, carry them to your house, and leave them there. I put a note through your letter box: '*You owe me £5*'.

Many philosophers have found this prosaic scene deeply puzzling. Familiar questions include the following: How can reflection on my desires and beliefs directly move me to act? Is the 'so' with which I introduce the action a genuine sign of a conclusion being drawn? In what sense *ought* I, or *must* I carry the potatoes if I reason this way? Would my failure to act thus be a failure of reason? Or a mechanical failure? Or an indication that an ingredient – an imperative-generating, motivating, inner push – is missing? These questions are the starting point for philosophy of action.

When one is attracted by these questions one's attention is typically drawn toward the individual and her psychological processes. What is going on inside my head as I reason thus? And how does that process generate action or reasons for action? The object of enquiry is the individual human subject, and the project is to connect various processes inside a Big Head (as Candace Vogler puts it) with an

doi:10.1017/S1358246119000171

intentional action that is the output of those processes.[1] One's questions become ontological and one's methods speculative. Though this enquiry often encourages introspection, it is notable that the form of explanation in which it issues will be essentially third-personal. The Holy Grail for this enquiry is an external specification of the connection that shows the relation between process (premises) and action (conclusion) to be not merely causal but rationalising. This is the framework within which much of contemporary philosophy of action operates.

One of the deep affinities between Anscombe and her teacher Wittgenstein is a quite staggering ability to resist this temptation to look toward the individual agent for answers to questions about the nature of practical reason and action. My topic in this paper is the philosophy of action that Anscombe makes available to us for use in ethics. It is absolutely central to understanding that philosophy that we appreciate fully the way in which the direction of Anscombe's attention differs from that of almost every other philosopher who has addressed the questions that are the starting point for philosophy of action.

2. Minds and The Mind

For Anscombe, the question 'What is intention?' is not a question about the states and properties of an individual or – worse – the inner workings of an individual mind. As she puts it in the opening section of her book *Intention* – it is rather a question about 'the character of the concept of *intention*'.[2] A question about the 'character of a concept' is not a question about the character of mental representation but a question about the sorts of patterns and abilities that make up a human life shaped by that concept, and about the social, institutional and empirical background that give those patterns their meaning and those abilities their point.[3] I will say more about

[1] Candace Vogler, *Reasonably Vicious* (Harvard: Harvard University Press, 2002), 45ff.

[2] G. E. M. Anscombe, *Intention* (Oxford: Basil Blackwell, 1957; 2nd edition, 1963), 1.

[3] See Peter Geach's *Mental Acts* (London: Routledge and Kegan Paul, 1957) for a Fregean analysis of the proposition that treats concepts in this way, viz. as abilities rather than representations. Note that Geach, Anscombe's husband, was writing this book while Anscombe was writing *Intention* and 'Modern Moral Philosophy'.

that in a moment. To answer a question about the character of a concept, one must attend to the *context of human life* within which *we employ* that concept, and to the sorts patterns of explanation and expectation that an application of the concept requires, imposes and supports. What is presupposed in the application of the concept of *intention?* – about an individual's past and present, about the society in which she lives, and about what will happen in the future?

I said that Anscombe's ability to keep her focus on this background was staggering because the temptation to turn one's attention toward an individual's mind – often one's own – when one's topic is *human psychology* is almost irresistible. But what Anscombe and Wittgenstein both recognised is that a version of Frege's anti-psychologist argument in logic applies here too.[4] As Frege de-psychologised logic, Anscombe and Wittgenstein de-psychologised psychology. Let me pause on that idea and use it to make clearer the object of Anscombe's – and Wittgenstein's – attention.

Frege said that his topic was 'the mind, not minds'.[5] He studied *The Mind* by studying and revealing the laws of thought. He insisted that the laws of thought are not like laws of nature; they are not 'psychological laws in accordance with which [mental process] takes place'.[6] So, for Frege, when one is studying the laws of thought one is not interested in how particular humans *in fact* think and reason – it is not relevant, for example, that most of us will infer *p* from *p*&*q* nor that attempting to entertain a contradiction causes psychological discomfort in all reasonable people. Nor is he concerned with the psychological processes – be they in the mind or in the brain, conscious or sub-conscious, personal or sub-personal – that attend thinking and reasoning and that one might discover by introspection or by empirical study. It is of no interest to Frege's study of the laws of thought that one does or does not feel a transition of thought in moving from antecedent to consequent to conclusion, nor that brain process XYZ is always found to attend an act of judgment. Rather, to describe the laws of thought is to describe a formal order in which anything, if it is a thought, will participate. To be a thought is to stand in logical relations to other thoughts, and the character of those logical relations can be described. To describe the structure of that logical space is to give the essence of thought. Anything that does not fit within that structure is not a thought, whatever an

4 Gottlob Frege, 'The Thought: A Logical Enquiry', *Mind* 65: 259 (1956), 289–311.

5 Op. cit. note 4, 289.

6 Op. cit. note 4, 289.

individual human being feels or experiences or determines by introspection or brain scans. This is what Frege means when he says he is undertaking a study of *The Mind* not of *minds*.

The Fregean idea of a law of thought, and the identification of thought's essence with the structure of logical space, take on a distinctive form in Anscombe's work, as they did in the later Wittgenstein's. This is because where Frege views language – the medium of thought – as an abstract symbolism, Anscombe and the Wittgenstein of the *Philosophical Investigations* picture language as a communicative tool, whose logic is shaped by and shapes the lives and actions of the humans who fashioned that tool for their own employment and to serve their collective ends. This organic and concrete conception of language means that the task of studying *The Mind* not *minds* requires one to attend to more than laws of logic; one must take as one's object human life shaped by concepts.[7] For Frege, to describe the structure of logical space is to give the essence of thought; for Anscombe and Wittgenstein, to describe the structure of human life (the human form of life) is to give the essence of thought and action. Frege's limits of thought – a boundary drawn from the inside when the structure of logical space is mapped – now become the limits of the intelligibility of a human life.

Because Anscombe takes as the object of enquiry the whole ambit of human affairs, she sees most other philosophers' attempts to address the topic of human action as mistaken not merely because they generate false theories but because they miss their subject matter entirely. They are studying *minds* but the proper topic for philosophy of action is *Mind*. She says of Davidson that his project of action explanation fails not because he cannot find a way to rule out deviant causal chains – though that is a failure too – but because he takes his object of enquiry, human action, as 'already given'.[8] He takes it, that is, that he can identify and individuate human actions, and can have a grasp of the difference between a human action and an involuntary gesture, or between a human carrying potatoes and a potato-carrying automaton, prior to and

[7] This characterisation of the way in which the Fregean idea manifests in Wittgenstein's later work is indebted to Cora Diamond, *The Realistic Spirit: Wittgenstein, Philosophy and the Mind* (Cambridge, Mass: MIT, 1995). See esp. 4–6.

[8] G. E. M. Anscombe, 'Practical Inference' (1972), Reprinted in her *Human Life, Action and Ethics* (Imprint Academia, 2005), 109–147. 110.

independently of having a grasp on what it is to give a reason for action.[9] But these entities and distinctions are not things to which he is entitled. His error is akin to supposing that one can identify an individual mental-item as a *thought* prior to identifying it as something that stands in inferential relations to other thoughts. For these physical happenings to be a human action (and not merely the movement of potatoes from one place to another by means of some organic matter) is for the happening to be characterisable in a way that locates it within a framework of reason, prediction, and action – in a way, that is, that locates it within the ongoing bustle of human affairs. So, in taking pre-philosophical intuition to entitle him to the category of *human action*, Davidson not only renders his investigation illegitimate, he – worse – precisely excludes the sort of enquiry that might yield a proper understanding of his topic. He excludes the enquiry that Anscombe undertakes in *Intention*: an enquiry into the formal order in which anything, if it is a human action, will participate, and which characterises the field of human affairs. If we return to the form of investigation of human action that I contrasted with Anscombe's above – the one that takes as its object of enquiry the individual human subject, her psychological states and processes and her intentional actions – we can add this: the individual 'agent' is also not something that can be taken as 'given' in the way that the Big Head investigation supposes.[10] This is one of the deep insights of Anscombe's 'The First Person'.[11]

3. Return to action

To return to my original deliberations as a grocer. We can now frame a new question: can we describe the background against which this sort of thinking and acting is possible, and by doing so can we start

9 This is a reference to the imagined society in Anscombe's 'The First Person' (in Samuel D. Guttenplan (ed.), *Mind and Language* (Oxford University Press, 1975), 45–65) who lack self-consciousness and the capacity for intentional action. See Rachael Wiseman, 'What am I and What am I Doing', *Journal of Philosophy* 114: 10 (2017), 536–550 for an expanded discussion of this point.

10 See, Michael Thompson, *Life and Action: Elementary Structures of Practice and Practical Thought* (Harvard: Harvard University Press, 2008) and Cora Diamond, 'Eating Meat and Eating People', *Philosophy* 53:206 (1978), 465–479 for different ways of showing, in this spirit, that *human* is not an empirical concept.

11 Wiseman 2017. Op. cit. note 9.

to reveal what is essential to practical thought? By 'possible' I do not of course mean *physically* or *psychologically* possible – though reflecting on the empirical conditions for the possibility of an instance of practical thought may help us to understand something about its essential character. By 'possible' I mean rather: what context and background are required for my thinking to so much as to be the kind of thinking that it is? This new question rejects the pressure to locate what is essential to this little scene inside my head and eschews the search for a connection between thought and action, inner and outer.

The answer begins, as Anscombe's *Intention* begins, with a grounding observation designed to situation our vignette in the context of an ongoing human history into which I – one grocer among many, past, present and future – will, for a short time, participate. *We have grown to the age of reason in a shared world.*[12] It is the fact that I have grown to the age of reason in this world, a world shaped by my fellow humans, that I am able both to pose this question – 'How shall I supply you with potatoes?' – and to draw on the tools of the language I have learnt to answer the practical problem I set myself. As Anscombe points out in *Intention*, it is also this fact that would allow me to say 'straight off' that you were supplying potatoes to me if I observed you carrying potatoes to my house and leaving them there.[13]

It is important to see that it is the shared world, the history of mankind (as Wittgenstein puts it), that carries the burden of holding together the conceptual relations that I draw upon when I pose to myself the question: what should I do, given that I want to supply you with potatoes? The connection between carrying potatoes to a place and leaving them there, and supplying potatoes, is located in the meaning of those descriptions, in the language that I use and we share, and in the shared world we inhabit.

The capacities that my mastery of our language encodes were shaped and reshaped by my kind: human animals with needs and interests that are characteristic of our species. Those needs and interests show up in the working of our language. 'Supplying' is not merely leaving stuff somewhere for another to find. A community of people who carried potatoes to houses and left them there, but who violently despised potatoes or had no institutions of commerce, exchange, nor any practice of the mutual provision of necessities, would not thereby be supplying potatoes. This absence of background would show up in the wider context – in the way that

[12] Op. cit. note 2, 8.
[13] Op. cit. note 2, 8.

individuals reacted to the potatoes that appeared on their doorsteps or to those who delivered them or in the wider rituals in which this behaviour was embedded. 'Supplying' is a way in which we make resources available to each other, in order that we may each have that which we need to live or want for pleasure. So, the description '*being supplied with* X' is completed with an 'X' that is wanted, needed or requested – only in very special circumstances would it be appropriate to say that I supplied you with a toenail clipping or a black eye. A cat does not supply her owner with a mouse and nor does a child supply his mother with her slippers because to act under the description 'supplying' is to stand in a relation to another that involves the sort of complexity and mutual recognition that animal-to-human or child-to-adult relations necessarily lack. This is not, of course, to say that a cat or a child cannot *bring* or even *give* a mouse or a pair of slippers.[14]

To learn the meaning of 'supply' – to learn to recognise when the concept applies and to be able to follow the order 'Supply X!' – is to learn, among other things, similarities and distinctions between supplying X and other activities like giving X, delivering X, providing X, making X available, and so forth.[15] Part of what someone who learns the meaning of 'supply' must know is what matters to humans – what sort of things they need and want. So a person who can employ this concept in practical thought and in judgment is someone who has at least a partial grasp on what sort of things are good or desirable for humans.

What one learns when one learns a concept, acquires a capacity, has of necessity a sort of incompleteness – this is an insight pursued to startling effect by Wittgenstein.[16] We acquire concepts, capacities, rules, by being shown examples. After a number of examples we

[14] We can always extend our concepts to include the activities of humans and children. Sometimes this extension is one we are compelled to make because we have discovered new facts. For example, learning about the complex social relations that exist among the higher primates may convince us that certain kinds of behaviour really is 'supplying'. Sometimes the extension is an 'as if' extension, as when we apply to our pets descriptions that their form of life can clearly not sustain ('The cat is negotiating with the dog about who gets to sleep in the basket'). Sometimes the case falls between the two, and here exists the space for conceptual innovation, aspect shifts, moral transformation and poetry.

[15] Compare the discussion of the concept of *length* in G. E. M. Anscombe, 'The Question of Linguistic Idealism (1976), reprinted in her *From Parmenides to Wittgenstein* (Oxford: Blackwell, 1981), 112–134. 117.

[16] Ludwig Wittgenstein, *Philosophical Investigations*, esp. §§138–242.

confront: 'and so on'. This 'and so on' is not shorthand for a finite list that is occluded for pragmatic or epistemic reasons. Rather, it marks gesture toward a standard of 'sameness' or 'similarity' that a normal learner will catch on to, but which cannot be articulated independently of the concept itself. This 'and so on' is tied to learning situations, so a conception of ordinary procedure, and relatedly of what is abnormal and exceptional is built into the grasp of the rule. But talk of what is 'exceptional' needs care. It would be an exceptional if I suddenly discovered I had won the lottery or if the roof fell in or if I received a phone call from the Queen. But none of these exceptional circumstances touches the relationship between the bringing and leaving of the potatoes and the supplying of the potatoes. What counts as 'exceptional circumstances' is internal to the meaning and significance of the description involved. It is here that disagreements can occur about what a person really did, and about whether the circumstances in which she acted are relevant not just our evaluation of her action, but to the descriptions under which it fell.

The connection between the description 'supplying you with potatoes' and 'carrying potatoes and leaving them at your house' cannot, then, be synonymity because exceptional circumstances can always mean that an activity that falls under the former description does not fall under the latter. Yet, the connection between the descriptions is not merely constant conjunction. Rather, carrying potatoes to a house and leaving them there is an exemplary case of supplying potatoes – it is one of the many cases of human action we might point to if we wanted to give the meaning of 'supplying' or to indicate what is normal and ordinary with respect to it. Even in cases of potato-carrying and leaving where the description 'supplying potatoes' is false, we might say: it has application here. The question: 'Is she supplying potatoes?' is salient and relevant as the question 'Is she organising a wedding?' is not. It is here that concepts like pretence, fraud and sham have their home.

We can represent the relation between 'carrying and leaving potatoes' and 'supplying potatoes' using a hypothetical: *If a then b*. Such hypotheticals encode our shared knowledge of what is and what can be done, and I, a human grown to the age of reason in this shared world, can make use of that knowledge when I use them to reason about how to do what I want to do.[17]

Let me pause to say something about the logical form of these hypotheticals. The connection between the descriptions is not synonymity but neither is it constant conjunction. The hypotheticals

[17] See op. cit. note 2, 50 and op. cit. note 8 for further discussion.

that I make use of in a piece of practical reasoning cannot have the logical form of existential generalisations. The relation is one that holds between descriptions of human action and it is a formal relation that tells us what those actions are and what are those actions. We must not try to represent the knowledge that these hypotheticals encode in the form:

> For every event (*e*), if *e* is *X carrying potatoes to Y's house and leaving them there*, then *e* is *X supplying potatoes to Y*

Such existential generalisations are false, which is bad enough, but to attempt to force our hypotheticals into this form is both a symptom of and an encouragement toward the sort of philosophical treatment of action that involves having one's attention in the wrong place. As a symptom, it reflects a misconstrual of the nature of the relata that the hypothetical concerns. In the quantified version the hypothetical statement ranges over entities that are specified prior to the application of the concepts that are our topic. It is as if you could pick out some event *e* prior to the specification of it under an action description, e.g., *carrying potatoes*. But this is precisely wrong and is a version of the error Anscombe finds in Davidson. This is to turn one's philosophical attention away from *The Mind* and onto *minds*.

Before I move on, I want to make one final comment about the institutions and social and cultural practices that provide the background to many of our concepts. This is an aside here, but it makes a point I want to have in place later, when we come to consider the subject-matter of ethics. What I want to add is this: just as many of our concepts have their point in the context of our institutions and social and cultural practices, so too our institutions and social and cultural practices have their point in the context of our needs and desires, and take their shape from the material conditions of our lives. These are things that in some aspects remain constant. Our instinct for the so-called 'four F's (flight, fight, food and reproduction) is characteristic of our species. The atmospheric pressure, the boiling point of water and the weight of this pen are the same now as in the past, and the same here as in America. But our lives – human lives – and the conditions in which they are lived do change, sometimes dramatically, not least because as our use of tools – and in particular, the tools of language – become ever more sophisticated, our interests and habitat can be altered and changed. Shifts across time, culture and geography in what we need and want and in the material conditions of our lives are to be expected for language-using creatures like us. This is one reason why – as Anscombe, Mary Midgley, Iris Murdoch, Alasdair MacIntyre and Bernard Williams each in different ways warn – once useful concepts can change from genuine capacities into dysfunctional habits or pathologies and once necessary institutions can become structures of injustice and oppression.

4. From psychology to ethics

What I have been saying is, as you may have spotted, an exploration and elaboration of Anscombe's discussion of 'brute facts' in her rightly celebrated paper 'Modern Moral Philosophy'.[18] You will remember that in that paper she says: 'It is not profitable at present for us to do moral philosophy. It should be laid aside at any rate until we have an adequate philosophy of psychology, in which we are conspicuously lacking'.[19] It is in consideration of this that Anscombe appeals to the relation of 'brute-relative-to'. In the remainder of this paper I want to start to think though how the reorientation I have described in philosophy of action provides the sort of philosophy of psychology that can provide a starting point for ethics.

Anscombe introduces the topic of brute facts in relation to Hume's puzzle.[20] She says that the troubling transition from 'is' to 'ought' makes an interesting comparison with the transition from 'is' to 'owes'. Hume's worry about the legitimacy of the former transition, she says, points us toward a kind of *relation* that is of significance to ethics. The relation is between levels of description of human action. Hume's worry is how a description of human affairs that employs only non-normative concepts can stand in this relation to a description that employs normative concepts, like 'ought', 'should' and 'must'. But Anscombe observes that the relation that Hume finds unintelligible is one that exists between descriptions of human affairs at many levels, not just between descriptions that employ only non-normative concepts and those that involve 'ought', 'must', 'should', and so forth. How does the fact that I carried potatoes to your house and left them there relate to the description 'supplying you with potatoes'? She writes:

> [I]t comes to light that the relation of the facts mentioned [viz. the fact that she ordered potatoes and the grocer supplied them] to the description "X owes Y so much money" is an interesting one, which I will call that of being 'brute relative to' that

[18] G. E. M. Anscombe, 'Modern Moral Philosophy', *Philosophy* 33:124 (1958), 1–19.

[19] Op. cit. note 18, 1.

[20] Op. cit. note 18, 3–4.

> description. Further, the 'brute' facts mentioned here themselves have descriptions relatively to which *other* facts are 'brute'—as, e.g., *he had potatoes carted to my house* and *they were left there* are brute relative to 'he supplied me with potatoes'. And the fact *X owes Y money* is in turn 'brute' relative to other descriptions – e.g. 'X is solvent'.[21]

What Hume puts his finger on is this: if we attempt to do moral philosophy without having understood this kind of relation we will be left mystified by the transition from 'is' to 'ought'. Anscombe's insight is that – at least part of – Hume's worry is not about the transition from 'is' to 'ought' but about the transition between levels of description of human action.

Returning to my moonlight job as a grocer. The fact that I carry potatoes to your house and leave them there is brute-relative-to the description 'supplying you with potatoes'. And the fact that I supply you with potatoes you ordered is brute-relative to the description 'You owe me for the potatoes'. So, here we have a fact is brute-relative-to a description that seems to be of interest to ethics.

Anscombe's reorientation in philosophy of action has given us the tools to articulate 'merely "factual"' descriptions that employ normative concepts like *ought* and *should, must.*[22] The hope was that this, in turn, would give the ethical a foothold in the human. It can seem, however, that this hope is short-lived because though we have introduced normative concepts it is not clear that the 'merely "factual"' 'ought', 'should' and 'must' can do the work that we want our normative concepts to do *in ethics*. First, the norms we have in play here do not transcend the institutions or practices in which they have their home. As Foot puts it: 'owes' is the sort of 'evaluative' concept, that 'belong[s] within an institution', and this means that if the institutions is a bad institution – an unjust one, we might say – then it may not follow that debts accrued in the context of that institution are debts one has a duty to pay – even though the description of the debt generates an 'ought' within the institutional context.[23] This recalls an observation we made earlier: institutions and practices that were once useful or sound can become instruments of oppression and injustice if facts on the ground change. Given this, norms that are internal to those institutions and practices cannot, it seems, be verdictive in the way that the norms of ethics seem to be.

[21] Op. cit. note 18, 3–4.

[22] Op. cit. note 18, 4.

[23] Philippa Foot, *Theories of Ethics* (Oxford: Oxford University Press, 1968), 11–12.

The second difficulty is that it seems that the 'merely "factual"' conceptions we have so far would provide me with reasons for action only if I there is something that I *want* that makes relevant to me those descriptions and gives me a reason to consider how I might make them true through my activity. Why should I use the hypothetical – *if I hand over this money I will pay what I owe* – if I am not interested in whether or not I pay what I owe? Why should I use it any more than I would use my knowledge – if I carry these potatoes to NN's house I will supply her with potatoes – when I have no interest or desire to supply NN with potatoes. But now we seem to have lost the foothold that ethics had. If these 'merely "factual"' descriptions have their point only within the context of man-made institutions – institutions that can be unjust, bad, or useless – and if the opportunity to make these descriptions true or false neither gives me a reason to act nor to refrain from acting – it seems we still have work to do before the philosophy of psychology that Anscombe gives us connects with the subject-matter of moral philosophy.

I wrote above of Anscombe's first warning at the beginning of 'Modern Moral Philosophy': 'It is not profitable at present for us to do moral philosophy. It should be laid aside at any rate until we have an adequate philosophy of psychology, in which we are conspicuously lacking'. Now is the time to remind ourselves of her second warning: 'the concepts of obligation and duty – moral obligation and moral duty, that is to say – and of what is morally right and wrong, and of the moral sense of "ought", ought to be jettisoned if it is psychologically possible'.[24] Now, the thought I want to explore in this final part of this paper is the following: that our feeling that we do not have enough in the 'merely "factual"' descriptions we already have is a symptom of the psychological hold that the idea of a 'moral sense of "ought"' has over us. We have enough already, I want tentatively to suggest, to 'do moral philosophy'. Though, of course, what 'doing moral philosophy' looks like now is going to be rather different to what we have been doing – or trying to do – before.

Here is the idea. Despite appearances, the framework we have – one which describes *Mind* not *minds* – is sufficient to generate the sorts of generic 'oughts' that are of interest to ethics. By 'generic' I mean: they are not relative to the particular desires or plans of the individual whose actions they concern. My idea – which I hope is close to Anscombe's idea – is that these generic 'oughts' are enough to

[24] Op. cit. note 2, 1.

characterise the subject-matter of ethics without us needing to appeal to a quasi-legal 'Moral Ought'. Let me try to bring this out.

Suppose someone asks, 'Why must I pay what I owe?' and consider two possible replies:

(1) You must pay what you owe because if you don't the grocer will never supply you with potatoes again

(2) You must pay what you owe because it would be unjust not to do so

These two replies look very similar, but Anscombe observes that despite their shared sentential structure, they have quite different logical forms. The first reply gives the individual who asks it a *reason for acting*. This reason will only interest the individual if the description of what will happen as a consequence of her failing to pay is one that she is interested in avoiding. Replies of this form offer a reason for acting that is specific to the individual who asks her question 'Why should *I* do it?'. As we might put it, the '*I*' in this question and the '*You*' in the reply introduce the particular individual who is deliberating about what to do.

Now contrast the second reply: You must pay what you owe because it would be unjust not to do so. In this answer the '*I*' in the question is treated by the responder as generic, akin to 'one' or 'we'. 'Why should *one* pay?' The answer contains the generic 'you': 'One shouldn't because it is unjust'. The phrase that follows the 'because' does not give an independent reason that is sensitive to the individual's idiosyncratic desires and beliefs, but rather characterises the action described in the first part of the statement as one that falls under a further description containing a vice term. The fact that the act would be unjust is not given as a further independent consideration, a reason for action, but is put forward as a characterisation of the action itself. The answer reminds the asker of a connection in the formal order that characterises human thought and action. Anscombe reserves the label 'logos' for an answer to the question 'Why?' that has this sort of generality.[25]

Recall Frege's project to describe the formal order in which anything, if it is a thought, will participate. In so doing, we noted, he traced from the inside the limits of intelligibility in thought. To answer a 'Why?' question by giving a logos is to draw attention to action's location at the limits of intelligibility in human life. This sounds rather grand, but it need not be; it is commonplace to say 'I

[25] G. E. M. Anscombe, 'Rules, Rights and Promises' in her *Ethics, Religion and Politics* Oxford: Blackwell, 1981), 332.

can't make sense of what she did', 'I don't understand his life', 'She seemed hardly human'. To employ the terminology that has been our topic today: the answer provides a reminder that the proposed action would be brute-relative-to a description of an action kind that we do not go in for: 'breaking a promise', 'contravening a rule', 'infringing a right', 'cheating', 'steeling', 'bilking'. These descriptions are ones whose meaning and point in our language is to mark out classes of activity that we, collectively in our language and our lives, recognise as of serious importance to human life going well – or badly – and they encode our shared knowledge of that fact. Here is an echo of Mary Midgley's brilliant insight: 'moral' is the superlative of serious.[26]

The idea, then, is that while an answer to the question 'Why?' which gives a *reason for action* can intelligibly be answered 'I don't care about that!', when an answer that gives a *logos* attracts this response the intelligibility of that answer is not to be taken for granted. When the 'you' in 'You mustn't because …' is generic, rather than individual, it makes an appeal to a standard of evaluation of the action in question that transcends the particular aims of the individual and makes reference instead to the *logos* of human action *as such*. An act of *carrying* can be evaluated as good or bad by reference to the individual's aims and goals in performing that act, and by reference to a standard case of carrying. Was it too slow, too ostentatious? Was the load carried to the right place, at the right time? Was it efficient and safe? But in evoking these descriptions in terms of virtue and vice – just, unfair, cowardly, and so forth – there is an appeal to an evaluation of the action by reference to a more general standard: the standard of good human action. *We don't do that, remember?* is the form of reply. This is where the ethical gets its foothold.

We may still raise, of course, a version of the worry that we had before, and I don't want to say that this worry can be easily dismissed. The worry from before was: 'shoulds' that are internal to institutions cannot be verdictive in the way that the oughts of morality are. The worry now is: 'shoulds' that are internal to the human form of life cannot be verdictive in the way that the oughts of morality are. What is one to say to that?

I don't quite know, but I want to try to give a sense of what is odd about that thought by recalling the depth of the connection between our form of life, the concepts that we have, and the things that we,

[26] Mary Midgley, 'Is "Moral a Dirty Word?', *Philosophy* 47: 181 (1972), 206. Midgley generously attributes this idea to Philippa Foot, 'The Philosopher's Defence of Morality', *Philosophy* 27 (1952), 103.

humans, want and need. Recall that to learn the meaning of 'supply' – to be able to employ that concept in thought and deed – is to know something about the sorts of things that humans might need or want. Our concepts have a point for us – they reflect our interests and goals – and learning a concept is, in part, learning that point. So, the limit against which a person comes here is not a limit in an arbitrary system of rules or 'mere' convention but the limit of our form of life. The concepts that we have record 'the history of mankind' and are tools that we have fashioned to serve our collective ends, our natural instincts and desires, in response to our environment. They are also the only means we have to navigate that world because what is to participate in the history of mankind is to grow to the age of reason in a world that is shaped by those concepts. Moral pioneers, individuals who live at the edges of intelligibility, do exist. We might call them the nihilists or saints or radicals. But their ability to pioneer, and through their actions to refashion our concepts, depends on the vast majority of us sustaining, in thought, word and action, the form of life into which we were born. On the whole, in the ordinary bustle of our day-to-day lives, we do keep our promises, honour our contracts, treat each other with compassion and justice. When we do something vicious, we often seek to demonstrate that exceptional circumstances undermine the description of what we did as such. Attempts to do so are often attempts to render our actions intelligible by rejecting the description of it as unjust, unfair or cruel in favour of one that reconnects it to human virtue: I was cruel to be kind, we say (meaning: what I did does not *really* fall under the description 'cruel'). If we – collectively, for a sustained period – ceased to operate broadly within the limits marked by these evaluative concepts, the result would not be a worse state of affairs but the chaos of a world in which there were no 'states of affairs' that we could recognise or describe, and nothing that we would recognise as human life and action.[27]

University of Liverpool
rachael.wiseman@liverpool.ac.uk

[27] Thanks to audiences at the University of Oxford, University of Liverpool and at the Royal Institute of Philosophy for helpful questions and comments. This paper would not have been possible without the benefit of Clare Mac Cumhaill's generous insights and stimulating conversation over several years.

Aristotelian Necessity

CANDACE VOGLER

Abstract

At the center of contemporary neo-Aristotelian naturalism is the thought that we can account for a great deal of ethics by thinking about what is needful in human life generally. When we think about practices like promising, virtues like justice or courage, and institutions that serve to produce, maintain, and help to reproduce well-ordered social life we can make some headway we consider the sense in which our topic makes some forms of human good possible and even, in some cases, actualizes the very good made possible thereby. G.E.M. Anscombe introduced this kind of thinking about ethics, which Philippa Foot named 'Aristotelian Necessity'. In this essay, I take a hard Look at Anscombe's work on the topic, and then consider her later insistence that crucial aspects of ethics could not be understood in these terms.

Introduction

At least as early as 1960,[1] Elizabeth Anscombe made arguments drawing on thought about things that are necessary in the sense that without them some good cannot be or come about, or some evil be expelled or avoided.[2] She drew this sense of the term *necessary* from Book V of Aristotle's *Metaphysics* – what she called Aristotle's

[1] I have in mind Anscombe's 'Authority in Morals,' read at a 1960 conference at Bec Abbey in Normandy, and first published in John Todd, editor, *Problems of Authority*, (London: Darton, Longman, and Todd, 1962).

[2] This gloss on the relevant sense of *necessity* is from St. Thomas Aquinas, *Commentary on Aristotle's* Metaphysics, Ch. 5, Lesson 6: Secundum modum ponit ibi, et sine dicit, quod secundo modo dicuntur necessaria, sine quibus non potest esse vel fieri bonum aliquod, vel vitari aliquod malum, vel expelli; sicut bibere pharmacum, idest medicinam laxativam, dicimus esse necessarium, non quia sine hoc vivere animal non possit; sed ad expellendum, scilicet hoc malum quod est infirmitas, vel etiam vitandum. Est enim hoc necessarium ut non laboret, idest ut non infirmetur aliquis. Similiter navigare ad Aeginam, scilicet ad illum locum, est necessarium, non quia sine hoc non possit homo esse; sed quia sine hoc non potest acquirere aliquod bonum, idest pecuniam. Unde dicitur, quod necessaria est talis navigatio, ut aliquis pecuniam recipiat.

doi:10.1017/S1358246119000237

'dictionary'.[3] And she later described the source passage from Aristotle as a 'pregnant remark'.[4]

In the early paper, her midwifery drew from the pregnant remark her thought about moral authority – the 'the authority to declare to someone else what is true – in this case what is right and what is wrong, and to demand that he accept what one says and act accordingly'.[5] It informed her discussion of the authority of the state where, again, authority is, as she puts it, 'a regular *right* to be obeyed in a domain of decision'.[6] More generally, it underwrites her account of rights and her account of rules. All turn on how some possibilities of good are created and then made actual through our understanding, deployment, and obedience to the dictates of what she called 'stopping modals'. She writes:

> I want to arouse interest in...what I'll call 'stopping modals'. These are of course negative; corresponding positive ones...we may call 'forcing modals'. The negative gets priority; it is I think more frequent than the positive, which restricts one's action to one thing. (Just as 'thou shalt nots' tend to leave you freer than 'thou shalts'.)[7]

She continues:

> 'You have to' and 'you can't' are the first words used by one who is making you do something (or preventing you), and they quickly become themselves instruments of getting and preventing action.
>
> After all, once this transformation has taken place, the following is true: in such a case you are told you 'can't' do something you plainly can, as comes out in the fact that you sometimes do. At the beginning, the adults will physically stop the child from doing what they say he 'can't' do. But gradually the child learns. With one set of circumstances this business is part of the build-up of the concept of a rule; with another, of a piece of etiquette;

[3] G.E.M. Anscombe, 'On Promising and its Justice, and Whether it Need be Respected *in Foro Interno*,' reprinted in Anscombe, *Collected Philosophical Papers of G. E. M. Anscombe, Vol. III, Ethics, Religion and Politics*, (Oxford: Basil Blackwell, 1981), hereafter, '*CP*', 15.

[4] G.E.M. Anscombe, On the Source of the Authority of the State,' in *CP* op. cit. note 3, 139.

[5] G.E.M. Anscombe, 'Authority in Morals, in *CP* op. cit. note 3, 43.

[6] G.E.M. Anscombe, 'On the Source of Authority of the State, in *CP* op. cit. note 3, 132.

[7] G.E.M. Anscombe, 'Rules, Rights and Promises,' in *CP* op. cit. note 3 100-101.

> with another of a promise; in another, of an act of sacrilege or impiety; with another of a right. It is part of human intelligence to be able to learn the responses to stopping modals without which they wouldn't exist as linguistic instruments and without which these things: rules, etiquette, rights, infringements, promises, pieties and impieties would not exist either.[8]

By tying our capacity to operate with stopping modals to human intelligence, and to the practices of human reason, Anscombe links the capacity to distinctively human goods. Rules, rights, and the like are linguistic instruments caught up in making possible such things as economic and legal systems, the moral education of children, peaceful modes of conflict resolution, good manners, and so on. In this sense, the capacity to use, understand, and follow the strictures at issue in stopping modals is, as Peter Winch put it, 'humanly necessary'.[9]

Anscombe's development of Aristotle's remark may be one of the most important aspects of her legacy in contemporary Anglophone practical philosophy. For, while Anscombe used her work on these topics in support of David Hume's famous observation that both the existence of such things as promises and the obligation to do one's word were 'naturally unintelligible', an *anti*-Humean form of contemporary ethical naturalism draws some of its inspiration, sustenance, and direction from Anscombe's work on this topic – a topic that Philippa Foot named 'Aristotelian necessity'.[10] Foot's work on natural goodness grows from this strand of Anscombe's thought, and some of Michael Thompson's work – to which Foot owes a special debt – can be read as a concerted effort to provide a more detailed, more thoroughly articulated, more advanced, and more clearly defended version of this strand of Anscombe's practical philosophy.

At the center of Anscombe-inflected neo-Aristotelian naturalism is the thought that we can account for a great deal of ethics by thinking about what is needful in human life generally. When we think about practices like promising, virtues like justice or courage, and institutions that serve to produce, maintain, and help to reproduce well-ordered social life we can make some headway in understanding both our topic and its *logos* or *ratio* if we consider the sense in

[8] G.E.M. Anscombe, 'Rules, Rights and Promises', in *CP* op. cit. note 3, 101.

[9] Peter Winch, 'Professor Anscombe's Moral Philosophy', in Lilli Alanen, Sarah Heinamaa, and Thomas Wallgren, editors, *Commonality and Particularity in Ethics*, (London: Palgrave Macmillan, 1997), 185.

[10] Philippa Foot, *Natural Goodness*, (Oxford: Oxford University Press, 2003), 15.

which our topic makes some forms of human good possible and even, in some cases, *actualizes* the very good made possible thereby. It is against the backdrop of thought about human life and what is good for the human as such that claims about Aristotelian necessity get some traction in this region of contemporary Anglophone practical philosophy.

I will focus on Anscombe. I will start by trying to disentangle different ways in which thought about Aristotelian necessity informs her practical philosophical writings, with special emphasis on her discussion of 'stopping-modals'. On the face of it, at least, very different kinds of negative considerations are at work in stopping-modals, according to Anscombe. I will try to say something about what these have in common.

Having tried to isolate what her varied examples share, I will consider how thought about human good gets caught up in discussion of stopping modals. Finally, I will turn to the cases where she thinks that appeal to what is generally needful in human life *fails* to help us understand the point or force of a family of key ethical considerations, even as she holds fast to the idea that the sphere of the ethical is the sphere of distinctively human life and distinctively human good.

2. Anscombe's Examples

Aristotelian necessity is a fairly broad topic, as Anscombe understands it. She gives a wide range of examples of stopping modals that express Aristotelian necessity, among them 'You can't wear that!' and 'You have to move your king'.[11] Unlike Aristotle's examples (needing to take a drug to relieve physical distress; needing to sail to Aegina to collect a sum of money) the special sub-class of interest to Anscombe does not point to some contingent facts independent of the stuff of the stopping-modal to trigger its applicability. Her stopping-modals seem to have three interrelated distinctive features in common:

1. The justification for 'you can't...' or 'you have to...' does not involve mention of any additional fact in support of the prohibition or prescription. If you 'can't' do such-and-such because it is N's to do (hence, you 'have to' let N do it), and this expresses N's right (or obligation), then the right (or obligation) is partly

[11] G.E.M. Anscombe, 'Rules, Rights and Promises', in *CP*, op. cit. note 3, 100.

constituted by the fact that it is not anyone else's place to do the thing in question. N's right (or obligation) is not an independent fact that can be adduced in support of the prescription or prohibition. Rather, the prohibition and prescription are joint aspects of N's right (obligation).[12]

2. The 'because'-clauses that one might attach to the prescription or prohibition – in this case, 'because N is the only one who has a right/obligation to do such-and-such' – do not provide extra reasons to do or forbear doing the thing in question.[13] Instead, they help to classify or thematize the stopping-modal/forcing-modal pair. The stuff of the 'because'-clause is, in the same sense – *dependent*. Anscombe writes: 'Let me now restrict the word 'reason' (in the context of action) to something independent which someone puts forward as his reason for what he does. And let me adopt the word 'logos' (I might also use 'theme') for the second half of 'you can't...because...' where the two halves are not independent. I shall say that there are various logos-types, and that the name of the general logos-type is an abstraction from many particular cases: a label which tells you the formal character of the stopping-modal'.[14]
3. Learning to deploy and abide by stopping-modals of a *logos*-type is learning both the concepts associated with the *logos*-type and the practical orientations that actualize the relevant *logoi*. The typical way in which this happens is through social interaction standardly governed in accordance with the relevant *logoi*. Recall Anscombe's remark about how this moral education works: 'With one set of circumstances this business is part of the build-up of the concept of a rule; with another, of a piece of etiquette; with another of a promise; in another, of an act of sacrilege or impiety; with another of a right'.[15]

[12] In a brilliant discussion of this topic, in the context of a larger exploration of Anscombe's practical philosophy than any I will attempt here, Katharina Nieswandt marks the crucial aspect by saying that rules, rights, and promises are necessarily 'self-referential'. See Katharina Nieswandt, 'Anscombe on the Sources of Normativity,' *The Journal of Value Inquiry*, 51 (2017): 141-163.

[13] If I understand him, this is part of what Roger Teichmann brings out in stressing that such "reasons" are categorical rather than hypothetical. See Roger Teichmann, 'Explaining the Rules', *Philosophy*, 77 (2002): 597-613.

[14] G.E.M. Anscombe, 'Rules, Rights and Promises', in *CP* op. cit. note 3, 101-102.

[15] G.E.M. Anscombe, 'Rules, Rights and Promises', in *CP*, op. cit. note 3,. 101.

> I take it that her list is a sample list of *logos*-types. Compare: 'one does not learn morality by learning that certain propositions – ethical ones – are true, but by learning what to do or abstain from in particular situations and getting by practice to do certain things, and abstain from others'.[16]

Our capacity to operate effectively with stopping-modals, then, is grounded in the order they help to provide in our shared social lives, and serves to help participants realize those very kinds of order in those very domains of decision.

How does Anscombe's work on stopping-modals connect to the way in which philosophers like Foot and Rosalind Hursthouse turn to thought about human nature to illuminate work on virtue, on human flourishing or happiness, and a host of other ethical concepts?

Recall that Anscombe remarked that the practical education at issue in deploying and abiding by stopping-modals counted as an actualization of basic human capacities: 'It is part of human intelligence to be able to learn the responses to stopping modals'.[17] We are the chatty animals – the rational ones. Anscombe takes a step in the direction of more recent extensions of her thought precisely by linking her exploration of stopping-modal/forcing-modal pairs to thought about discursive human reason. And her discussions of rules and rights – generally, and in the specific context of her discussions of authority – make direct reference to common human good – to what is generally needful in human life, in a way echoed by more recent neo-Aristotelian work.

For example, when invited to locate the source of the obligation to do one's word – the sense in which I do not merely risk *being* reproached if I break my promise, but *deserve* reproach – Anscombe points out that it is generally needful in human life to get other people to do things, and that this need dramatically outstrips anyone's power to get others to do his will because they love him or fear him. 'Thus,' she writes, 'such a procedure [as promising] is an instrument whose use is part and parcel of an enormous amount of human activity and hence of human good; of the supplying of both human needs and human wants so far as the satisfaction of these are compossible. It is scarcely possible to live in a society without encountering it and even being involved in it'.[18]

[16] G.E.M. Anscombe, 'Authority in Morals', in *CP*,op. cit. note 3, 47.

[17] G.E.M. Anscombe, 'Rules, Rights and Promises,' in CP, op. cit. note 3, 101.

[18] G.E.M. Anscombe, 'On Promising and its Justice, and Whether it Need be Respected *in Foro Interno*', in *CP*, op. cit. note 3, 18.

Of moral authority, she writes: '[The authority to declare what is right or wrong, virtuous or vicious], however distasteful it may be, is a sort of authority that can hardly be denied to exist by the most recalcitrant moral philosopher. For it is exercised by people in bringing up children; and if there is such a thing as authority of a commanding kind at all, or if there is such a thing as a right, this authority and this right can hardly be denied, since it is quite necessary, if children are to be brought up, that their bringers-up act as if they were exercising such authority; and since what is a necessity can hardly fail to be a right, so anyone who wants to bring children up must have this right'.[19] The requirement that we bring up children, of course, is perfectly general. No society is possible without meeting the requirement, and the bringing-up of children is what makes it possible for children to come into their own as the maturing, discursively reasoning, social animals that they are born to be.

In her discussion of the authority of the state, by a similar token, she argues that the right of civil authority to back up its strictures with coercive force, although it must have some standing in custom, cannot be merely a customary right. She argues that people in general need protection against violence, and also protection in law against violation of their customary rights. Partly because we are vulnerable to personal violence, partly because different systems of customary right can clash within a single complex society, and partly because we have come increasingly to inhabit complex societies, we need the kind of civil authority that is lodged in the state. That authority is nothing other than the state's claim to our regular obedience in, for example, matters of the establishment, promulgation, and enforcement of positive law. Of course, the state can forfeit its right to our obedience if it fails to discharge the tasks for the sake of which we need civil authority, and it can overreach its authority in some areas if it enshrines or extends a customary right – say, through legislation – beyond what one might call a reasonable limit. Winch imagines a case in which a society uses queueing as a mechanism of fair access in many contexts and a government eager to penalize queue-jumping by imposing strict penalties on jumping the queue as one possible instance of overreach.[20]

What matters for my purposes is that in all of these cases, Anscombe adverts to Aristotelian necessity as a way of arguing *for* a right, a rule, an institution, a practice, and the sorts of practical dispositions might actualize these in the lives of practitioners *without*

19 G.E.M. Anscombe, 'Authority in Morals', in *CP*, op. cit. note 3,. 43.
20 Op. cit. note 8, 187-189.

appeal to particular customs, or instances of positive law, or contract, or pure principles of Reason that might seem to operate independently of the business of specifically human life. By the same token, appeal to Aristotelian necessity can give some leverage in arguing that what is taken to be a customary right could, actually, count as a customary *wrong*.[21] Anscombe, then, finds in perfectly general thought about what is needful in human life a source of support for *some* substantive ethical claims, and a *check* on others. The sort of justification at issue on both sides is instrumental. Uses of stopping-modals are *instruments* for creating and actualizing possibilities for human good. We *need* virtues in order to live well. Some forms of authority are *required* in human life if we are to manage to do the things that we must. And so on. Aristotelianly necessary matters in Anscombe's practical philosophy are collective means to common ends – where the 'commonality' points to shared human nature, rather than to some amalgamated measure of private interests that happen to crop up in any particular group of human beings. Part of what Aristotelian necessity can sometimes explain is *why* some such interests might crop up in many members of a particular group of human beings – for example, interests in marrying or making contracts or raising children

We can quarrel with Anscombe's justification of the state – noticing, for example, that the reach of the modern state dramatically exceeds the reach of, say, a Lockean umpire state. We can doubt the extent of the authority of bringers-up of children. We can notice that Anscombe does not argue that individual people will tend in general to go along with any of it, even if the justification for the relevant forms of obedience rests in what is humanly needful. In short, we can raise any number of concerns about her substantive use of thought about what humans in general need to provide such justifications. But the basic form of argument she develops in these specific contexts has been undeniably attractive to many philosophers working in contemporary neo-Aristotelian ethics. And while I do not think that she should, or even *could*, accept every such development of her teaching, for better or worse, her teaching has inspired an entire school of contemporary Anglophone moral philosophy. This is part of the reason that I want now to have a look at her sense of the points where thought about Aristotelian necessity fails to illuminate crucial aspects of the ethical.

[21] G.E.M. Anscombe, 'On the Source of Authority of the State,' in *CP* op. cit. note 3, 145.

3. 'Mystical' Value

In a recent essay, directed primarily to Foot's account of natural goodness, Anselm Müller traces out Anscombe's concern about attempting to rely upon thought about Aristotelian necessity to capture the whole of morality.[22] Müller stresses that the kind of justification that Anscombe offers is fundamentally instrumental in character. The good or point of the virtues, rules, rights, institutions, and social practices that Anscombe finds in appeals to what is generally needful in human life sees the objects thereby justified as instruments for satisfying these general needs – as ways of promoting or actualizing human good. The justifications are, in a peculiar sense, utilitarian, although the 'beneficiary' of the good in questions is not in the first instance an individual, or a group of individuals, or a mass of human individuals. The good in question is, as I mentioned, in a special sense, *common* good, where common good need not be the good of any arbitrarily large collection of individual human beings.

On Müller's reading, Foot attempts to use Anscombe-style thought about Aristotelian necessity to reach all the way down to particular individuals facing particular practical situations. This is, he thinks, why she seems to take it that a 'Why should I be moral?' question will cease to arise once we have fully appreciated the character of natural goodness. Because Foot ties morality explicitly to rationality, it looks like a 'Why be moral?' question, when pushed, will slide toward something on the order of a 'Why be rational?' question, and there are well-known arguments to the effect that it is hard to see how such a question ever could be given a sensible answer.

Although Anscombe explicitly links her discussions of stopping-modals and forcing-modals to general concern over human intelligence and the practices of human reason, she *does not take* this extra step. More than this, she comes to reject the suggestion that all important points about the virtues and their exercise can be grounded in thought about what is humanly needful.

Müller puts her point this way:

> Anscombe...came to argue that not all virtue can be understood as serving our well-being. Or rather, since virtue belongs to the human form of life so that all virtuous conduct is part of our well-being: that some of virtue's requirements can be said to 'serve' a good

[22] Anselm Müller, ''Why Should I?' Can Foot Convince the Sceptic,' in John Hacker-Wright, editor, *Philippa Foot on Goodness and Virtue*, (London: Palgrave MacMillan, 2018), 151-185.

> human life only in the sense that satisfaction of these requirements is an ingredient – not an instrument – of human good.
>
> Where a virtuous practice cannot count as virtuous because it serves an aspect of human well-being other than the practice itself, we cannot explain its goodness in terms of Aristotelian necessity. Otherwise, the functionality signified by this term could not supply is with grounds for, e.g., viewing generosity and reliability, but not vindictiveness and arrogance as virtuous motivational patterns.[23]

Anscombe argued that central aspects of virtue, for example refusing to engage in murder as a means or an end, could not be understood in terms of Aristotelian necessity. Müller's gloss on her refusal to seek a grounding for the prohibition on murder in Aristotelian necessity is, I think, right. Anscombe's writing on the topic takes a less abstract tack.

Given that the one wronged by murder is, in the first instance, the victim, Anscombe writes:

> If someone is wronged, he has a right which is violated. But the wrongfulness of murder seems to be the basis of the right, rather than vice versa, because (a) there is not a simple right to life, but rather a right not to be murdered, and (b) if there were a certain right to life upon which the wrongfulness of murder is based, it would be difficult to see why it should not be waivable.
>
> The prohibition on murder is indeed a great charter right to all of us, but it is the prohibition that comes first, and not the right.[24]

She goes on to argue that the aspect of human nature at issue in the prohibition on murder is something on the order of the spiritual nature of human beings, a source of supra-utilitarian value.

In other writings, she brings together this thought with specifically theological concerns about our ultimate end. We may be unwilling to follow her that far. But she does, I think, supply is with grounds to be suspicious of the general extension of her thought about Aristotelian necessity to cover the whole field of morality.

University of Chicago
vogue@uchicago.edu

[23] Op. cit. note 22, 162-163.

[24] G.E.M. Anscombe, 'Murder and the Morality of Euthanasia', in Mary Geach and Luke Gormally, editors, *Human Life, Action, and Ethics: Essays by G. E. M. Anscombe*, (Exeter: Imprint Academic, 2005), 266

Volunteers and Conscripts: Philippa Foot and the Amoralist

NAKUL KRISHNA

Abstract
Philippa Foot, like others of her philosophical generation, was much concerned with the status and authority of morality. How universal are its demands, and how dependent on the idiosyncrasies of individuals? In the early years of her career, she was persuaded that Kant and his twentieth-century followers had been wrong to insist on the centrality to morality of absolute and unconditionally binding moral imperatives. To that extent, she wrote, there was indeed 'an element of deception in the official line about morality'. In this paper, I shall explore her early alternative: a system of merely 'hypothetical' imperatives, imperatives that depend on the motivations of particular individuals. Could so contingent a system deserve to be termed a morality? How revisionary a proposal was this, and how serious its costs? And how might we reconcile ourselves to a morality stripped of what she called the 'fictions' that surrounded it? Foot's early answer, tentative and exploratory, remains of interest, long after she herself abandoned it.

> [...] our freedom is not just a freedom to choose and act differently, it is also a freedom to think and believe differently, to see the world differently, to see the different configurations and describe them in different words. Moral differences can be differences of concept as well as differences of choice. A moral change shows in our vocabulary. How we see and describe the world is morals too [...] Iris Murdoch[1]

1. Philippa Foot and the Amoralist

'It is often felt,' wrote Philippa Foot in 1972, 'even if obscurely, that there is an element of deception in the official line about morality'.[2] The official line about morality – articulated in its most influential form by Kant – was that 'moral judgements cannot be hypothetical imperatives'. That is to say, the 'ought' in a genuinely moral

[1] Iris Murdoch, *Existentialists and Mystics: Writings on Philosophy and Literature* (London: Penguin Books, 1999), 73.
[2] Philippa Foot, 'Morality as a System of Hypothetical Imperatives', in *Virtues and Vices* (Berkeley: University of California Press, 1978), 167

doi:10.1017/S1358246119000249

judgement is not conditional: if I think that a certain person ought, *morally*, not to lie, then I do not then have to follow that up with the many advantages to him of not lying. The idea is, I think, supposed to be a *conceptual* point about the moral ought. If we are conceiving of the oughts in our judgements to another person as distinctively moral, then, as Foot put it, 'we do not have to back up what we say by considerations about his interests or his desires'.[3] This, she said, had long been thought 'an unquestionable truth'. Her influential paper 'Morality as a System of Hypothetical Imperatives' sought to show it was not: certainly not unquestionable, and very possibly not a truth.

The nerve of the paper consisted in her unKantian proposal that we needn't divide human motivation into what is done for the sake of the moral law and what is 'merely' selfish or hedonistic. Where would that leave those who do charitable things, ingenuously enough, because they care about a particular someone who would benefit from the charity? Or those who are truthful out of love for truth, or just because they love liberty?[4] Was it really such a problem that a person of this kind did these things 'merely' because he cared – about other people, or particular causes? Foot summarised the objection thus: 'But what if he never cared about such things, or what if he ceased to care? Is it not the case that he *ought* to care?'[5]

Moralists of the Kantian kind wanted, needed, to say yes: the mere fact that a person *happened* to care couldn't be enough. There had to be a more basic demand *to* care, and one that applied, without exception, to everyone. A morality with room for exceptions seemed to leave the foundations of morality to the tender mercies of particular psychologies. It left room for the possibility that there were those who had no moral duties, because they didn't care about the right things in the first place. It didn't matter if there were such people. It would be enough to undermine the authority of morality were it admitted, in principle, that there might be. An exemption for some would amount to an amnesty for all. If I found the demands of morality onerous (as we all do at one point or another), it would be enough, for me to be freed from them, to stop caring, if I could, about the things that generated the demands in the first place.

As she later clarified, Foot had not 'wanted to reject morality itself', only to expose 'the fictions surrounding morality'.[6] There could be a

[3] Op. cit. note 2, 159.
[4] Op. cit. note 2, 165.
[5] Op. cit. note 2, 166.
[6] Op. cit. note 2, 174.

morality, and one still deserving the name, purified of these fictions, a morality based not on a universally binding and unconditional moral law, but on simple human solidarities. To those who feared 'defection from the moral cause', she urged that there wasn't yet cause for panic. As she memorably concluded the essay in which she made this point, 'Morality as a System of Hypothetical Imperatives', 'the people of Leningrad were not struck by the thought that only the *contingent* fact that other citizens shared their loyalty and devotion to the city stood between them and the Germans during the terrible year of the siege'.[7] Her claim has the flavour of someone pointing out the painfully obvious. What a peculiar thing to worry about: that people who 'thought of themselves as volunteers banded together to fight for liberty' would be any less likely to stay the moral course than those 'persuaded by talk about the authority of the moral law'.[8] Put that way, the traditional philosopher's anxieties seemed absurd, almost the projection of a pathology: as if caring for other people were any less powerful a spur to morality than the rational recognition of the special authority of the moral law.

Does this more modest thing deserve the name of morality? Foot couldn't see why not, though she allowed that there might be those whose understanding of the word 'morality' simply ruled out such concessions. On their view, if there is such a thing as morality, it is a system of categorical imperatives, unconditionally binding. But why adopt such a picture when there is another available, one that makes up for its loss of universality with a more realistic picture of human psychology?

Foot would come in later life to reject her conclusions in this paper, even to rue them. She had, she later thought, been excessively optimistic. She had hoped that even on her picture of morality, one could explain that *everyone* 'could have reason to do good actions and avoid bad ones, whatever one's aims or desires'.[9] But her friend and colleague Warren Quinn put it to her that she, like most philosophers, had been getting things back to front: 'What would be so *important* about practical rationality if it could be rational to do despicable actions?' She came to agree with him that she had been wrong to seek foundations for morality in a theory of practical reason. 'One shouldn't think that morality must pass the test of

[7] Op. cit. note 2, 167; emphasis in original.

[8] Op. cit. note 2, 167.

[9] The quotation is from her interview with Alex Voorhoeve in Alex Voorhoeve, *Conversations on Ethics* (Oxford: Oxford University Press, 2009), 102.

rationality, but rather that rationality must pass the test of morality'.[10] The theory she came to embrace was in its essence Aristotelian: where she had, 'brashly', interpreted moral judgements as amounting, ultimately, to claims linking our actions to our desires, she came to think that 'moral propositions are about the natural goodness of a human will'.[11] Morality was grounded in a picture of natural goodness and defect: interpret our moral judgements as being about *that*, and morality is seen to have objective foundations of the sort Kant had sought, unconditional and binding.

In a late interview, she describes her career as a slow movement away from the various forms of positivism that marked moral philosophy in her youth, views on which moral judgements amounted to little more than the expression of attitudes one tries to get other people to share. The central problem with such views, she later remarked, was that

> there is no way, if one takes this line, that one could imagine oneself saying to a Nazi, 'But we are *right*, and you are *wrong*', with there being any substance to the statement. Faced with the Nazis, who felt they had been justified in doing what they did, there would simply be a stand-off. And I thought, 'Morality just cannot be subjective in the way that different attitudes, like some aesthetic ones, or likes and dislikes, are subjective'. The separation of descriptions from attitudes, or facts from values, that characterized the current moral philosophy [sc. 1950s] had to be bad philosophy.[12]

Philosophers have been divided about the shift, with philosophers of a broadly Humean cast of mind disappointed that Foot abandoned the sensible subjectivism of her youth.[13] Her mistake, as they would have it, was to see it as a *problem* that not everyone, on her early view, could have reason to do good things and avoid the bad. Or, what comes to the same thing, that she saw the possibility of a fully rational 'amoralist' – someone who denies 'that he has any reason to trouble his head over this or any other moral demand' – as a philosophical challenge to be overcome, rather than a fixed fact about human life that presents a practical hurdle to work around.

[10] Op. cit. note 9, 102.

[11] Op. cit. note 9, 101; 'brash' is her word.

[12] Op. cit. not 9, 92.

[13] The phrase is from David Wiggins, 'A Sensible Subjectivism?', in *Needs, Values, Truth* (Oxford: Clarendon Press, 1998), 185–215.

2. Talking to and about the amoralist

Foot's career saw her adopt the full range of available positions with respect to the old question: why be moral? The 'why' in the question is naturally understood as a demand for a reason: what *reason* have I to be moral, to care about the good of others, and for their own sake rather than because caring about them may on occasion conduce to my own good? The basic structure of the question has the general structure of inquiry famously recommended by Descartes: one casts out any beliefs or attitudes that one has grounds for doubting, work backwards to what is indubitable, then work outward from the indubitable to reinstate those of our old beliefs and attitudes that we can now show to deserve to stand. However, to put it very briskly, morality is far from indubitable; its claims can and frequently are doubted, indeed resented. So, one asks, reasonably enough, for a reason to be moral. Now, the only thing one may not doubt when asking for reasons is rationality itself. To ask for a *reason* to be rational is, surely, already to concede the point, to presuppose the worth of that whose worth one purports to doubt. And so, rationality seems to provide an Archimedean point from which we hope, if we can, to provide that dubitable thing, morality, with foundations.

This Cartesian procedure can be described in a less abstract, less solipsistic, way too. Reasons can be sought in isolation, but they are also *demanded* in encounters between people. Western philosophy's original amoralist was just such a one: Plato has him appear in various guises, most famously, as Callicles in the *Gorgias* and Thrasymachus in the *Republic*. Callicles and Thrasymachus are difficult figures, full of sound and fury, anxious to win in a contest with Socrates more than they are to discover the truth.[14] Their aggressiveness makes them excellent guides to the human psychology surrounding the problem, if confusing guides to its basic structure. Plato's best, and least emotive, attempt to illuminate the problem appears when Glaucon and Adeimantus in the *Republic* present the amoralist case as devil's advocates. Being well-brought-up young men from a good (and prosperous) family, they remain within the world of morality – or, to put it less anachronistically, justice – and are genuinely

[14] For a useful general discussion of these figures, see Rachel Barney, 'Socrates' Refutation of Thrasymachus', in *The Blackwell Guide to Plato's Republic*, ed. Gerasimos Xenophon Santas (Oxford: Blackwell Publishing, 2006), 44–62; also, Bernard Williams, 'Plato Against the Immoralist', in *The Sense of the Past: Essays in the History of Philosophy*, ed. Myles Burnyeat (Princeton: Princeton University Press, 2009), 97–107.

moved by its demands, but would like Socrates nevertheless to vindicate those demands to a notional sceptic. In their mouths, our question 'why be moral?' appears as the question, 'Is justice more than an instrumental good?' Or, to put it more bluntly, ought we to be just even if – *per impossibile* – we might be unjust with impunity? Why be good if we can be bad and get away with it.

The challenge of Glaucon and Adeimantus is a challenge *to* Socrates: someone (pretending to be) outside the world of morality, but within the world of rationality, is inviting someone who is within the world of morality to make the case for being there. The 'case' must be an argument, a rational case. Appropriately given what is being argued for, no threats are allowed, nor rhetorical subterfuges. The argument is to be had out in the sun.

The dramatisation of the argument – presenting the amoralist as a flesh-and-blood individual with a mind of his own, not as an intellectual spectre – has the considerable advantage of encouraging both moralist and amoralist to play fair in their arguments. If they cheat or falter, their opponents will notice. And this will mean that a victory for either side, or indeed a stalemate, counts for something. It can be a solace to moralists, or a further spur to the scepticism of the amoralist. Moreover, it might show us something true, important yet non-obvious about the possibilities and limits of reason itself.[15]

This point was put elegantly in a book published in 1972, the same year as Foot's paper. Bernard Williams wrote of the amoralist, in the opening pages of *Morality: An Introduction to Ethics*, that if 'morality can be got off the ground rationally, then we ought to be able to get it off the ground in an argument against him'. The point wasn't actually to persuade a real person of this kind: one may not exist, and any that do exist may be unwilling to listen, or too irrational to recognise the force of a decisive argument. Nevertheless, 'it might seem a comfort to morality if there were reasons which, if he were rational, would persuade him'.[16]

Williams's formulation of the problem expresses, as he elsewhere put it in his remarks on Kant's moral philosophy, a distinctly modern inflection on the ancient problem, 'fed by real features of moral experience and by demands and hopes, dimly felt, for that experience to be coherent and honorable in the conditions of

[15] For a thorough and insightful introduction to the history of the problem, see Alison Hills, *The Beloved Self: Morality and the Challenge From Egoism* (Oxford: Oxford University Press, 2010).

[16] Bernard Williams, *Morality: An Introduction to Ethics* (Cambridge: Cambridge University Press, 1972), 4.

modernity'.[17] The anxiety that morality might, some or all of the time, be what Thrasymachus thought it was, viz. another name for being a mug, is a real feature of human experience, brought on by what is surely a ubiquitous human fear: of being a dupe. But mere exhortations to see virtue as its own reward, in the style of a sermon, whether from priest or Socrates, will hardly do once doubt has set in. One wants more, a picture both 'coherent and honorable', that is to say, an argument that can appeal to our (modern, post-Enlightenment) sense of ourselves as, above all things, rational.[18] If the rational amoralist is compelled, by rational principles he does – indeed, must – accept, to embrace the demands of morality, then those of us who accept those demands are far from beings mugs or dupes. We have, despite the tauntings of the Thrasymachuses of the world, been not credulous but rational all along.

Like Foot in this period, Williams was pessimistic that the demand for such an argument could possibly be met on these terms. Even the best arguments against the amoralist, he thought, eventually committed the same fallacy: that of begging the question. To say that the amoralist is depraved, cruel, narcissistic or whatever, is to presuppose the legitimacy of the very moral categories he rejects. To say that the amoralist could not consistently will that everyone be an amoralist like him is very likely true (what could such a society even look like? Could a community of amoralists even be a *society*?); but it is also dialectically irrelevant. The demand to 'universalise' one's moral judgements, as Kant put it, is surely a demand that the amoralist can reject without obvious irrationality. Kant famously disputed this, but the contention that rationality requires universalisation needs arguing for and can hardly be simply assumed in this context.[19] So what is left that might compel the perfectly rational amoralist to see the inescapability of morality?

Well, nothing. With quick enough footwork, the rational amoralist can dodge any argumentative bouncer the moralist hurls his way. But – and here Williams pointed to the silver lining – this wasn't a

[17] Bernard Williams, 'Fictions, Philosophy, and Truth', *Profession*, 1 January 2003, 40.

[18] This point about the modern self is put memorably, and satirically, by William James in section VII of his lecture, 'The Will to Believe': '... he who says, "Better go without belief forever than believe a lie!" merely shows his own preponderant private horror of becoming a dupe. He may be critical of many of his desires and fears, but this fear he slavishly obeys'.

[19] For a classic (and underappreciated) discussion of these difficulties, see Don Locke, 'The Trivializability of Universalizability', *The Philosophical Review* 77, no. 1 (1968): 25–44.

particularly happy or comfortable place for the amoralist to be. For one thing, the amoralist couldn't crow about his apparent invincibility, certainly not in any terms that were distinctively moral. He could not (truthfully, consistently) declare himself to be, for instance, *courageous*, a term that belongs to the world of morality that he rejects. So, he could not – to return to the cricketing metaphor – be got out, but nor could he score. The consistently amoralistic position is a dangerous place to be, every human encounter fraught with temptations to lapse into conventional morality. Morality (like society) is, in theory, escapable, but usually at a considerable cost.

Having conceded the battle in its most philosophical form, Williams went on to claim back the lost moral territory as a problem in human life. What might a flesh-and-blood amoralist look like, he wondered – at any rate, an amoralist who is not simply a pathological case, a psychopath – who is real, but not typically an aspirational figure for those harbouring doubts about the authority of morality. 'Some stereotype from a gangster movie might come to mind, of the ruthless and rather glamorous figure who cares about his mother, his child, even his mistress'.[20] But to bring the mother, the child, the mistress on to the scene immediately disrupts the simple picture of pure, cold, egoistic rationality. To care for those particular other people – however little he cares for anybody else, however little he expresses that caring in terms of abstract moral considerations – suggests that 'he has the notion of doing something for somebody, because that person needs something'.[21] He is actuated to act, however 'intermittently and capriciously', by the thought '"they need help", not the thought "I like them and they need help"'.[22] And to have this thought is already to have given up on the pure variety of amoralism: 'there is no bottomless gulf between this [sc. the gangster's] state and the basic dispositions of morality. [...] To get him to consider their situation seems rather an extension of his imagination and his understanding, than a discontinuous step onto something quite different, the "moral plane"'.

As Williams saw it, the philosopher's original mistake had been to pick up a fight with the invincible (but spectral) opponent when there was a realistic and entirely vincible opponent to contend with. The pure rational amoralist is not a realistic alternative for anyone; the psychopath is not an *attractive* alternative; what that leaves us with is a not a sharp line between the moral and the amoral, but a spectrum

[20] Op. cit. note 16, 10.
[21] Op. cit. note 16, 11
[22] Op. cit. note 16, 11.

of possibilities: from caring, somewhat unreliably, for the interests of particular others, to caring for the interests of everybody. The problem is not solved in its original form – so much is clear – but the problem has been replaced by another, more tractable but no less important. We are no longer anxious about what we might say to the imaginary amoralist, but rather what we might say *about* him, to each other. As he later put it, 'The justification he [sc. the philosopher] is looking for is in fact designed for the people who are largely within the ethical world, and the aim of the discourse is not to deal with someone who probably will not listen to it, but to reassure, strengthen, and give insight to those who will'.[23] As Williams described it, the audience for justifications of morality was not the amoralist pounding at the gates, but the amoralist within, that is to say, within us all.

3. Mitigating the aporia

What shall we call such an argumentative strategy? The original hope had been, as we might put it, for a *demonstration*, a rational pathway from amoralism into morality. In panic at the difficulty of producing such a demonstration, we might be tempted into catastrophising, or into a gloomy or cynical embrace of the amoralist extreme. But both Williams and Foot seem to be proposing a middle way. There is space between these extremes for insisting, in a principled rather than desperate or defensive way, that the amoralist's apparent victory is in fact pyrrhic. Call this strategy that of deflation, or better, *mitigation*.[24]

Williams had credited Kant with conceiving, insightfully, of the challenge for the moral philosopher as that of showing that the central elements of moral experience could be coherent and honourable in the conditions of rationalism and scepticism characteristic of modernity. The catastrophising response, as I have called it, is that of conceding that the sense of an absolutely, unconditionally and universally binding moral obligation cannot be shown to be coherent or honourable under the sceptical gaze. Incoherent because not

[23] Bernard Williams, *Ethics and the Limits of Philosophy (With a Commentary on the Text by A. W. Moore)*, Reissue (Abingdon: Routledge, 2006/1985), 26

[24] I borrow the term 'mitigation' from Tim Button, *The Limits of Realism* (Oxford: Oxford University Press, 2013), 161 and *passim*, who uses it in connection with questions of metaphysical realism.

consistent with a plausible theory of what reasons are and where they come from; dishonourable because to persist in living out a morality of categorical imperatives is an exercise in systematic (self-) deception.[25] But as Foot tried to show, why take *that* element of moral experience – the categorical imperative – as the central element, with which the whole caboodle must stand or fall?

Strategies of this sort are often termed, in our contemporary philosophical demotic, as cases of 'biting the bullet'. The metaphor has something to commend it: the expression arises after all (my dictionary has it) 'from the old custom of giving wounded soldiers a bullet to bite on when undergoing surgery without anaesthetic'. The gruesome metaphor may well be appropriate here: to find reasons to carry on living the moral life without the support of the categorical imperative exerts some of the same psychological pressures as must surely have afflicted Victorian church-goers in the throes of religious doubt. We need the bullet to bite on because the alternative, to put it no more dramatically than that, is to scream.

But the phrase is also misleading to the extent that it suggests that the adoption of such 'mitigating' views is supposed to count, at least a little, against the premises that led us to them. Neither Williams nor, in this period, Foot, seemed to think of their views in this way. To do so would be to treat Kant's view of what is central to moral experience as authoritative, a fixed point in our theorising about morality. Foot and Williams prise that question – what, if anything, is essential to the experience of morality? – back open. They ask what in our moral experience actually stands in need of vindication. As Williams sees it, the answer could just as plausibly lie in a Humean conception of the sources of morality, not in the experience of categorical obligation but rather in the natural sympathy of human being for human being, a sympathy that can be extended, though who knows how far, and not necessarily by rational means. Should this come as a disappointment? Why should it, when after all, as every parent (and teacher and therapist and politician) knows, changes of mind – or as we might more

[25] Nietzche's notorious remarks in *Twilight of the Idols* about English moral thinkers are relevant here: 'They have got rid of the Christian God, and now think that they have to hold on to Christian morality more than ever [...] In England, every time you take one small step towards emancipation from theology you have to reinvent yourself as a moral fanatic in the most awe-inspiring way'. (Friedrich Nietzsche, *Nietzsche: The Anti-Christ, Ecce Homo, Twilight of the Idols: And Other Writings*, ed. Aaron Ridley and Judith Norman, trans. Judith Norman (Cambridge: Cambridge University Press, 2005), 193–4.

evocatively put it, changes of *heart* – are seldom induced by mere argument.

Foot had, as we saw earlier, a different way of addressing the sense of disappointment a would-be defender of morality might naturally feel at the modesty of the Humean conclusion. Disappointment and panic: 'panic at the thought that we ourselves, or other people, might stop caring about the things we do care about'.[26] The appeal of the categorical imperative consisted partly in its promise to give us 'some control over the situation'.[27] A crux of the many early modern debates between moral 'rationalists' and 'sentimentalists' was, after all, the question of whether an account of morality grounded in human sentiment provided it with far too contingent a grounding. It is to this old concern that Foot responds when she tells us, 'it is interesting that the people of Leningrad were not similarly struck by the thought that only the contingent fact that other citizens shared their loyalty and devotion to the city stood between them and the Germans during the terrible years of the siege'.[28]

The example sticks out conspicuously from the page and the philosophical literature in its historical specificity and vividness. But one may think it ill chosen. Even in 1972, the siege of Leningrad was remembered as Stalin and his successors had decreed it should be: a tale of innocents ennobled by the fortitude with which they bore the death, disease and starvation that the siege brought. But it has come to be known since the era of *glasnost* that the tribulations of the siege, like tribulations of other terrible wars, did not (simply) ennoble their victims. People were known to sell their bodies for an extra ration of sawdust-filled bread; the sufferings were by no means equally distributed among the population; 1,500 arrests were made for cannibalism. Diaries of survivors unearthed in Soviet archives have since shown that the ultimate effect of the severe malnutrition of those months was an extreme apathy. As one survivor put it, they began to exhibit 'the indifference of the doomed', just as much to those of their friends, neighbours and children as to their own. 'The best way to survive', one of them chillingly wrote, 'was to draw an even tighter ring around oneself'.[29]

[26] Op. cit. note 2, 167.
[27] Op. cit. note 2, 167.
[28] Op. cit. note 2, 167.
[29] A harrowing recent work of scholarship on the siege, Alexis Peri, *The War Within: Diaries from the Siege of Leningrad* (Cambridge, Massachusetts: Harvard University Press, 2017), recounts these stories and others yet worse.

Does the grim truth of the siege, rather than the Party-approved romance, put paid to Foot's hopefulness? Does the behaviour of the Leningraders confirm what the rationalists have long said about the unwisdom of basing morality in human sentiments, sentiments so painfully apt to dissolve when the going gets tough? It is not clear that it does. For one thing, it is a simple fallacy to infer from the fact that human beings do terrible things in terrible conditions to the conclusion that these terrible things show us something deep about what we are 'really' like.

As Williams put it, it would be a sloppy ethologist indeed who based conclusions about the natural behaviour of lions, say, from their behaviour when caged and starved for weeks, and a poor physiologist who decided that human skin is 'naturally' like it is after exposure to twelve hours of blazing sun. 'If someone says that if you want to see what men are *really* like, see them after they have been three weeks in a lifeboat, it is unclear why that is any better a maxim with regard to their motivations than it is with regard to their physical condition'.[30]

Moreover, as Foot might have urged, the rationalist can derive no comfort from these facts. If human sympathies gave out under such conditions, so did any consciousness of the authority of the categorical imperative. 'Perhaps,' Foot had memorably concluded, 'we should be less troubled than we are by fear of defection from the moral cause; perhaps we should even have less reason to fear it if people thought of themselves as volunteers banded together to fight for liberty and justice and against inhumanity and oppression'.[31] Volunteers, she had said, as opposed presumably to conscripts, a powerful redescription of the Kantian view in a manner that precisely inverts its own self-conception.

The sense of obligation, as Kant saw it, came from deeply within; that was why actions done from the motive of duty counted as 'autonomous', and therefore, possessed a special moral worth.[32] Foot's metaphor suggests that the sense of obligation could be experienced equally as a burden, an imposition from the outside, the voice of military recruiters pressganging the unwilling into service. Equally, actions done from natural sympathy could feel like the expression of what is mostly deeply one's own. Moreover, if the question is

30 Op. cit, note 16, 9.

31 Op. cit. note 2, 167.

32 For a classic discussion, see Barbara Herman, 'On the Value of Acting from the Motive of Duty', *The Philosophical Review* 90, no. 3 (1981): 359–82.

about what can sustain motivation in tough times, than one might answer: if the volunteer spirit couldn't survive the weakening of natural sympathies, it isn't clear why it would have been any likelier to weather the weakening of the sense of obligation. The same sorts of circumstances, of pain, disease and starvation, are surely apt to weaken both to the same degree. More precisely, there seems no way to say, in advance and *a priori*, that the one source of motivation was any likelier to persist in extreme circumstances than the other.

4. Styles of voluntarism

The force of Foot's strategy consists in good part in this feat of rhetorical redescription. Other moral philosophers in this period saw morality as, in some sense, voluntary, a matter not of vision or discovery or acknowledgement but of choice.[33] Jean-Paul Sartre, in his 'Existentialism is a Humanism', certainly took such a view; so, nearer home, did Foot's colleague and the frequent target of her early critical papers in the 1950s, RM Hare. Hare, a survivor of the Siam 'Death Railway', had had a harrowing experience of the second World War, and his voluntarism had nothing flip or glib about it.[34] The moral philosophy he developed from the late 1940s was an attempt to show the essence of morality to consist in the universalisability of moral judgements, a feature of the 'logic' of moral language, in particular, of the word 'ought'.[35] In endorsing a moral judgement, one could not be speaking only for oneself and one's interests: to judge that someone ought, morally, to do something, was to judge that *everyone* similarly situated ought to do so as well.[36]

The figure that haunted Hare's philosophy was what he called the 'fanatic'. The fanatic was someone whose principles met Hare's every logical test – in short, that they could be universalised without

[33] For a wide-ranging and profound discussion of the contrast and affinities between these ways of conceiving of morality, see Iris Murdoch, 'Vision and Choice in Morality', *Proceedings of the Aristotelian Society: Dreams and Self-Knowledge* Supplement no. 30 (1956): 32–58.

[34] See R. M. Hare, 'A Philosophical Autobiography', *Utilitas* 14, no. 3 (November 2002): 269–305, and Ved Mehta, *Fly and the Fly-Bottle: Encounters with Contemporary British Intellectuals* (London: Weidenfeld & Nicolson, 1963), 46–57 and *passim*.

[35] See R. M. Hare, *The Language of Morals* (Oxford: Oxford University Press, 1952).

[36] See R. M. Hare, *Freedom and Reason* (Oxford: Clarendon Press, 1963).

contradiction – but ended up with a worldview that was, to those who did not share it, repugnant. The logic of moral language by itself couldn't stop a fanatical Nazi from thinking that to be Jewish was to deserve death. It couldn't stop him from persisting in the belief even after being invited to consider that it was the merest accident of birth that made him a German and Gentile. 'It is possible', Hare said, 'for a man to come sincerely to hold an ideal which requires that he himself should be sent to a gas chamber if a Jew'. But this was not, he insisted, a *reductio ad absurdum* of the position that had led him to this conclusion. Rather, said Hare, 'That is the price we have to pay for our freedom'.[37] The freedom in question was the freedom to give ourselves an absurd, and self-destructive maxim: nothing in the nature of rationality could take away that freedom from us.

Freedom, choice, decision, the will: these words gave to what presented itself as a detached theory, of what morality simply is, its characteristic *mood* of seriousness and tough-mindedness. The mention of freedom seems reminiscent of Foot's insistence that there was nothing to regret or fear in moral commitment being a contingent matter. In both cases, reason and logic can only take us so far with the amoral or fanatical outliers. In both cases, the limits of rational argument are, at second if not first blush, not tragedies to be mourned. They are, rather, emancipations and opportunities, for the individual, and perhaps challenges to be tackled co-operatively in society. But the *mood* in Foot is radically unlike that in Hare. Hare's voluntarism is, above all, *lonely*, as befits a philosophy arrived at – as Hare reported – in the loneliness of the prisoner-of-war camp.[38] Foot's argument for her voluntarism is not simply, as we might now say, metaethical. Her argument urges that there is something to be said for her view about the status of ethics from within ethics itself, from a particular ethical point of view.[39]

[37] Op. cit. note 34, 111.

[38] Op. cit. note 34.

[39] For an ingenious recent argument in this vein, see Max Khan Hayward, 'Immoral Realism', *Philosophical Studies* 176, no. 4 (2019): 897–914. Similarly, see these remarks by Amia Srinivasan, whose first sentence nicely echoes Foot's own motivations for her adoption of a kind of ethical realism: 'Those who think that Realism is the only morally sound meta-ethics are often motivated by the belief that the most important thing is to be able to condemn atrocities as always and everywhere wrong. Anti-Realists prefer to think that people are ultimately answerable, not to abstract principles or divine commands, but to each other. We should take this view seriously [...] because it is ethically attractive in its own right'.

Foot's voluntarism, while it lasted, was *social*, and the freedom she prized the freedom to see ourselves as social creatures, whose obligations are obligations *to* our fellow creatures, not to reason. Not me, alone with my conscience and rationality, but us – 'banded together', pursuing shared aims in tandem. Why does it matter that these aims are, as one might say, 'merely' contingent?

That is not a merely rhetorical question. And Foot herself would come to worry that it did matter. On the voluntarist picture, she came to think, if those who had fought against the Nazis thought of themselves as in the right, *tout court* and not just by their own lights, there would be no 'substance to the statement'. And the conceptual freedom it relied on opened up other, and disturbing, possibilities: that we might exercise that freedom to conceive of ourselves as outlaws fighting for injustice and unfreedom. The challenge for all subsequent moral philosophy has been precisely this: what grounds have we for hoping that people will not choose to conceive of themselves this way? What distinguishes our hope from mere optimism, or worse, complacency?

There may be no way of answering this question in advance. Williams and the young Foot put their hope in human beings, in the human ability to be led by natural sympathies to use their freedom in ways more, rather than less, conducive to many of the demands of morality. They thought a morality consisting in people answerable not to the moral law but to each other was morality enough. Like others who put their trust in human beings, they were taking a risk that brought with it the possibility of disappointment and catastrophe.[40] It may be too early to say if they were misguided.

University of Cambridge
nk459@cam.ac.uk

(Amia Srinivasan, 'In the Long Cool Hour', *London Review of Books*, 6 December 2012.)

[40] For a useful discussion of the growing pessimism in Williams's thought on these matters, see Paul Sagar, 'Minding the Gap: Bernard Williams and David Hume on Living an Ethical Life', *Journal of Moral Philosophy* 11, no. 5 (24 September 2014): 615–38.

Virtues as Perfections of Human Powers: On the Metaphysics of Goodness in Aristotelian Naturalism

JOHN HACKER-WRIGHT

Abstract
The central idea of Philippa Foot's *Natural Goodness* is that moral judgments belong to the same logical kind of judgments as those that attribute natural goodness and defect to plants and animals. But moral judgments focus on a subset of human powers that play a special role in our lives as rational animals, namely, reason, will, and desire. These powers play a central role in properly human actions: those actions in which we go for something that we see and understand as good. Many readers of Foot resolutely ignore what she says about the human good being *sui generis* and obstinately continue to read her as advocating a version of naturalism grounded in empirical study of human nature. One might wonder how else it could count as a naturalistic view unless we could square the view with nature as studied by the empirical sciences. In this paper, I propose a metaphysical response to this question: help can come from turning to recent defenses of Aristotelian essentialism. Foot's naturalism can square with nature as interpreted through the lens of Aristotelian essentialism. On such a view, the virtues are perfections of human powers including reason, will, and desire.

1. Introduction

The central idea of Philippa Foot's *Natural Goodness* is that moral judgments belong to same logical kind of judgments as those that attribute natural goodness and defect to plants and animals. They are all judgments of natural normativity. These judgments situate a living thing, say, a giraffe, against the background of its form of life, *the* giraffe. A giraffe lacking one or more of its ossicones is a defective giraffe, since, under normal circumstances for a giraffe, such a defect will impede it from living the characteristic life of its kind. On Foot's view, moral judgments likewise situate individual human beings against the background of our kind, the human being. But moral judgments focus on a subset of human powers that play a special role in our lives as rational animals, namely, reason, will, and desire. These powers play a central role in properly human actions: those actions in which we go for something that we

doi:10.1017/S1358246119000250

see as good.[1] Through a moral defect, I may be unable to go for what I see as good: for instance, through weakness of will, I may be sidetracked into doing something that I judge to be bad. These powers, when they are functioning well, are precisely my active powers to pursue the good deliberately, and so how I deploy those powers characterizes me as an agent in a way that physical talents or defects do not.

It would be a mistake to think that in putting moral judgments into the same kind of judgments of natural goodness and defect in other living things, Foot is offering us a way to resolve moral questions scientifically, by filling out our picture of human nature with further empirical research. She points out differences between how we understand non-human animals and how we understand our own form of life. Situating our capacities for reason, will, and desire against the background of the human form of life is not like seeing that lacking ossicones is a defect in a giraffe. Whereas we can study how the absence of one or both ossicones affects the ability of a giraffe to live its characteristic life in normal circumstances, we do not obviously get the same sort of guidance by examining the impact of the absence of courage on a human being. If it turned out that human beings lacking courage lived longer lives or more reported more contentedness with their lives, we nevertheless need not accept that this should cause us to revise our idea of what makes for a good human being. In fact, Foot emphatically denies that the goodness of the human will is a matter of biology and asserts that the human good is sui generis.[2] For example, she argues that while sterility is certainly a physical defect in humans and animals alike, the choice not to have children is not ipso facto a defective choice.[3]

Many readers of Foot resolutely ignore what she says about the human good being sui generis and obstinately continue to read her as advocating a version of naturalism grounded in empirical study of human nature. One might wonder, how else could it count as a naturalistic view unless we could square the view with nature as

[1] As opposed to 'acts of a man' which can include mindlessly scratching one's beard or incontinent acts. See Aquinas *Summa Theologiae* 1a2ae, 1, 1, and John McDowell, 'The Role of Eudaimonia', in *Essays on Aristotle's Ethics,* ed. Amélie Oksenberg Rorty (Berkely: University of California Press, 1981) 361.

[2] Philippa Foot, *Natural Goodness* (Oxford: Oxford University Press, 2001) 51. Hereafter 'NG'.

[3] NG op. cit. note 2, 42.

studied by the empirical sciences? If she insists that the human good is sui generis, might not a more textually sensitive objection might question whether, given what she says, she still counts as a naturalist? If the human good is sui generis, as Foot claims, then it might seem that our nature is not after all playing a substantial role in determining the goodness of choices: she is not according it a 'speaking role'. This raises the question, if normativity comes apart from our nature, then in what sense is it a naturalistic view? And that raises the further question of where we are supposed to get guidance in determining the human good, if not from empirical study of human nature. In this paper, I propose a metaphysical response to these questions: help can come from turning to recent defenses of Aristotelian essentialism. This will help us to get clear on how Foot's view can count as a version of naturalism and how we might get guidance from her theory in working out the nature of the virtues. We can take up Foot's approach as a version of ethical naturalism because we are by nature animals with powers that include reason, will, and desire: these are natural powers of human beings. These powers are variable in that they can take on further qualities, including virtues and vices. The virtues are perfective of human powers. There is therefore a sense in which the human good is sui generis and also a sense in which it is an outgrowth of our nature, when we take nature to include distinctively human powers that can be perfected. On this view, moral virtues perfect our appetitive powers and morally good acts represent their complete actualization. This view provides some guidance in that further reflection on the nature of human powers and the formal goals of our powers would cast more precise light on which qualities are in fact virtues.

In making this argument, I am going beyond Foot's own views by entertaining the revival of a broader range of Aristotelian ideas than she ventured to advocate. Foot's Wittgensteinian methodological commitments limited her to offering a conceptual framework or logical grammar for moral judgments, eschewing realist commitments. So, her naturalism might be called a logical naturalism. She is content to argue that there is a common logical structure to natural normative judgments in non-humans and moral judgments in the human case. My aim is to advocate for extending Foot's logical naturalism in light of recent defenses of Aristotelian essentialism and the related issue of powers in metaphysics. It is through consideration of this work that we can make a case that the powers, defects, and goodness that we attribute to individual organisms by way of natural historical judgments, including human beings, are a bona fide part of nature, and not merely something we posit as an upshot of the mode of representation appropriate for living things. Moreover, on such a view, powers are part of nature generally, not just human or animate nature. It's just that human powers are distinctively rational. As a result, we get a picture on which there really are forms of life instanced in individual living things, with determinate natures, and that these individuals can be good or defective instances of their kind. Through metaphysically informed reflection on human powers, we can also hope to come to greater insight into the virtues.

In what follows, I will outline the grammatical and analytic methodology of Foot and Thompson. This method yields a categorial framework that is necessary for speaking intelligibly about living things. Yet it is also has some limitations. Nothing in their account gives us a methodology for distinguishing our separate powers, including our appetitive powers. To fully appreciate our appetitive powers, I argue that we need a methodology like that employed by Aquinas in the *Treatise on Human Nature* and the *Commentary on De Anima*. We also need to embrace a realistic conception of form and finality. Appreciating the distinctiveness of our appetitive powers is crucial to properly understanding central aspects of human morality; we must see ourselves as oriented toward particular sensible goods and attempting to bring our orientation toward those goods into line with our idea of what it is to live well. Hence, we must see ourselves as having perfectible sensitive appetites, appetites that can take on qualities that are the moral virtues. Of course, we need not embrace the details of the Thomistic account of moral psychology, but the methods and some features of Aquinas' account have much to offer as a starting point, or so I will argue.

I conclude by contrasting my realist views on virtue with John McDowell's approach to virtue as second nature, which he offers as a way of filling out Foot's views. McDowell rejects a reading of Aristotle on which the latter is appealing to human nature to underwrite his idea of what it is for a human being to live well[4]; not only does he reject this as a reading of Aristotle, he rejects the idea of constructing standards in ethics out of the facts of nature as 'bad metaphysics'.[5] There may be bad metaphysics involved in many such attempts, but with a plausible essentialist view of nature, the project isn't doomed as it seems to McDowell. I will argue that metaphysical assumptions about 'disenchanted nature' as a passive law

[4] John McDowell, 'Two Sorts of Naturalism' in *Mind, Value, and Reality* (Cambridge, Mass.: Harvard University Press), 168.

[5] Op. cit. note 4, 187.

governed realm are behind McDowell's rejection of the project. Further, I will argue that we must endorse some neo-Aristotelian metaphysics to fill out the idea, embraced by McDowell, that we can be said to 'actualize ourselves as animals' through the development of the virtues compatibly with nature as understood by modern science.[6]

2. From logical to realist naturalism

As mentioned above, Foot takes herself to be offering a framework that renders explicit the 'real logical grammar' of moral judgments.[7] She is here evidently using the term 'grammar' in Wittgenstein's sense, on which it refers to the logical structure of the appropriate uses of words in various practical contexts, counteracting a philosophical tendency to abstract words from those contexts. It is a central part of Wittgenstein's philosophical methodology to conduct 'grammatical investigations', which is the exploration of the various ways in which a term is appropriately used, contrasted with artificial philosophical uses of the term in question.[8] Foot takes up this approach herself in her treatment of evaluations in general and moral judgments in particular. Following Peter Geach, Foot argues that the real logical grammar of goodness, counteracts artificial philosophical treatments of 'good' such as those found in statements like 'pleasure is good' wherein the evaluative predicate floats free. 'Good' does not function as a predicative adjective. So, such a statement is 'rarely appropriate', Foot thinks, and it invites fruitless philosophical speculations about non-natural properties or special attitudinizing in non-cognitive accounts. She writes, 'Judgments of goodness and badness can have, it seems, a special 'grammar' when the subject belongs to a living thing, whether plant, animal, or human being'.[9] She thinks that the exploration of that grammar can

[6] John McDowell, *Mind and World* (Cambridge, Mass.: Harvard University Press, 1994), 78.

[7] NG op. cit. note 2.

[8] As Marie McGinn states, 'The idea of a grammatical investigation is central to Wittgenstein's later philosophy, and it is the key to understanding his work'. See *The Routledge Guidebook to the* Philosophical Investigations (London: Routledge, 2013) 15. See also Marie McGinn, 'Grammar in the Philosophical Investigations', in *The Oxford Handbook of Wittgenstein,* Oscar Kuusela and Marie McGinn (eds) (Oxford: Oxford University Press, 2011).

[9] NG op. cit. note 2, 26.

yield insight into goodness as it is used in moral contexts. In her explication of that grammar, she relies on the work of Michael Thompson, who is much more explicit about his methodological commitments, which he names 'analytic' or 'Fregean Aristotelianism'.[10]

Thompson investigates life, action, and practices through analyzing the logical form of thoughts that apprehend each of these objects. Although his investigation 'has something like a metaphysical character',[11] he distinguishes his investigation from a straightforward metaphysical investigation in that the distinctions he draws, for example between living and non-living, are distinctions among different forms of thought and not drawn directly from the things that are thought about.[12] In the case of living things, he argues it is a mistake to think that living things are just like non-living things, except in that they feature some distinctive properties, such as growth, having DNA, or self-movement. He argues that each of these proposed marks of life is subject to counterexamples, and so builds a case that it isn't any property that distinguishes the living from the non-living; life cannot be given a real definition on his view. Rather, our talk about living things employs a distinctive categorial framework. If there were a property or set of properties picking out living things from non-living things, a single form of judgment would fully embrace both cases, and what would pick out something as alive would be that certain claims would be true of it that can be formulated in propositions with the same form as that instanced in describing a non-living object. 'My cat has four legs' would be much like saying 'my car is red'. But this is not the case, according to Thompson; my thought about my cat employs a distinctive logical form, on his view. I am not inferring from some set of properties it has to the fact that it is living, but from the first employing a distinctive categorial framework in order to understand it as alive and to understand my cat as the bearer of legs in the relevant sense. Hence, we find in this domain a different way that the subject of judgments about living things relates to its predicates. For instance, from the fact that cats have four legs, and this is a cat, it does not follow that this cat has four legs. Judgments of living things have a distinctive 'non-Fregean' form of generality, such that general claims can be true of them despite their not describing even the most statistically common features of that form of life.

[10] Michael Thompson, *Life and Action* (Cambridge, Mass.: Harvard University Press, 2008), 13–22. Hereafter 'LA'.

[11] Op. cit. note 10, LA 5.

[12] Op. cit. note 10, LA 13.

The subject of what Thompson calls 'natural historical judgments' is something that is, on his view, necessary to the representation of things as alive, with this form of generality. The generality is attributed to the life form, e.g., the domestic housecat, which is then instanced, no doubt imperfectly, in the features and activities of particular cats.

It follows from this approach that we don't acquire the concept of life and living thing from observation and generalization. If there are no empirical properties that distinguish the living from the non-living, then of course we cannot form the concept by induction from instances that bear the appropriate properties contrasted with those that do not. Rather, Thompson believes that there are 'irreducibly diverse but interrelated capacities that find their seat in our intellects' that enable us to grasp different forms of being.[13] Though the content of our thoughts about living things comes from experience, the categories whereby we grasp living things as such are a priori and part of the power of thought itself. The concepts that Thompson arrives at to characterize the categorial structure of such thinking, including 'life-form' and 'natural historical judgment', are 'supplied by reflection on certain possibilities of thought or predication' rather than by experience.[14] They are pure a priori concepts, on his view.

For Foot's ethical naturalism, Thompson's analysis of the representation of life has the important result that our representation of something as living features species-dependence.[15] This means that any case of representing an individual as an organism requires situating that individual against the background of its kind. The reason this must be so is that in taking something to be alive we are taking at least some of the occurrences surrounding it as non-accidental and agential. If something happens to an organism whereby some matter gets into it and happens to further its metabolic processes it has not eaten, though perhaps it is nourished. When an animal eats it takes in something that at least appears to it to be the sort of thing from which it derives nutrition for that purpose; it is a non-accidental and active process. To see such a process, we must see it as acting in a way that characterizes something of its kind, and this brings in a normative dimension; such processes can go awry. Something being a cat is a sufficient explanation for its having four legs; the distinctive generality of natural-historical judgments

13 Op. cit. note 10, LA 17–18.

14 Op. cit. note 10, LA 20.

15 Op. cit. note 2, NG 27.

allows for the statement that cats have four legs to be true while we are looking at a cat with three legs. We then register the cat in front of us as having a defect and may wonder how this came about. For these reasons, Thompson thinks that his Davidsonian swamp double who arises from a lightning-bolt and perfectly mimics his actions 'is not so much as alive'.[16] *Ex hypothesi,* what is happening in the swamp double is purely accidental; there is no way for it to be defective in any respect because it does not belong to any kind, instead being 'a mere congeries of physical particles'.

Foot and Thompson both argue that this logical structure applies equally to the case of human beings. When we represent human beings in claims about them, we cast ourselves against the background of a form of life, the human being. Yet, as Thompson is especially at pains to emphasize, our relation to this life-form is unique in that our relation to it is necessarily not mediated by observation. Here he draws an analogy between the I-concept and the concept human understood as the life form I bear. No observation could establish that the figure in the mirror is me in the absence of an a priori I-concept; that is, nothing could bring it about that I connect that image with an image of myself in the absence of such an a priori concept, because it is no empirical feature or set of features of the image that make it an image of me. I must have such an a priori concept and be able to apply it in a thought such as, 'I've looked better'. Likewise, there are no empirical features of human beings that makes them bearers of the life form I bear; rather, I come into contact with the life form I bear primitively, albeit implicitly, in having thoughts about myself. Thompson describes his line of thought as follows:

> In the self-conscious representation of myself as thinking, as in all my self-conscious self-representation, I implicitly represent myself as alive, as falling under life-manifesting types. And in bringing myself under such types I bring myself under a life form... Self-consciousness is thus always implicitly form-consciousness.[17]

This distinctive relation that we bear to our own life-form is crucial to Foot's naturalism, though she does not emphasize this in her own writings. On Thompson's understanding, we cannot get ourselves

[16] Op. cit. note 10, LA 20.

[17] Michael Thompson 'Apprehending Human Form', in *Modern Moral Philosophy*, ed. Anthony O'Hear (Cambridge: Cambridge University Press, 2004), 68.

into view, describe ourselves, or so much as be aware of ourselves as thinking without situating ourselves as members of a life form that features some norms. This includes norms concerning what it is to reason and act well. Those norms, whatever they are, are norms that reveal our conception of what it is to live well qua human. These norms do not come to us from without, from observation, but are embedded in our a priori self-conception that is at the basis of our self-consciousness, according to Thompson. These norms are my norms if anything is mine. Thompson's thereby embraces a sort of *life form internalism,* according to which when we act deliberately and not in weakness of will, we necessarily demonstrate our conception of what it is to live well qua human.

On Thompson's view there are certain features of the human life form that are incontestable inasmuch as they are necessary components of a self-conscious form of life. It is instructive to contrast Thompson's methodology as an analytic or Fregean Aristotelian with the approach to self-knowledge found in Aquinas, who of course also draws on Aristotle. Aquinas writes:

> ... [the] soul's acts and powers are distinguished by their different objects only when the objects differ *qua* objects – i.e., in terms of the object's formal nature (*rationem formalem*), as the visible differs from the audible ... in cognizing the soul we must advance from things that are more external, from which the intelligible *species* are abstracted through which intellect cognizes itself. In this way, then, we cognize acts through objects, powers through acts, and the essence of the soul through its powers.[18]

This follows a methodological principle from Aristotle to the effect that 'actualities and actions are prior in account to potentialities'.[19] The idea is reasonable since we can only know potentialities, if there are any, through their actualizations, and since potentialities are distinguished through being directed toward their distinctive acts. In Aquinas' methodology, as with Thompson's, we come to know our powers through acts directed at objects, which are differentiated not materially, but formally. In Thompson's methodology, as distinct from Aquinas', this is carried out in the first instance within the domain of intellectual judgments, delineating distinctive objects

[18] *A Commentary on Aristotle's* De Anima, trans. Robert Pasnau (New Haven: Yale University Press, 1999), 162.

[19] *De Anima,* Christopher Shields (trans.) (Oxford: Oxford Universty Press, 2016) at 415a18–20.

(e.g., living things versus inanimate objects) through analyzing the distinctive forms of thought that apprehend them, arriving at irreducible capacities for thinking about living things that reveal something about the powers of our form of life.

Thompson's methodology is necessary for getting at the grammatical forms pertinent to living things and their associated pure concepts; I will assume his claims about these forms are correct. My question is whether Thompson and Foot have an adequate philosophical interpretation of these categories. As I noted above, Thompson counts these concepts among the 'irreducibly diverse but interrelated capacities that find their seat in our intellects'. The irreducibility of these powers is demonstrated by their purity and the irreducibility of the correlative judgments: as Thompson argues in detail, they can't be boiled down to standard Fregean judgments with ceteris paribus clauses or to Fregean judgments with second-order quantification. Given that such judgments are necessary to self-representation, there is a transcendental necessity to the attribution of a power of thought including the capacity for the representation of living things, on Thompson's view. I can't think of myself as thinking without representing myself as a form of life with the capacity for thought. Hence, I must take myself to be a form of life with at least this power if I am aware of myself as thinking of anything at all. As Thompson himself puts it, this argument has an 'unwholesome Cartesian' flavor.[20] My concern is that this approach imposes a divide between powers that we must take ourselves to have on pains of not being able to represent ourselves as thinking, and powers that we merely represent ourselves as having without such transcendental necessity. There are, after all, acts that we apparently engage in that are not intellectual acts, and these acts seem not to be function of our cognitive powers alone. For example, we appear to be animals with appetitive powers that target particular material objects as good. Goodness in this sense is traditionally taken to be something that appears to us as an upshot of possessing appetitive powers. For Aquinas, these apparent goods are sufficient grounds for attributing a separate appetitive power. The objects of my sensitive appetites are formally distinct from the objects of my intellect or my senses, even when I desire the same object that I also sense and cognize. As Aquinas puts it, 'An object of both apprehension and appetite is the same in subject, but differs in character (*ratione*). For it is apprehended insofar as it as it is a sensible or an intelligible being, whereas it is the object of appetite

[20] Op. cit. note 17, 67

insofar as it is suitable or good'.[21] In other words, the intellect and the senses can contemplate objects without taking them to be good, but the appetites target objects as good or averse, or as threats to attaining a good or avoiding an evil. On Aquinas' standard, then, the senses, intellect, and appetite are distinct powers, since their objects are formally distinct, and there are further distinctions to be drawn within each, as the intellect, senses, and appetites all collect further distinct capacities, that can be separated based on further formal distinctions among their respective objects.

Aquinas' conception of 'formal nature' of course extends further than Thompson's, because it is not merely logical form. If I see some tofu, say, and it inspires an appetite in me, there is a relation between its nature, its form, as a piece of tofu, and my own, bodily animal nature, my senses and appetites, such that I situate it under the formal nature of goodness and love it, where this simply means that I am inclined toward the possession of the good, the eating of the tofu.[22] Aquinas could see the appetites and the passions that correspond to them as powers that are actualized in specific ways through movements that bring them to completion. For Aquinas, these aspects of our nature cannot be grasped without attributing powers to things, including our own bodies, and in so doing, we are attributing form and finality to them; we must take them to be in the things thought about in virtue of their bodily nature, both in the appetitive animal body and in the desired thing that satisfies those appetites.

My complaint is that Thompson's methodology does not, by itself, give us a framework for sorting out claims about powers other than those that are necessary to the capacity for self-consciousness. Aquinas, by contrast, provides such a framework, albeit one that depends on metaphysical claims that Thompson seems unwilling to venture. To illustrate, when I desire a piece of tofu and aim at attaining it, I represent myself as desiring tofu. I must take myself to have powers of thought to so represent myself. Yet, do I take the desiring of tofu to be a result of the power of representation, that is, an upshot of my cognitive powers, or part of a separate power? Thompson, on my reading, does not give us an approach to this question. And this question is important – is my excessive desire for tofu a cognitive defect – so that the problem is that I am representing myself in a certain way? That would seem to be clearly mistaken; the problem is with another power, the appetites, which, *ex hypothesi*, prompt actions in conflict with my conception of acting well qua human being.

21 *Summa Theologiae,* Ia 80, 1 ad 2.
22 *Summa Theologiae*, Ia IIae 36, 2.

Getting the appetites into view in a way that they can figure as needed in an Aristotelian framework requires this more expansive conception of form and a metaphysical commitment to realism about it. It requires, I think, conceiving the content of our representations of living things as having powers that feature formal and final causation on a physical level, and using these as a basis for distinguishing powers in much the way that Aquinas does in the *Treatise on Human Nature*. That is in part a matter of translating the features that Thompson finds in on the logical level of representation back into the physical world. Thompson finds concepts including organism, organ, vital operation, and life-form, which he collectively terms 'vital categories' to be irreducible logical categories.[23] My claim is that they are *not only* that, and stopping there, with laying out a categorial framework for living things, would leave us with an incomplete self-understanding. Thompson's restrictions appear to issue from a worry about embracing an 'egregious organicist metaphysics' and a view that the inanimate physical world is to be understood as a realm of law and passive matter. Yet this picture of nature is increasingly coming under challenge from those committed to essentialist accounts of the physical world on which there are kinds with dispositions to act in certain ways that define their intrinsic natures, and these are their causal powers.

It is crucial to frame this issue in a way that brings Thompson's categorial framework into contact with the metaphysical claims in order to make headway. Recent work in neo-Aristotelian metaphysics has treated life in a way that does not integrate Thompson's categorial framework. For example, Edward Feser and David Oderberg defend a scholastic conception of life on which it is defined by 'immanent causation'. This is 'causation that originates with an agent and terminates in that agent for the sake of its self-perfection'.[24] Nutrition, here, would be a paradigmatic case of immanent causation; an organism photosynthesizes or eats for the sake of maintaining its form, that is, for the sake of self-perfection. This is to be contrasted with transient causation: which is causation that terminates in something other than the origin of the cause: one rock knocking another off a cliff, for example.[25] Thompson's argument shows that this

[23] Op. cit. note 10, LA 48.

[24] David S. Oderberg, 'Synthetic Life and the Bruteness of Immanent Causation', in *Aristotle on Method and Metaphysics*, Edward Feser (ed) (Basingstoke: Palgrave Macmillan, 2013), 213.

[25] Edward Feser, *Scholastic Metaphysics* (Heusenstamm: editiones scholasticae, 2014), 90.

definition cannot stand on its own. That is because the notion of self-perfection contains a reflexive term, and, as Thompson points out, 'the whole problem is already contained in the reflexive'.[26] That is, the reflexive conceals an assumption concerning the relevant entity that is to perfect itself. Consider Thompson's analogous case concerning self-movement, another mark of the living: he contrasts a bird flying out of a stadium of its own accord versus a bird that has been mistaken for a fast ball and is flying out of a stadium having been struck by a bat. Which one is self-movement? Intuitively it is the first, but as Thompson points out, 'if A moves B, then the mereological sum of A and B in some sense moves itself, or some of itself'.[27] In other words, the batter and bird together form a self-moving system. The determination of the relevant entity, the organism, depends on establishing the natural historical judgments against the background of which we can pick out a living thing as such and attribute flight to that thing. Thompson would therefore deny that we can pick out living things as individual material objects distinguished from inanimate objects through possessing a property or mark of engaging in self-perfective acts; we must have recourse to a life form, as captured in natural historical judgments, in order to pick out an individual living thing, and to see what happens in it as self-perfective action.

My suggestion, then, is that human beings are a distinctive sort of living thing with specific causal powers, that is, distinctive self-perfective powers. We require Thompson's categorial framework to get ourselves into view as living things. Within that framework, we need, in addition, something like Aquinas' criterion to get our individual powers properly into view.

3. Appetitive powers and virtue

Awareness of oneself as having a desire is a deployment of the sort of form consciousness discussed above. To understand myself as having a desire I must understand myself as a living thing. As Anscombe says, 'a primitive sign of wanting is trying to get'.[28] A little before that she states, 'one cannot describe a creature as having the power of sensation without also describing it as doing things in accordance with perceived sensible differences'. These remarks situate a living

[26] Op. cit. note 10, LA 45.
[27] Op. cit. note 10.
[28] G.E.M. Anscombe, *Intention* (Oxford: Blackwell, 1963), 68.

thing against a wider context which represents it as featuring sensory and appetitive powers. In my own case, my awareness of wanting something situates me under a certain kind with such capacities; wanting and trying to get are things that characterize that form, even if my particular wants are rather idiosyncratic. Part of my form consciousness is pure, on Thompson's view. I must have a pure conception of a living thing, he believes, and of the concept of 'the life form I bear'. As with recognizing one's image in the mirror, a self-conscious desire is immediately attached to an I-concept; I don't observe a desire and then attach it to myself, but rather my desire involves me and directs me, in the case of what Aquinas terms 'sensitive appetites', to something in my sensory field or imagination. So, part of what I am aware of in desiring something is the pure form-consciousness that frames my form of life as something with a capacity for wanting and trying to get.

On the Thomistic view that I am advocating, we should understand our sensitive appetites as the function of a power separate from our powers of representation. That is because the objects those acts concern differ formally. The intellect's powers culminate in an act of cognition that abstracts from the particularity of the object of my cognition, and the psychological particularities of my occurrent grasp of the object of my cognition; it is something I can repeat under different circumstances faced with different particulars that fall under the same universals, grasped under different psychological conditions. It is repeated by others, in different bodies with different psychological contexts. In other words, sensed particulars might occasion an episode of cognition and it occurs in a particular embodied rational animal, but the cognitive act aims at something that goes beyond those particulars. By contrast, my hunger is sated by some particular bit of matter that I sense, ultimately being subsumed into my form, not by mere apprehension and cognitive appreciation of the tofu's form. My appetites therefore relate me as a concrete particular to other concrete particulars as such; indeed, it relates me to some of them as goods. The appetites in question are sensitive appetites in that they follow sensing something.[29] Our bodies respond to what we perceive through the senses; there is physical change in us that responds to the perception of something desired or some threat to something desired. These changes initiated in us through sense apprehension Aquinas labels the passions; though they begin passively, in apprehension, each passion is the active bodily course of an appetite playing out in relation to a particular apprehended object inciting that appetite. The appetites relate to sensed

[29] *Summa Theologiae*, Ia 81, 1

particulars in a distinctive way, as goods. The appetites are a power to go for the good as it is manifest in the sensible world.

All of this occurs in an individual organism against the background of natural historical judgments that pick out an individual organism with powers of sensation and appetite that define natural norms for an organism of that sort. If I have a nagging appetite for what I know to be motor oil, there is clearly something defective about my appetites. Of course, the desire may persist in light of my recognition that it is leading me to something that is not genuinely good. Desires can thereby manifest in various ways; I can be plagued by an unwelcome desire, or I can identify with my desires as leading me to something genuinely good, and this is part of the form consciousness that is necessary for self-consciousness. Those desires that come unwelcome are represented as defective in the sense of being something not directed to a genuine human good. Most of us probably have some desires that show up in this way; these are desires that we wish to be rid of, and we may undertake to do so, say, through resolve and repeatedly acting to resist promptings of the desires. In so acting, we are working to transform the appetites, and positing that they can take on different qualities. These qualities are the subject matter of virtue ethics: they are the *hexeis* or *habitus*. In undertaking to bring our appetites into accord with our conception of what is good, our picture of the proper human life, we are positing that the appetites can take on these different qualities, virtues and vices.

Our attempts to transform our appetites imply that those appetites are *variable causal powers*, to use Brian Ellis' terminology.[30] More specifically, they imply that my appetites might be shaped through reason to acquire states that are a function of my choices. This is a core thesis of Aristotelian virtue theory: my appetites can be brought under a principle through my choices. In Aquinas' terminology, the habitus that are moral virtues and vices are principles of the movement of the sense appetites. Developing such a principle is a distinctive sort of change that belongs uniquely to the appetitive powers of a rational animal. There are other changes that my appetites can undergo that are oblique to these changes. My appetites grow and diminish with age and health. From one day to the next, I may have a taste for fish, tofu, or leafy greens, all of which are wholesome and preserve good condition in moderate amounts. To introduce a distinction from Aristotle, these changes in my appetitive powers

[30] Brian Ellis, *The Philosophy of Nature: A Guide to the New Essentialism* (Montreal: McGill-Queen's University Press), 28.

are merely alterations. But the change that occurs in bringing my appetites into accord with a principle that embodies my conception of the good is something I will conceive as a perfection. It is indeed a perfection if my conception of the human good is correct.

In my view, this interpretation of our form of life involves registering a desire and attributing it to a distinct power. There is a bit of metaphysics involved here: it goes beyond pure form consciousness and offers a metaphysical interpretation of that form consciousness that posits appetites as a power, belonging to me as a human being, but distinct from my intellect. It is difficult to see how we can avoid such a self-interpretation. As Aquinas points out, the appetites contribute 'something of their own'.[31] This is their independent capacity to grasp and present particular sensed things as good; reason cannot, on its own, relate to particular sensed objects as good. That is, there would be no reason to go for anything sensed apart from an appetite for it. Reason can, however, take an independent stand on what the appetites present to it as good or bad. Thus appetites 'clash with reason as a result of our sensing or imagining something pleasant that reason forbids, or something unpleasant that reason demands'. These are everyday phenomena that support the Aristotelian interpretation that there is a distinct appetitive power.

That this power is perfectible is likewise a seemingly inevitable part of our interpretation of human form. Take the example of Mary from Julia Annas' 'Virtue Ethics and Social Psychology'. Mary treats her colleagues respectfully, but humiliates waiters in restaurants, yells at her son's soccer coach, and is rude to shop owners.[32] Let us say Mary recognizes that her behavior in restaurants, shops, and the soccer field is bad, and aims to get better. If Mary is to get so far as to be continent about her irascible behavior in these contexts, this must surely require a transformation of her appetites. If acting considerately in all of those contexts is indeed part of her conception of the good, she must regard her inclinations to the contrary as foreign intrusions that she would undertake to rid herself of. She must aim to bring her appetites into conformity her conception of how it is best to live.

[31] *Summa Theologiae*, Ia 81, 3 ad. 2

[32] Julia Annas, 'Virtue ethics and social psychology,' *A Priori*, 2, 20-34. These paragraphs condense an argument that is carried out more fully in my 'Moral Growth: A Thomistic Account' in *The Theory and Practice of Virtue Education*, Tom Harrison and David Ian Walker (eds) (London: Routledge, 2018).

To suggest that this is impossible or rare, as some philosophical situationists do, is to embrace a significant limitation on our moral agency: we cannot hope to ever fully desire what we claim to think of as good. But this isn't just a limitation on our desires, it is also a sort of cognitive limitation: a limitation on our ability to relate to the good as presented in the particulars of our existence. Mary could have a cognitive grasp on the importance of showing compassion to others, and yet not have the ability to desire to treat her waiter with compassion; for that reason, she would not be able to appreciate the particular goodness of that act of compassion, even if through self-control, she is able to bring it about that she acts in conformity with a rule. Of course, Mary may end up saddled with recalcitrant desires. But it is crucial for her to undertake to change her appetites, and there are reasons to see it as a process that takes time. As Aquinas points out, habitus change in rational animals requires more than one act. As he writes:

> ...reason, which is an active principle, cannot wholly dominate an appetitive power in one act. For the appetitive power is inclined in different ways and to many things, whereas reason judges in a single act that this should be willed for these reasons and in these circumstances. Consequently, the appetitive power is not at once wholly controlled so as to be inclined like nature to the same thing for the most part, which is proper to a habitus of virtue.[33]

So, the nature of the appetitive power is such that it cannot be determined all at once to what is good, as discerned by reason. It takes time to perfect one's appetites, and no definite amount of time can be specified: hence, Mary should not all at once resign herself to recalcitrance if the appetites prove obstinate to change. Instead, she must continue to act on right reason, hoping her desires will come into alignment with her choices over time. For it is through acts that we change our appetites. On Aquinas's view, reason, as the active component of the soul, acts on the appetites as a passive component, producing a quality. As Aquinas puts it 'the habitus of virtue is produced in the appetitive powers [i.e., the will and the sense appetite] as they are moved by reason'.[34] Hence, it is not a distinct process that Mary would have to undergo to change her appetites, but rather a persistence in acting against contrary desires so as to bring about, eventually, appetites in conformity with her conception of the good.

33 *Summa Theologiae*, Ia IIae 51, 3.
34 *Summa Theologiae*, Ia IIae 51, 2

4. Virtue and the Metaphysics of Powers

On the basis of these mundane but crucial features of our moral experience, I am arguing for a more metaphysically robust interpretation of human form than Foot or Thompson avow. Virtues are perfections of our appetitive powers, and so, these powers are in an important sense naturally directed to morally good acts. Those acts are the completion of the appetites as the sort of thing they are: they perfectly actualize them in that they are the attainment of what they are powers to do. Yet, as a power that is rational by participation there is another sense in which this does not happen naturally. For our appetites to attain their perfection they must take on qualities that come from reason and so are not simply there as a matter of course; rather, they require the exercise of rational agency to be developed. This can make it seem as though reason is setting standards quite independently of our so-called first nature. Foot describes virtues as consisting of '(a) the recognition of particular considerations as reasons for acting, and (b) the relevant action'.[35] But which considerations should count? Those that make the will good, which on Foot's view includes the sort of considerations that are taken into account by agents who possess justice, courage, temperance, and charity, among others. As Michael Thompson interprets Foot, she does not want to justify these claims, but rather takes them to be self-validating. As he writes:

> The human form of life is one in which considerations of justice, for example, characterize a sound practical reason. But this is not something we properly discover from a close study of human life.... That we operate with these thoughts is thus a part of what makes these thoughts true.[36]

Let us call the *strongly sui generis* reading of the human good; it is an understanding of the project of naturalism that one can find in John McDowell, Thompson, and Foot on Thompson's interpretation. By contrast, I want to argue that the study of human life does yield substantive results. There seems to be some evidence that Foot herself thought along these lines, as when she says thing like 'the evaluation of the human will should be determined by facts about the nature of human beings and the life of our own species'. The view that I am advocating might be called *weakly sui generis* in that I hold that

[35] NG op. cit. note 2, 13.

[36] Michael Thompson, 'Three Degrees of Natural Goodness,' http://www.pitt.edu/~mthompso/three.pdf.

there are distinctive standards that apply to human beings qua rational animals, and yet essential features of human beings as rational animals, including our appetitive powers, determine what it is for us to be good qua human beings.[37]

Part of the reason this latter interpretation of Foot's project may not seem to be open is due to blinkered metaphysics. If we can't think of finality in nature, we of course can't think of our desires as having an independent finality, that is, a finality independently of aims that we deliberately take up. One could think that appetites take on finality only through being integrated into intentional action, but I want to say that appetites have their own completion as a separate power, and their completion is essential to human excellence. That completion occurs when appetites take on the virtues as principles of their movement and then achieve their aim in morally good acts. We can, of course, act contrary to the finality of our appetites; for example, we can deliberate poorly about what constitutes the proper fulfillment of our appetites. Yet, I would like to say, for example, that there is such a thing as temperance that holds across human kind; it is, of course, contextually sensitive, such that there is a certain small amount of water to drink on an expedition in the Sahara, and another larger amount among the abundant freshwater lakes of Canada, but that the contextually appropriate mean, however much water that is, is the proper fulfillment of human appetites. It may be up to reason to determine what the mean is, but it is not up to reason to determine that whatever the mean is, that is the end of our appetites.

In affirming this, I am advisedly taking up a position that was not very long ago taken to be obviously out of bounds. Bernard Williams, to take one famous example, railed against the idea of an 'inner nisus'

[37] In a study of John Finnis' natural law theory, Mark Murphy draws a parallel distinction to my own between a weak and strong grounding in human nature. On the weak grounding interpretation of natural law theory, human nature does not impact what counts as good, but only our ability to access goods. So, if human nature were different, say, our if we lacked some intellectual capacities, we might not have access to some things that are goods, say an understanding of nature. On the strong grounding view, human nature actually explain why certain things are good. In terms of my distinction, the strongly sui generis view parallels the weak grounding view, since the good can come apart from facts about our nature, whereas the weakly sui generis view corresponds to the strong grounding claim. See 'Self-Evidence, Human Nature, and Natural Law', *American Catholic Quarterly,* LXIX, 3 (1995), 471–484. Thanks to Micah Lott for pointing out the parallel between my distinctions and Murphy's.

toward virtue in his 1986 *Ethics and the Limits of Philosophy*. Yet even some time before Williams wrote dismissively of these ideas, powers and finality were enjoying a revival in metaphysics and philosophy of science. As far back as 1970, Rom Harré argued that there is nothing occult about the idea of powers, and that they are in fact central to an adequate epistemology of science.[38] To ascribe a power to something is to tell us what it will do because of its intrinsic nature. Molière's mockery of the *virtus dormitiva* is undeserved. Instead of the fatuous pseudo-explanation is supposed to be, it in fact says something substantive: that the sleepiness observed after the ingestion of opium is to be attributed to the intrinsic nature of the opium. This claim leads us to a scientific investigation of what it is about the constitution of opium that gives it this power. Further, on the view of some powers theorists, including Edward Feser and David Oderberg, powers capture aspects of causality that cannot be captured by a counterfactual analysis. Powers capture what causality *is* rather than its consequences.[39] Oderberg argues that in order to account for efficient causality, we must make an appeal to finality:

> Final causes are the *precondition* of the very possibility of any efficient causality. If fire burns wood but not pure water, if beta particles can penetrate a sheet of paper but not a sheet of lead, this can only be because the agents are ordered to some effects rather than others: they each have their own finality, which restricts the range of their effects (while still having various kinds and degrees of indifference within the range).[40]

In other words, effects are a function of the nature of the things involved in the causal interaction, and their powers are due to their constitution. Nancy Cartwright argues that the powers or capacities make better sense of the methods of the sciences than Humean approaches. We proceed scientifically, she thinks, by attributing powers to things, positing that these powers are behind the effects that we witness. Hence, there are reasons from both metaphysics and philosophy of science to affirm the existence of powers in nature, and no reason to hold the prejudice Williams and others harbor toward the view. All I mean to do here is to suggest that this prejudice

[38] Rom Harré, 'Powers', *The British Journal for the Philosophy of Science,* 21, 1 (1970), 81–101.

[39] Op. cit. note 25, 62.

[40] David Oderberg, 'Finality revived: powers and intentionality', *Synthese,* 194 (2017), 2396.

is unwarranted, and to point to a potentially fruitful collaboration between neo-Aristotelian metaphysics and neo-Aristotelian ethics.

Specifically, taking our departure from this essentialist view of nature for developing a neo-Aristotelian ethical naturalism allows us postulate that virtues perfect our first nature, and reject the strongly sui generis reading of the human good in favor of the weakly sui generis view. Take John McDowell's understanding of Aristotle. On McDowell's view, Aristotle conceives of ethics as an autonomous set of rational requirements that result from an upbringing that imparts an ethical outlook: an upbringing that gets us to see certain considerations as reasons for action. This *Bildung,* as McDowell styles it, imparts a second nature, operating within the realm of law yet not determined by its demands. Whereas nature controls the behavior of non-rational animals, the acquisition of a second nature frees us to answer to demands that are not given by nature, and 'to step back from any motivational impulse one finds oneself subject to, and question its rational credentials'.[41] Through this reshaping of our motivational impulses, we ourselves acquire a freedom vis-à-vis the demands of nature, and our motivational responses are reshaped in accordance with what we rationally affirm: what is initially a passive, contingent upshot of our biological nature becomes, as a result of *Bildung,* a reflection of a conception of living well qua human being. Our desires thereby reflect our spontaneity as rational beings rather than our passive determination as natural beings.

McDowell rejects a reading of Aristotle according to which his aim is to 'construct the requirements of ethics out of independent facts about human nature'.[42] He casts this reading of Aristotle as an 'historical monstrosity' because it attributes to Aristotle an anxiety about the status of reasons to which he was immune, because he lacked the modern conception of nature as a realm of law. What is bizarre about McDowell's argument is that if Aristotle's understanding of nature is not that of a realm of law, then what 'constructing the requirements of ethics out of independent facts about human nature' would mean for him would also be quite a different thing that it means to someone pursuing such a project today in light of a Humean conception of nature. So, what McDowell must mean is that those readings of Aristotle (he cites Williams) take him to be doing something we obviously cannot do because we reject his conception of nature. McDowell wants to save Aristotle from doing something that would be cogent given his understanding of nature,

[41] Op. cit. note 4, 118.
[42] Op. cit. note 6, 79.

but not ours. If this is correct, the anachronism may be McDowell's: he is trying to defend Aristotle from criticism for a project that he didn't undertake: squaring ethics with nature conceived as a realm of law. Instead, Aristotle's project may indeed be that of squaring the requirements of ethics with nature, not as a passively obedient realm of law, but as a realm of active powers, which is the project that I want to defend in our contemporary context.

It is worth pointing out features of McDowell's account that are rendered either incoherent or trivial given his strongly sui generis stance on the human good. McDowell says that the educational process of *Bildung* is 'an element in the normal coming to maturity of the kind of animals we are'; '*Bildung* actualizes some of the potentialities we are born with';[43] 'our mode of living is our way of actualizing ourselves as animals' or 'exercises of spontaneity belong to our way of actualizing ourselves as animals'.[44] What does such talk mean in the absence of a conception of nature as containing powers that stand to be actualized? These claims are all made from the standpoint of someone who has acquired the relevant upbringing: perhaps it is a matter of using traditional philosophical vocabulary to shower praise on what one has been brought up to praise. They simply mean: 'our mode of living is good, according to our mode of living'. If they are supposed to mean something more than this, then it raises important questions of how these supposed potentialities we possess are part of the realm of law, which is exactly the sort of question that McDowell invokes the idea of second nature in hopes of silencing.

In light of an essentialist conception of nature, we can instead take these claims straightforwardly to be true. Virtue perfects us as the kind of thing we are by perfecting powers that are essential to us as rational animals. Placing virtue within nature in this way bridges the gulf between second nature and first nature in a more straightforward way. Instead of attempting to shut the questioning down as misplaced, this program offers the promise of a direct answer. As Brian Ellis states:

> ...the power of agency is not something unique to human beings, or other living creatures. It is a pervasive feature of reality. This is not to say that human agency is not something rather special; it clearly is. On the other hand, it is not as alien to the essentialist's view of the world as it is to the Humean one.[45]

43 Op. cit. note 6, 88.
44 Op. cit. note 6, 78.
45 *Philosophy of Nature,* 141.

As Ellis sees it, the essentialist's conception of nature has the potential to bring the manifest and scientific image together by showing that human rational powers are in many ways like the things we find elsewhere in nature. That is, like powers in inanimate things, human rational and appetitive powers have intrinsic natures that dispose them to realize themselves in certain characteristic ways. Unlike inanimate powers and even the variable causal powers of complex systems, human rational powers are also metapowers: powers to change their own dispositional properties.[46] Of course, understanding those sorts of powers would be a central question as part of a productive collaboration between neo-Aristotelian metaphysics and neo-Aristotelian ethical theory. Yet, if I am right, this is the direction that we need to go in order to fund a full-blooded realist ethical naturalism.

We should see the human good as a matter of perfecting appetitive and intellectual powers that we really have. The perfection of the appetites consists in their taking on qualities whereby they respond to our environment in a way that exhibits a principle of reason: they reflect our conception of the good as they reach out to sensible particulars. The human appetites are by nature aimed at morally good acts, and find their ultimate fulfillment therein. When we acquire virtue, we are acquiring states that allow us to fully realize our nature. In making this argument, I take myself to be going beyond the Wittgensteinian grammatical project started by Foot and the Fregean Aristotelianism of Thompson, but in a way that is very much indebted to their project. The point I'm making is that their vital-ethical *Categories* needs supplementation with a new, essentialist *Metaphysics* that bridges our moral judgments to a natural world inhabited by rational animals.

Department of Philosophy, University of Guelph
jhackerw@uoguelph.ca

[46] Op. cit. note 30, 143.

Depicting Human Form

CLARE MAC CUMHAILL

Abstract
This paper involves constructive exegesis. I consider the contrast between morality and art as sketched in Philippa Foot's 1972 paper of the same name, 'Morality and Art'. I then consider how her views might have shifted against the background of the conceptual landscape afforded by *Natural Goodness* (2001), though the topic of the relation of art and morality is not explicitly explored in that work. The method is to set out some textual fragments from *Natural Goodness* that can be arranged for a tentative Footian 'aesthetics'. I bring them into conversation with some ideas from Iris Murdoch to elucidate what I think the import may be, for Foot, of depicting human form.

1. Preamble

The subject of this paper is art and morality in Philippa's Foot's monograph *Natural Goodness*, a surprising topic perhaps since Foot seems not to mention this area in that mature work. Instead, we find a 1972 paper, included in the 2002 collection *Moral Dilemmas*, entitled 'Morality and Art', which, in the preface, Foot tells the reader she has included only 'hesitantly', the reason being that she was less able to speak, in her words, 'more robustly' of the objectivity of moral judgments there than she was in later work. It seems that such was her dissatisfaction with the paper that she didn't include it in an earlier volume of essays where chronologically speaking it belongs – *Virtues and Vices*, published in 1978.

It is true that as Foot's life progressed she came to speak more and more 'robustly' of the objectivity of moral judgment, arriving at her most robust formulation with the conception of *natural goodness* that the title of her monograph refers to. The Foot Archives at Somerville College contain an earlier draft called *The Grammar of Goodness*, a title which would have remained apt. Foot is concerned with forms of evaluative judgment and in particular with the peculiar grammar of forms of evaluation of *living things*. A good deer is one that can run swiftly; a good owl is one that can see in the dark. A deer or owl that cannot do such things is defective insofar as they cannot do what creatures of their kind do.

doi:10.1017/S1358246119000274

The word 'good' applied this way is used *attributively*, not *predicatively*. Foot jokes in a footnote of the 1972 work that she used to explain this contrast by holding up a torn scrap of paper for her interlocutors to see. Like the adjectives 'large' and 'small', the use of 'good' in most contexts isn't intelligible independently of consideration of what the noun to which it is attributed picks out. A small elephant is only small *as elephants go* – we cannot say that it simply is small. Likewise, a scrap of paper is not simply good or bad. Foot recalls that an offer to pass the paper around to check whether or not it *is* good would rouse a laugh, a recognition of the grammatical – and logical – absurdity.

With this invitation to check, Foot means to target a *predicative* use of 'good' that G.E. Moore draws attention to in his 1903 *Principia Ethica*. Moore thinks that goodness is a property which is 'out there' and which is intuitable – we can recognise and contemplate it, hence Foot's invitation to check. But goodness, for Moore, is non-natural. It cannot be identified with or reduced to natural properties. Instead he lists the pleasures of human interaction and the enjoyment of beautiful objects as 'good' in this predicative sense, saying that 'it is only for the sake of these things – in order that as much of them as possible may at some time exist – that anyone can be justified in performing any public or private duty. They are the *raison d'etre* of virtue.'[1]

By 2001, Foot had her own way of making sense of the most important reason for virtue's being. Just as a good deer needs to be swift, the good human needs the virtues – for instance, in order to do what humans do, courage is often needed, as is kindness, honesty and, as Foot emphasises and which many theorists leave off their list, a willingness to receive good things. The virtues, though important, are not my topic in this paper; instead see the contribution of John Hacker-Wright to this volume. For now, we need only note that by *Natural Goodness* Foot had found her way to speaking *robustly* of the objectivity of moral judgment because she had discovered a normativity that is *natural* insofar as it is necessitated *by the kind of animal we are*, and so is grounded neither in subjective attitudes, nor in social conventions or in rules or principles of the sort that are created by our linguistic practices. But when she was writing 'Morality and Art' in the early Seventies, she was still on her journey towards robustness. The task of that 1972 paper was to compare moral and aesthetic judgements. My task is in this paper is to attempt a bit of exegetical extrapolation – or construction.

[1] G.E. Moore, *Principia Ethica* (Cambridge: Cambridge University Press 1903/1922), 189.

By *Natural Goodness*, Foot's views on moral judgment have changed. My question is: How might she have treated the comparison between moral and aesthetic judgment from that later perspective, or indeed the broad topic of art and morality at all? There are glimmers on the topic of art in the text of *Natural Goodness* that invite this strategy. I'm going to lift them from the text so as to set out one way in which theorising on Foot's naturalism could go. And in particular, I want to show that looking at things in the way I suggest can help to deflect a criticism that can be laid against Foot of a certain kind of conservatism.

So, here's the plan for the paper. First, I'm going to set out the 1972 contrast. Then I'm going to offer a closer synopsis of Foot's later view before moving on to my constructive project in the second half of the paper. There I will set out some textual fragments from *Natural Goodness* that I think can be arranged for a tentative Footian 'aesthetics'. I bring them into conversation with some ideas from Iris Murdoch to elucidate what I think the import may be, for Foot, of depicting human form. I demonstrate this in the last part of the paper by drawing attention to two passages from the final pages of *Natural Goodness*.

2. Getting started: Strain or fiction?

Foot starts her 1972 paper by delimiting her terrain. She says she will not ask whether moral considerations are relevant when judging art. She says she will not argue, with G.E. Moore that aesthetic experience is an intrinsic good that ought to be pursued for its own sake.

Like Foot, I have started by mentioning Moore, but not quite to leave him aside. It's well-enough known that some of Moore's views on ethics and aesthetics influenced the Bloomsbury group. In a 1908 letter we find Virginia Woolf writing to Clive Bell, author of the formalist manifesto *Art* and husband of her sister, painter Vanessa Bell:

> 'I am splitting [my] head over Moore every night, feeling ideas travelling to the remotest parts of my brain, and setting up a feeble disturbance hardly to be called thought. It is almost a physical feeling, as though some little coil of brain unvisited by any blood so far, and pale as wax, had got a little life into it at last.'[2]

[2] Virginia Woolf, 1908, quoted in S. P. Rosenbaum, 'The Philosophical Realism of Virginia Woolf', in S.P. Rosenbaum ed. *English Literature and British Philosophy*, (Chicago: Chicago University Press, 1971), 319.

Literary critic Patricia Waugh comments: 'Rarely has reading analytic philosophy appeared so erotic, so close to the body'.[3] Here we have a picture of ideas being *in-corporated*. But if Moore's aesthetics proved animating or vivifying in this way – some little coil of brain has got life into it at last – the content of his aesthetics Waugh finds more 'eviscerated'. Though Moore thinks we should admire the corporeal expression of the mental qualities of those we have affection for – something Bloomsbury also went in for – his conception of aesthetic experience or consciousness is neither bodily, nor situated or historical. A diagnostic introduced in the last chapter of the *Principia*, 'The Ideal', helps us see this.

Moore instructs: we are to consider things as if they existed by themselves *in absolute isolation* and to ask whether their mere existence is good – 'good' being used here in a predicative sense. Those things that survive absolute isolation include, he thinks, the states of consciousness involved in aesthetic experience and in the appreciation of what is beautiful in Art or Nature.

Such isolationalism might be thought the pinnacle of art-for-art's sake, a movement that Iris Murdoch discards in her 1959 paper 'The Sublime and the Good' as 'flimsy' and 'frivilous', and with which she associates with Bloomsbury. 'Art is for life's sake....' – she writes – 'or else it is worthless'.[4] I show a little later to what extent Foot would agree.

After leaving aside Moore, Foot shares a hunch, something that tallies with her broadly Wittgensteinean method – we often find her drawing attention to feelings of malaise, a sense of queerness that is the mark of something philosophically suspect (recall the laugh that the scrap of paper roused). Her hunch is this: 'there is some element of fiction and strain in what we say about right and wrong, while our appraisal of aesthetic objects is relatively free from pretence'. This is a contrast that she thinks has, to borrow her way of speaking, *something behind it*. She sorts three dimensions of difference which I'll call *Contingency*, *Relativity*, and *Inescapability*. Let us go through each of these briefly.

Start with *Contingency*. In the two papers from the late Fifties which made her name – 'Moral Arguments' and 'Moral Beliefs' –

[3] Partricia Waugh, 'Beauty rewrites literary history : revisiting the myth of Bloomsbury.', in *The recovery of beauty : Arts, Culture, Medicine.* (Basingstoke: Palgrave Macmillan, 2015), 108–128.

[4] Iris Murdoch, 'The Sublime and the Good', in P. Conradi ed. *Existentialists and Mystics: Writing on Philosophy and Literature* (New York: Penguin), 218.

Foot urges that moral judgments are not simply subjective. They can't be likened to cries like 'ow' or 'alas' or even declarative expressions like 'How nice!', which can be sincere or insincere but not true or false. But we want to be able to say that certain moral judgments are true or false.

Admitting this much, however, still leaves open what makes a given moral judgment true. Perhaps I can conjure up moral principles by myself, *for* myself, self-prescribe how I am to act. Foot demonstrates that such a view would allow for bizarre prohibitions against, for instance, *'walking up to an English door, slowly'* (I mustn't do that) or *'looking at hedgehogs by the light of the moon'*. Instead, morality must have some connection with securing benefit and removing harm. And to the extent that it does it must be objective. Still, for the 1972 Foot, an uncomfortable degree of subjectivity remains, best explained by example. A conception of morality as connected with benefit and harm fixes it that the killing of human beings is objectionable. Nonetheless – and here I quote from a footnote in the 1972 paper – 'there is a genuine choice as to whether or not to count as a human being, with the rights of a human being, what would become a human being but is not yet capable of independent life'.[5]

This is an example of *Contingency*. Though there may be fixed starting points in moral disagreement – even a *definition* of good and bad, as connected say with benefit and harm – there may be 'play' in the system, as she calls it. But where there is such play, we may wind up tracing back to and leaning on the strength of mere conviction; we may wind up wanting to say that something 'just is' right or wrong, thereby giving the impression of some kind of authority standing behind our conviction. But here is the fiction, Foot thinks. The strain or uneasiness we may feel is the sense that there *is* nothing behind our 'just is' proclamations. Aesthetic judgment is different; the notion of contingency doesn't get a foot-hold. It's not obvious what it could be for two people to agree on all the *aesthetic* facts relevant to appreciation – the starting points – and then disagree in their appreciation to the extent that discussion backtracks to bare 'just is' statements, with the spectre of some kind of authority behind them.

Relativity. It follows from the assumption of contingency that there may be *some* moral judgments for which a relativistic account will be right for where there is 'play', mere conviction – or attitudes

[5] Philippa Foot, 'Morality and Art', in Moral Dilemma (Oxford: Oxford University Press, 1972), 7.

or feeling – may stand behind certain assertions. Foot gives some examples of relativity from outside ethics. *Clothes are said to be elegant; someone is good-looking; letting yak's butter go rancid before floating it on tea, gives a delicious flavour.*

No one will deny the relativity of such statements, says Foot. 'It would quite obviously be ridiculous for us to say that our opinions about the Tibetan's tea is correct and theirs mistaken'. It involves, in her words, '*no compromise of our own*' to grant that a Tibetan uttering a sentence meaning 'Rancid yak's butter gives a good flavour to tea' is saying something true. But a compromise of our own is involved if we grant that 'it is right to do X' is *true* when said by some person even though, were *we* to say it, it would be false.

In the case of the flavour of tea on at least one reading, to refuse to acknowledge that a Tibetan uttering the sentence meaning 'Rancid yak's butter gives a good flavour to tea' is saying something true belies, thinks Foot, a fictional belief that one's own taste is superior. The same is true in morals. In morals, we don't tend to allow a modest relativism – or compromise. But where there is contingency, and where compromise is ruled out, the fiction of superiority lurks nearby, something about which we may feel uneasy. In contrast, when it comes to art, if we have something to say in criticism of the art of, for example, a different age – perhaps that it is 'melodramatic' or 'florid' – we offer reasons in support of our claims but we don't insist that we must somehow be right. To grant that the Eighteenth century reader might have been saying something true in describing Samuel Richardson's *Pamela* as 'riveting' involves no compromise of our own should we find the narrative voice 'dull' and 'overbearing'. And here Foot adds something that I find striking:

> 'Sometimes recognition or appreciation fails. But then we are increasingly likely to think of the matter like that, and not to condemn what we do not understand or like'.[6]

Inescapability is a theme that haunts Foot. We tend to think of moral judgments as committing, or inescapable – for some moral considerations are overriding. Moral judgments pertain to choice or action, something Foot thinks Hume gets right. But the amoralist is, we might say, an *escapist* – where we treat moral judgments as having a kind of inescapablity with respect to choice or action, he does not; though he may recognise the demands of morality, he does not act on them. This invites a distinction with the *immoralist* – the

[6] Op. cit. note 5, 15.

immoralist does not recognise the constraints of the ethical at all. I return to the immoralist at the end of the paper.

The 1972 Foot is worried primarily about what we might say to the amoralist. We might try to convince him that he *should* act this way or that. What she feels, however, is the ineptitude, the complete inefficacy of *this* 'should'. For why should he? She has not yet found a form of natural necessity that grounds the real inescapability of certain moral judgments. At the moment, inescapability is felt but without any identifiable grounds.

By comparison, aesthetic judgments are escapable – we are free to retract, revisit, reframe prior leanings. Aesthetic evaluations don't pertain to action choice – and perhaps with practical rest comes a certain amount of evaluative abandon.

3. Bees and me

In this part of the paper, I move on to the late Foot. To recap my strategy: I'm attempting constructive exegesis. In *Natural Goodness,* Foot doesn't say anything much, or very explicit, about the contrast between aesthetic and moral judgments or on the topic of art and morality. But her views on morality have changed. How might she have treated the topic from her later viewpoint?

To begin, let's note in more detail what has changed by 2001 with respect to *morality*. Foot picks up work by Michael Thompson, itself a development of some Anscombian strands of thought, and which offers Foot a way of articulating a conception of the human life-form to which she will attach her *attributive* 'good'. For Thompson, the form of life of a kind of living thing is captured by a series of what he calls *natural historical judgments,* where these are judgments expressed by statements of the sort that might be narrated on a natural history TV program. They have forms like 'The S have/does F'; 'S's do F'; 'This is how things go with an S: they do F'.

For instance: swordbills have a beak longer than their body – as each long flower blooms, it gives the swordbill a fresh supply of food all to itself; Saiga antelope give birth to twins so their numbers grow rapidly just when grass is plentiful; the glass frog[7] leaves its eggs on stones close to waterfalls. Such statements are unquantified and non-empirical. There is no particular swordbill that has, all to itself, the deepest draft of nectar from the longest

[7] I have adapted some natural historical judgments from those narrated in David Attenborough's Planet Earth II.

flowers. Often the lifeform term in the grammatical subject appears with the definite article – *the* glass frog. Such judgments are also *atemporal* – though saiga antelope are born when grass is plentiful there is no *particular* past, present or future time *at* which *the* saiga is born.

Foot assumes, like Thompson, that a cache of such natural historical judgments characterises the human life form and that it is in light of *that form* that judgments of natural goodness or defect can be made. A 'good' human can do what creatures of their kind do, where, as I noted at the outset, this requires the possession of the virtues - humans need virtues like bees need stings, Foot would say. And since practical rationality involves acting well – as Foot puts it in a 2003 interview, it involves taking the right things as reasons[8] - morality becomes part of practical rationality. What we have reason to do is grounded in our human nature.

With this new model of moral evaluation, gone, it might be thought, are the feelings of uneasiness and strain that the earlier Foot detects; they are replaced instead, with relief and maybe even the joy of the naturalist. Humans are returned to the natural world of bees and plants. But not for long. Our reflective capacities transmogrify, and are essential to, human ways of going on. By the end of *Natural Goodness*, the feeling is different, darker. Foot considers Nietzsche's immoralism; she describes it as 'poisonous', a description I will return to.[9] Before that, we can ask how *Relativity*, *Contingency*, and *Inescapability* now look against the backdrop of this new conceptual scene.

First, note that *Relativism* with respect to moral judgment no longer involves compromise. All it involves is an innocuous kind of cultural relativism which allows that the human form of life is exemplified at different times and places, habitats even, in different ways.

Contingency too is transformed. The starting point for ethics is now a life-form concept, *human*, a concept that makes relevant natural historical judgments that say how things are and ought to be with an individual of that kind. To hesitatingly revisit my earlier example, it does not strike me that Foot would say now, as she did in 1972, that 'there is a genuine choice as to whether or not to count as a human being, with the rights of a human being, what would become a human being but is not yet capable of independent life'.

[8] Philippa Foot, 'The Grammar of Goodness: An Interview with Philippa Foot', *The Harvard Review* of Philosophy XI (2003), 32–44.

[9] Philippa Foot, *Natural Goodness* (Oxford: Oxford University Press), 113.

The later Foot might rather say: in conceiving of some bit of matter as something that can 'become a human being' one brings it under the concept human, and lets it be the grammatical subject of natural historical judgments that together make up the natural history of the life form human. *The human begins as a cluster of cells*. Of course, this leaves open whether the same rights extend – at the same time – to every individual organism that shares in the human form of life, but it seems that it does not leave open whether *this individual* falls under the concept human. Critically, though, the idiom of 'play' survives in *Natural Goodness*. She writes: 'I have very little idea of how much 'play' there will in the end turn out to be, how many grey areas'.[10] I will return to *Contingency* later and with it *Inescapability*.

So, how does aesthetic judgment fare from the explanatory perspective of natural goodness?

I want to say first off that there is no reason to think that Foot would have changed her mind about *their grammar* – aesthetic judgment involves attitudes and feelings. At the same time, however, were Foot to have revisited the themes of the 1972 'Morality and Art' explicitly in *Natural Goodness*, I can imagine that the *strategy* according to which she would have charted the comparison would have changed – this is what I'm going to demonstrate next.

4. Art, secondary goodness, still-life

In making her 'Fresh Start' – the name of the chapter at the beginning of *Natural Goodness* – Foot says that the goods that 'hang on human cooperation' also hang on such things as respect for art. It might be wondered why and how goods that hang on human cooperation also hang on art. Foot does not say what this connection could be. I have a go – and here I am beginning the constructive part of the paper.

Elizabeth Anscombe says we have ways of getting each other do things that do not depend on force. Promising is an example of such co-operation. While force is indexed broadly to the present, *now*; promising brings about its effects in the future. Anscombe calls the kind of necessity that promising brings about Aristotelian necessity. Foot mentions self-interest as an Aristotelian necessity; self-interest is necessary for humans since, once grown, *we* are better placed than anyone else to look out for ourselves and for our futures. Though the word 'time' does not appear in the index of

10 Op. cit. note 8, 23.

Natural Goodness, *care* for the future is, I think, a kind of virtue for Foot; sensitivity to time and a suitable kind of temporal orientation, for oneself, one's children or dependents, is part of natural goodness, as is, we might imagine, care for the form of life itself and the variety of ways in which it can be instanced at places. She often mentions hope.

Further, although atemporal, natural historical judgments often contain time references to temporal phases of various sorts – circadian, seasonal, developmental (at night, the moongoose forges; in spring the black bear lazes by its den; the human infant puts objects into its mouth), these temporal phrases and words are, we might say, part of the *superficial* grammar that articulates a life-cycle. But this is distinct from having a kind orientation in time that is part of the life form itself and which the natural historical judgments that characterise the life-form collectively express or *show*.

So, with this notion of an Aristotelian necessity in sight, we might ask: Does art involve a way of getting people to do things that does not depend on force, where this may involve respect for the normative status of art? I'm going to draw on Iris Murdoch's aesthetics to defend this possibility though the idea I want to explore is slightly distinct, if compatible – it is the idea not that we have ways of getting people to *do* things that depends on art, but that we have ways of getting each other to *see* things that depends on art, where seeing for Murdoch is a precursor to doing. Murdoch writes that we can only act in the world that we can see.[11]

In Murdoch' aesthetics we find at least two ways of homing in on the idea that we have ways of getting each other to see things which hangs on art. First, let us return to Gordon Square – where this paper was first read – though at an earlier time. In her essay 'Old Bloomsbury' in *Moments of Being* (1976), Woolf depicts a way of going on that was characteristic of the members of the Bloomsbury group, but which is mundane and familiar:

> 'We sat and looked at the ground. Then at last, Vanessa, having said....that she had been to some picture show, incautiously used the word 'beauty'. At that, one of the young men would lift his head slowly and say, 'It depends what you mean by beauty'. At once all our ears were pricked. It was as if the bull had at last been turned into the ring. The bull might be

[11] Iris Murdoch, 'The Idea of Perfection', in P. Conradi ed. *Existentialists and Mystics: Writing on Philosophy and Literature* (New York: Penguin), 329.

'beauty', might be 'good', might be 'reality'. Whatever it was, it was some abstract question that now drew all our forces .... Often we would still be sitting in a circle at two or three in the morning.'[12]

Murdoch sees the kind of triangulation that exists between at least two individuals, here a group, and an artwork, here a picture show, as having epistemic significance. Words are used in contexts. I can learn something about your scheme of concepts in the context of a shared object of attention. For instance, with reference to the picture-show I can learn something about what *you* think is 'mediocre', or 'ingenious' or 'derivative' since you will help me see where and why, for you, such words apply and we can thereby get the measure of where we diverge and overlap.[13]

Second, Murdoch gives a certain explanatory role to the *form* of the artwork. For instance, the novel, a narrative artwork, yokes together elements from our shared form of life in a coherent way. And if it is *great* art, for Murdoch, it will be realistic. Realism in art, like realism more generally is, for her, a *moral* achievement. But in this respect, the great artwork is, for Murdoch, a bit like a lens. In depicting patterns of human life in a realistic way, those patterns are made more salient to us when we turn away from fiction to reality; they come to 'stand out', they are lifted out of the maelstrom of existence otherwise full of contingency and seeming to lack point. And if it is great, it will foreground, now using *Foot's* idiom, what is serious not trivial in human life, though this is not to say that what is serious cannot be found in the most humdrum realities. What is serious for Foot is what matters in a human life; its goods. Yet if great art is like a lens for Murdoch – and, to be clear, this is my way of framing things – it is also like a mirror. The artwork, she says, is a 'cracked object'. In writing about the novel in *Metaphysics as a Guide to Morals* she tells us that:

'The novel is a discursive art...The novel, in the great nineteenth-century sense, attempts to envisage if not the whole of life, at any rate a piece of it large and varied enough to seem to illuminate the whole, and has most obviously an open texture, a porous or cracked quality... . The object is as it were full of holes through which it communicates with life, and life flows

[12] Virginia Woolf, 1976, 'Old Bloomsbury', in S.P. Rosenbaum ed. *A Bloomsbury Group Reader* (Oxford: Basil Blackwell, 1993), 362–63.

[13] For detailed discussion, see Anil Gomes 'Iris Murdoch on Art, Ethics, and Attention', *British Journal of Aesthetics* 53/(2013), 321–337.

> in and out of it. This openness is compatible with elaborate form. The thing is open in the sense that it looks toward life and life looks back.'[14]

I cannot explore this passage adequately here, but suggest only that it chimes with perhaps the most quoted of lines in Murdoch's entire philosophical corpus: 'Man is a creature who makes pictures and then comes to resemble those pictures' – this is from her 'Metaphysics and Ethics', published the same year as Anscombe's *Intention*. It is also statement that at once recalls the form of the *natural historical judgment. Man is a creature who makes pictures*; 'The S does F'. Making pictures is something we, humans do, where 'picture' may be read on a cultural and historical scale to involve myth – the epic pictures we need but can be held captive by, a theme Mary Midgley's meta-philosophy constantly and brilliantly returns to.[15] *And then comes to resemble those pictures*. 'This is how things go with an S: they do F'.

Of course, we might wonder what it is to *resemble* a picture and again there is much to say. But for now, and for the purposes of this paper, I only note that resembling cannot mean copying which would involve interpretation and the possibility of mistake. In her long essay – or short book – *The Fire and the Sun,* Murdoch, writing on the *Timeaus*, comments 'a good man does not copy another good man, playing him as an actor plays a role....'[16] Her own philosophy agrees. The only sense in which one can copy a villain is by performing instances of actions that *are villainous*. But, if so, resembling a picture is not a matter of copying: it is a matter of *being* what is depicted. Here we might be reminded of the closeness that Woolf's thought comes to Moore's on reading him – his thoughts are incorporated.

Returning to Foot then I think we can so far light on a negative claim, though not before adding a further detail to the picture I am assembling.

In 1972, Foot says that in cases of good conduct, benefit does not usually accrue to oneself, or at least self-benefit is irrelevant – and it is precisely this fracturing of benefit from which the amoralist

14 Iris Murdoch, *Metaphysics as a Guide to Morals*, (London: Chatto and Windus, 1992) 96.

15 For instance, see Mary Midgley 'Philosophical Plumbing' *Royal Institute of Philosophy Supplement* 33 (1992), 139–151.

16 Iris Murdoch, 'The Fire and the Sun', in P. Conradi ed. *Existentialists and Mystics: Writing on Philosophy and Literature* (New York: Penguin), 436.

wants to escape. In contrast, the fruits of good art *are* garnered by the one to whom the good – the interest and enjoyment of the artwork – will come. But from the perspective of *Natural Goodness*, elaborated in this Murdochian frame, this no longer seems the case; the goods of art range wider. This might at once be thought to point to a crude *functional* account of art - the propensity of formal artworks to hone our attentive capacities, to allow for the co-ordination of divergent evaluative perspectives and so on. This might suggest too that art is at best only of *instrumental* value, but Foot, I think, offers us a distinctive way of conceiving this relation – and this is the second glimmer I want to shore up from *Natural Goodness*.

It is easy to overlook natural goodness, Foot thinks, because we make so many evaluations of *non-living things* in the natural word – she mentions the soil and weather, but also artefacts made by animals - the nests of birds and beaver's dams, and, in the human case, houses and bridges. But the goodness of these things she thinks is only *secondary* – their goodness is only intelligible in the context of the life form in which they play a part. Specifically: '*they contribute to the way things can go in the life of the species*.' It is tempting to see art, if not quite having the artefactual status of at least many houses and bridges, then as expressions of our creative capacity that are at least akin to these things. But, if so, we can think of art too as possessing a kind of secondary goodness.

Some clarifications. Importantly, evaluations of secondary goodness when applied to art or representation are not quite aesthetic evaluations though evaluation of aesthetic quality may be a component feature of the assessment of secondary goodness. Nor is such evaluation straightforwardly suggestive of an ethicism or aestheticism about art. Ethicism is broadly the idea that the moral outlook endorsed by an artwork is relevant to its *aesthetic evaluation*. In aestheticism there is no such link. Whether Foot would hold either of these I cannot say but at any rate the evaluation of secondary goodness is evaluation of a different kind. Things that have a secondary goodness *contribute to how things go in the life of the species*. I think we can leave it highly indeterminate how art contributes to how things go in the life of the human animal. That things do go some way or other however brings into view the third comment I want to consider.

In evaluating how things contribute to how things go in the life of the species, we are concerned with the life-form *as it is now* – not with how it could be. For one, the idea that the human life-form itself could be 'better' or 'worse' assumes the predicative use of 'good' that Foot wants to head off. Besides, she also tells us, using the language of art, 'it is only insofar as 'stills' can be made from the 'moving picture' of the evolution of the species that we can have a natural history of the life of a particular kind of living thing' at all.[17] And here she comments on what she sees as a gap in Michael Thompson's account.

The gap she sees is this. Not just any proposition that has the *natural historical form* let's say – the superficial grammar of such judgments - should figure in the set of natural historical judgments that tell us how a good *X* should be. Here's her example: 'The blue tit has a round blue patch on its head', but supposing blue-tits being so coloured plays no part in the life of the blue tit, the grey-headed blue tit in my garden need not be defective. On this understanding, what plays a part is just what is needed *to live* the life of a particular kind of thing. And here Foot shows us that there can, in fact, returning to our earlier discussion, be a little 'play' in the system – a creature that can live the life of a blue tit need not have a blue-coloured head. Likewise, there may be many different ways in which *what is needed* to live the life of a particular kind of thing can be met. These two points I think help waylay the charge of a certain kind of conservatism that can be laid against Foot. For instance, in a recent and illuminating paper Tom Whyman writes that Foot articulates a notion of the human good as 'univocal' and 'ultimately unchanging – something that every human being, who has ever existed, is subject to in ethical reflection in exactly the same way'.[18] But Foot, I think, allows for change – there is the still and there is the moving picture – *and* she allows for variation – the natural historical judgments that go to make up the 'still' must have teleological import but what is needed to live the life of a particular kind of living thing can be met in different ways.

It seems then that we can finally circle back to *Inescapability* and *Contingency*. We now have an explanation for the *inescapability* we may feel with respect to moral judgment. To act well, even if we don't on occasion, issues from our human nature, and this explains too in what sense *Contingency* is transformed. At the same time, once we admit the Murdochian natural historical judgment into the 'still' that constitutes our natural history, this picture becomes complicated. For just as a characteristic kind of orientation in time is expressed, or shown, by our natural history, so does it contain a latent dynamism which hangs on the pictures we make of ourselves and

[17] Op. cit. note 9, 29.

[18] Tom Whyman, 'Radical ethical naturalism', *Philosophy and Social Criticism* 44/2 (2018) 159–178.

on their secondary goodness. In the last part of the paper, I draw these ideas together by glossing some of Foot's closing remarks in *Natural Goodness*.

5. Depicting human form

Earlier I said that Foot describes Nietzsche's doctrines as 'poisonous'. In what ways are they poisonous? According to Nietzsche's view, as cast by Foot, there are no right or wrong actions *considered in themselves*. But, here, and I let Foot's voice take over:

> 'human life, unlike the life of animals is lived according to norms that are known and taken as patterns by those whose norms they are. So, we have to teach children what they may and may not do...the norms to be followed must be largely formulated in terms of the prohibition of actions such as murder or theft....[U]nlike the members of other species, humans, having the power of abstract thought can consider they own ways of going on. We humans have ourselves developed and can criticise our own practices. We can ask whether human life might be better conducted if Nietzsche's doctrines were taught. But then we must think about how human life could be carried on'[19]

The norms to be followed that involve prohibition are what Anscombe calls 'stopping modals' – they are of the form 'you mustn't do *X*', 'you can't do *X*', where *X* may be filled in by something that it *is* in the power of a human animal to do; thieve or lie or murder even. That adults teach children such norms is part of our natural history and again a certain kind of orientation in time is expressed by our instructing our children in this way. But since living according to such norms is what we humans do, a human that flouts these norms is defective.

A Nietzchean immoralist is *more* than defective however. Since it is part of human life that norms expressed using stopping modals are taught to children, a view that doesn't treat the actions that can take the place of *X* as prohibited *in themselves*, would be, *were that view taken up*, inimical to the human form of life going on. It is in this sense, then, that Nietzsche's doctrines are poisonous – they fail to have secondary goodness. I have so far cast the Wittgensteinean frame of Foot's thinking on these matters in terms of epistemic feelings – hunches, feelings of malaise. But in this final page of *Natural*

[19] Op. cit. note 9, 114.

Goodness, there are echoes of the rule-following argument – the possibility of human life going is internal to the human life form itself.

So, does this mean, finally, that we should not countenance poisonous doctrines – or, as Hume would cast, it morally vicious artworks, a question Foot explicitly does not broach in her 1972 paper? I'm not sure Foot would say so, but in a postscript, she gives an example which might suggest that the taking of certain kinds of objects as objects of aesthetic appreciation is defective:

> 'Goethe told his secretary Eckermann of a certain Englishman who, owning an aviary, was so struck one day by the beautiful appearance of a dead bird that he straightaway had the rest killed and stuffed. Hardly a crime! And yet there was *something wrong* with that man'[20]

For a Moorean isolationist, the mere existence of states of aesthetic appreciation is good and the more such states exist - as 'killing the rest' might engender – the better. The problem with absolute isolationism however is that it demands the de-historicisation of the work. But – more critically – it also assumes that the act of contemplation of such isolated objects is itself de-historicised, floating free from any background. And perhaps the evaluative escapability of aesthetic judgment tempts this picture. This, I think, is what Foot would find dangerous.

Works of art and philosophical doctrines appear against a background – they are Murdochian 'cracked objects', full of holes, '[they] look toward life and life looks back'. Foot is writing against a background where the aesthetic pull of Nietszche's depictions of human form were mirrored in the historical events that she took as the background for all of her philosophy from 1946 on, and she too recognises too their allure. But she also recognises her task as philosopher. Again, feelings creep in. When criticising Nietszche, she feels herself a surveyor reducing a glorious countryside to its contours – 'or like someone telling the Sirens they are singing out of tune'.[21] But like Midgley, Anscombe and Murdoch, she sees that this is work that needs to be done. If art is for life's sake, then so is

[20] Op. cit. note 8, Postscript.

[21] Philippa Foot, 'Nietzche's Immoralism', in *Moral Dilemmas* (Oxford: Oxfrod University Press, 2002), 158.

philosophy. Or to paraphrase Foot: We were seduced once. Who's to say we will not be again?[22]

Durham University
clare.maccumhaill@durham.ac.uk

[22] This paper was given at Gordon Square, on 15th March 2019, as one of the Royal Institute of Philosophy London Lectures on Anscombe, Foot, Midgley and Murdoch. I am very grateful to my Durham colleagues Joe Saunders, Andy Hamilton and Ben Smith for comments on a draft. I am especially indebted to Rachael Wiseman for endless and illuminating discussion on these and related themes.

Love and Unselfing in Iris Murdoch

JULIA DRIVER

Abstract
Iris Murdoch believes that unselfing is required for virtue, as it takes us out of our egoistic preoccupations, and connects us to the Good in the world. Love is a form of unselfing, illustrating how close attention to another, and the way they really are, again, takes us out of a narrow focus on the self. Though this view of love runs counter to a view that those in love often overlook flaws in their loved ones, or at least down-play them, I argue that it is compatible with Murdoch's view that love can overlook some flaws, ones that do not speak to the loved one's true self. Unselfing requires that we don't engage in selfish delusion, but a softer view of our loved ones is permitted.

1. Introduction

> I am looking out of my window in an anxious and resentful state of mind, oblivious of my surroundings, brooding perhaps on some damage done to my prestige. Then suddenly I observe a hovering kestrel. In a moment everything is altered. The brooding self with its hurt vanity has disappeared.[1]

This passage in *The Sovereignty of the Good* is one of the most famous in Iris Murdoch's oeuvre. In it, so much of her thought is conveyed. The kestrel is beautiful. The perception of that beauty takes her out of herself because the kestrel's beauty, its goodness, exists apart from her own interests. Taken out of herself, she has a clear perception of reality, of Beauty, of the Good. This is an example of a process or instance of 'unselfing'. Unselfing is a very important component to Murdoch's thought. It is through unselfing that we come to acquire knowledge of the Good, and make ourselves morally better people. It is through unselfing that we acquire virtue. Indeed, several commentators have noted that one of the distinctive features of Murdoch's philosophy, writing as she was in the mid 20th century, is her pursuit of an answer to the question 'How do we make ourselves morally better?' *We need to know the Good*, and this

[1] From Iris Murdoch, *The Sovereignty of the Good*, (Routledge Classics, 1970), 82.

doi:10.1017/S1358246120000028

will elude us if we remain psychologically isolated. In this essay I try to achieve a grasp of unselfing as Murdoch sees it and then discuss what I perceive to be potential shortcomings of the account. I also explore how unselfing as clear perception relates to love. I disagree with how many have read Murdoch on love, but arrive at an interpretation that I am happy to endorse: the tension between 'seeing clearly' and 'love' can be resolved by noting that love responds to the other person's true self, which one can perceive without being aware of some of that person's flaws.

2. Our Flawed Character

I have previously written about Murdoch's distinctive brand of particularism, which happened to stimulate, and be a part of, dissatisfaction with the way the Moral Philosophy was conducted in mid-20th century Oxbridge. But, of course, her unhappiness was not limited to methodological issues. She, as well as Philippa Foot, had come through WWII believing that morality is real, it *must* be real. We are not simply booing Hitler when we condemn him. We are committed to the truth of the claim 'Hitler was evil'. Further, it is important that Hitler be identified as 'evil'; to simply say that what Hitler did was morally wrong, while true, leaves out too much detail. It leaves out the scope and depth of his wrongdoing. We are better able to understand the moral dimensions of the world around us when we use the thicker evaluative terms. This is another form of particularity. In the case of Murdoch, one can understand the world this way if one becomes imbedded in various details of one's experience – and if one has the capacity to look at the world in what the early moral philosophers referred to as a 'disinterested' way – that is, where the goodness is perceived independently of the viewer's own interests.

History contains ample evidence that human beings are flawed, and that those flaws get in the way of our virtue. Murdoch shared with Foot the view that virtues correct for defects of human nature, though their views on how this worked were quite different. Foot does so in her account by holding that virtues are correctives:

> ... they are *corrective*, each one standing at a point at which there is some temptation to be resisted or deficiency of motivation to be made good. As Aristotle put it, virtue is about what is difficult for men....one may say that it is only because fear and the desire for

> pleasure often operate as temptations that courage and temperance exist as virtues at all.[2]

In Foot, however, there is no appeal to an overarching Good the apprehension of which leads to virtue. She did not have the same systematic view of virtue held by Murdoch. Murdoch was a Platonist and on her view virtue was a way of seeing reality. As many other writers have noted her work is literally filled with allusions to Plato's Cave. Characters move out of the world of shadows and into the light. In *The Nice and the Good*, one character literally leaves a cave as a more enlightened person. One of the primary characters of the novel, John Ducane, has entered Gunnar's cave on a rescue mission, only to be trapped with the person he was trying to save:

> He thought, if I ever get out of here I will be no man's judge. Nothing is worth doing except to kill the little rat, not to judge, not to be superior, not to exercise power, not to seek, seek, seek. To love, and to reconcile and to forgive, only this matters. All power is sin and all law is frailty. Love is the only justice.[3]

Indeed, Ducane is in a position to destroy someone's career, and then decides not to do it. The novel ends with many acts of reconciliation amongst the characters. It also illustrates another feature of unselfing: putting things in the right perspective. An important feature of the analogy or identification between beauty and the good is the significance of perspective in both. In spelling out his own account, and making use of the analogy, David Hume notes that one of the things we do is we correct for imperfect perspectives and this allows for consistency in our judgements of beauty.[4] For Hume it was important for us to pick a fixed point of reference so that everyone, in effect, was talking about the same thing when they made judgments of beauty as well as moral virtue. For Murdoch, though, it wasn't a matter of being able to communicate effectively with others, it was a matter of getting it right, of our judgements matching the world. The value of a work of art, the value of the world, the value of beautiful things in the world – all of this has nothing to do with *my* interests. Or even, with anyone's interests. This is a rejection of the sorts of considerations that Hume found important in our

[2] Philippa Foot, 'Virtues and Vices' in *Virtues and Vices* (Oxford: OUP, 1978) 1–18.

[3] Iris Murdoch, *The Nice and the Good* (Penguin Books, 1968).

[4] David Hume *A Treatise of Human Nature,* ed. David Fate Norton and Mary Norton (Oxford: Oxford University Press, 2007).

perceptions of beauty. Hume had the view that the pleasures we felt were often due to the utility we perceived in an object or character trait. And, certainly, Utilitarians had the view that considerations of utility were what provided moral justification. Murdoch was rejecting this view, which was how some of her colleagues viewed morality, as serving our interests. Ducane, in Gunnar's Cave, came near death. It is a literary trope that coming close to death can change a person's perspective, enlarge it. In Ducane's case, it gave him a better sense of what was truly important. It is not retribution, but love and understanding.

To see another person justly we may need to adopt the perspective, or become clearer on the 'context' that another person is living in. Moral psychologists refer to this as a kind of empathy in that it involves another meta-cognitive skill – that of taking the perspective of another person. This skill is important in our interactions with others, since if we cannot see another's perspective they will be a mystery to us. But there is another kind of empathy as well. We might care about others and want to see the world from their point of view as a matter of understanding them sympathetically.

This way of seeing reality, the virtuous way, simply as a matter of contingent fact does correct for flaws of human nature related to ego, but that isn't a defining feature of virtue. In a world without any temptation, there still could be virtue. It is just that, given the reality of our fallen nature, clear perception *would* dispel the self-interested fantasies we conjured up to preserve our own egotism. In 'On God and the Good' Murdoch, though not a Freudian herself, finds a Freudian view of human nature 'realistic':

> Freud takes a thoroughly pessimistic view of human nature. He sees the psyche as an egocentric system of quasi-mechanical energy, largely determined by its own individual history, whose natural attachments are sexual, ambiguous, and hard for the subject to understand or control. Introspection reveals only the deep tissue of ambivalent motive, and fantasy is a stronger force than reason.[5]

Unselfing, then will involve close attention, and in understanding others we need to pay close attention in such a way as to 'share' their contexts. This is difficult to do. She explicitly notes that often we cannot do this. Yet, there is much that indicates that unselfing is not accomplished via force of will. That doesn't support the phenomenology she appeals to in many cases. Instead, it is a kind of

[5] Op. cit. note 1, *The Sovereignty of the Good*, 50.

letting go of our egocentrism in the presence of beauty. This is why she uses the example of seeing the kestrel. She is sitting at a window, brooding over a slight to her dignity, and making no attempt to escape those thoughts. But she was *open to* the escape the kestrel supplied. In that case, there is no force of the will at work. On the other hand, this can run counter to other things that she says about unselfing, for example, that it requires moral imagination and effort. This describes the famous M case, since in that case the mother-in-law is presented as someone who is *trying* to attend to her daughter-in-law charitably. The case is set up in the context of M's relationship with her daughter-in-law, D. M begins with a very low opinion of D. Though she thinks that D is basically 'good hearted' she also thinks that D lacks 'dignity' and 'refinement' and 'tiresomely juvenile.' However, M is also reflective, and begins to reconsider.

> M tells herself 'I am old-fashioned and conventional. I may be prejudiced and narrow-minded. I may be snobbish. I am certainly jealous. Let me look again.' Here I assume that M observes D or at least reflects deliberately about D, until gradually her vision of D alters.[6]

M is quite clearly *trying* to look at D more clearly. M is *trying* to correct for her excessive conventionality. But there need not be any contradiction. We can hold that she is really open to both ways of attending: being open to the world, and trying to see it more clearly. Her use of 'attention' can be understood to include both. She notes in *The Sovereignty of the Good* that attention is '…a just and loving gaze directed upon an individual reality. I believe this to be the characteristic and proper mark of the moral agent'. However, there are pitfalls to the 'trying' element, which will be discussed later in the paper.

Though it may be hard to properly attend, we can do it sometimes. When we come to genuinely appreciate a person, for example, and, in other cases, to *love* someone, we can do this. Love enables us to thwart our tendencies towards self-involvement, selfishness, fantasy, and illusion:

> It is in the capacity to love, that is to see, that the liberation of the soul from fantasy consists. The freedom which is the proper human goal is the freedom from fantasy, that is the realism of compassion. What I have called fantasy, the proliferation of blinding self-centered aims and images, is itself a powerful

[6] Iris Murdoch *The Sovereignty of the Good* (Routledge, 1970) 17.

> system of energy, and most of what is often called 'will' or 'willing' belongs to this system. What counteracts the system is attention to reality inspired by, consisting of, love.[7]

In her novel, *The Sea, The Sea,* the main character, Charles Arrowby, is someone who is enormously self-centered and self-deceived.[8] Arrowby tells himself that he has 'abjured' the magic of the stage, and London, in order to rusticate in a cottage, Shruff End, so as to devote himself to becoming good. However, the novel details just how extraordinarily bad Arrowby is at becoming good. He is a master of self-deceit. He deceives himself about the love of a woman, Hartley Finch, who he has not seen in decades. He concocts elaborate and ill-advised plans to bring them together. He believes himself in love, though he utterly fails to clearly see the object of his love.

Charles Arrowby is certainly an exaggerated character, but he exhibits an uncomfortable truth: that we are prone to telling ourselves comfortable stories in order to preserve our own good view of ourselves. Some of the early sentimentalist writers on morality, such as Shaftesbury and Hume, often noted that we, unlike animals, have the ability to engage in meta-cognitive reflection, and that this is what allowed us to be self-regulating. We have a need to be able to withstand *our own scrutiny*. If we saw moral ugliness in our own characters, we would be moved to change. Murdoch, however, was worried about our meta-cognitive capacities responding not to reality, but to comfortable stories we tell ourselves so that we *can* bear our own scrutiny. Fantasy insulates us against suffering and self-recrimination.

Unselfing, then, is a matter of seeing the world with clarity, inspiration in beauty, attending to others with loving appreciation in such a way as to overcome our egoistic tendencies. However, Christopher Mole has pointed out a possible problem with this view. It seems to leave out something that we do think is important for moral development: *some* attention to our own mental states. Consider one of his cases:

> … a man is wondering whether he should tell his wife about a minor indiscretion in his past. He recognizes that keeping the secret is a way of being untrustworthy and so he resolves to tell the truth. What moves him is the realization that he does not want to be the kind of person who would continue to lie. The

[7] Op. cit. note 5.
[8] Iris Murdoch, *The Sea, the Sea* (Penguin Books, 1980).

> distinctive feature of this form of moral reasoning is that the terms of evaluation it employs indict the agent rather than the act.[9]

Indeed, as Mole points out, Murdoch herself points out instances of self-criticism. In the case of M, discussed earlier, she describes M, the mother-in-law as 'intelligent and well-intentioned person, capable of self-criticism'. Mole notes that of all of her characters, John Ducane exemplifies the character caught up in self-reflection and self-criticism, and the pitfalls associated with them. From *The Nice and the Good*:

> What Ducane was experiencing, in this form peculiar to him of imagining himself as a judge, was, though this was not entirely clear in his mind, one of the great paradoxes of morality, namely that in order to become good it may be necessary to imagine oneself good, and yet such imagining may also be the very thing which renders improvement impossible, either because of surreptitious complacency or because of some deeper blasphemous infection which is set up when goodness is thought about in the wrong way. To become good it may be necessary to think about virtue, although unreflective simple people may achieve a thoughtless excellence. Ducane was in any case highly reflective and had from childhood quite explicitly set before himself the aim of becoming a good man.

Earlier I tried to establish that attention can be both an openness to reality, as well as more active. It can also involve a *trying* to see. In the above passage, though, we see Murdoch alluding to the pitfalls of self-study, of trying to see oneself. Recall also, in the earlier quote from *The Sovereignty of the Good* regarding Freud's 'realistic' view of human nature, she alludes to his very pessimistic views on introspection. Trying to attend to the self may necessitate thinking of oneself as unattentive first, since this needs to be established first if one is to be motivated to improve – and this opens the door to distorting psychological influences again. Mole tries to dissolve this tension by holding that for Murdoch, when we are attempting to become good, we cannot achieve that through *pure* introspection. We need contact with the world, with external reality:

9 Christopher Mole 'Attention, Self, and *The Sovereignty of the Good*,' in *Iris Murdoch: A Reassessment*, ed. Anne Rowe (Palgrave Macmillan, 2006), 75.

> Even when introspection succeeds in being honest and astute, the features of ourselves that we learn about through introspection are features that are morally salient only on account of their relationships to things outside the self. Introspective meditations do not bring us into a proper relationship with the world, and they do not tell us whether we are in a proper relationship with the world. It is careful understanding of the world that reveals our failures of virtue as failures. If one takes our moral character to be partially constituted by the ways in which we attentively interact with the world, then one can hold that character traits are primary bearers of intrinsic value without thereby making one's own properties a focus of concern in one's pursuit of goodness.[10]

Mole seems to be interpreting Murdoch as holding that it is pure introspection that is inimical to self-improvement. However, critical reflection on ourselves does involve considering our relation to the world – to what is genuinely Good. It is this contact with reality that allows us to see our failures, the mismatch between ourselves and the world. It is the world that provides the standard of Good.

Another possibility that Mole does not consider is that Murdoch is alluding to another well known paradox: the paradox of hedonism. Suppose it is true that our proper aim is to achieve happiness, or pleasure of the right sort. Given various plausible assumptions about how we and the world work it would seem like this theory gives us self-defeating advice, because if one actively seeks happiness one will stand less of a chance of actually achieving it. The best way to be happy is not to adopt a strategy of constantly looking for it. Instead, one should be *open to it* as one lives one's life normally. All of the things we associate with happiness, including loving relationships, are not to be sought out as a means to that happiness. When I love another person, I love that person for themselves. That's where the story ends. I do not love someone *because I want to be happy*, though if I do love someone that will be a part of my happiness. So perhaps the resolution of Murdoch's paradox is that when we try to be good without an *appreciation of the good*, which we can achieve by being open to its presence in our lives, we will fail. I ought not seek out my own virtue, but pay attention to what is around me, be open to it, and thereby achieve virtue. As Mary Midgley writes in *Beast and Man*, the pleasure one gets at seeing beauty, in the kestrel, is 'self-forgetful' – what ties being open to

[10] Op. cit. note 8, 83.

beauty and trying hard to see it is this self-forgetting.[11] By self-forgetting she doesn't mean that the virtuous person forgets the things that have happened to her in the past. Instead, she 'forgets' a false view of the importance of the self.

In any case, however this paradox is to be resolved, if it can be, it is relevant to other things that Murdoch claims for clearly seeing, for loving attention.[12] What about Love? Love does take us out of ourselves in the ways that Murdoch outlines. But part of what it is to be in love with someone and to care for them for their own sakes is to also take a careful look at oneself. When I love someone I need to take a long look at myself. Love might not justify a relationship all on its own. Am I someone who is really good for the person I love? Does my character warrant love in return?

Thus, there is a good case to be made for the fact that eliminating self-reflection also conflicts with the development of moral character. After all, how *disinterested* can I really be if I want to improve *myself*, as Ducane does? Even if I relax, and take the world as it is, just by following that advice I am still trying to improve *myself*. In fact, it seems likely that my main worry should be my own character, and not improvement of the character of others.

Further, there is a distinction between seeing clearly and overcoming our egoistic tendencies. Someone might press the point that love may at least sometimes involve a *failure* to see clearly, even if it always involves a thwarting of our egoistic instincts. Self-deception isn't always of Arrowby's sort. Self-deception is not always deceiving myself *about myself*, or in such a way as to flatter my self-image. A parent, for example, arguably has more reason to overlook at least minor flaws in their children than strangers do. And by 'overlook' I mean that the parent is not taking on board the entirety of what the evidence supports. Perhaps, for example, the evidence supports the judgement that Donald's child is not even a mediocre scholar. It may still behoove Donald, as a parent, to have a somewhat better assessment of the child. This may be very important for the child's development and improvement.

This is true for other close relationships as well. There's something to the saying that 'Love is blind'. Of course, it ought not be too blind, so as to overlook serious failings. But some flaws ought not register.

11 Mary Midgley, *Beast and Man* (New American Library, 1978), 359.

12 Samantha Vice criticizes Murdoch for the erasure of self in her 'The Ethics of Self-Concern,' in *Iris Murdoch: A Reassessment*, ed. Anne Rowe (Palgrave Macmillan, 2006), 60–71. Mole is trying for a reconciliation between two strands he sees in Murdoch's work.

One phenomenon of love is that we often feel compelled to make sincere excuses for the person we love, so that others are aware of how we see them.

This issue is taken up by Susan Wolf in her study of *The Philadelphia Story*.[13] There she argues that Murdoch did not seem to have a 'positive light' view of love, of the sort I have sketched in the previous paragraphs. Instead, love involves loving the other in spite of their flaws, in full awareness of their flaws. Thus, there is no incompatibility at all between seeing clearly and love. This is illustrated in the plot of *The Philadelphia Story*. The film is about love and misadventure. Tracy Lord is a socialite who is about to marry for the second time. She divorced her first husband, Dexter Haven, because of his flaws. She felt he drank too much, though his drinking was in response to her low opinion. Her fiancé is George Kittredge. Kittredge has idealized Tracy, made her perfect.. In the end, she breaks off with George. After seeing her drunk and being carried by another man, rather than his mind turning to charitable interpretations of the evidence, he presumes the worst. He has little confidence in her. Tracy, instead, marries Dexter again. Dexter knows what she is really like, and he has confidence in her loyalty. Dexter also is well aware of the flaws that she really does have. And, Dexter loves her in spite of her flaws. As Wolf notes: '...Dexter's love is the truest and best love Tracy (or anyone) can have...' precisely because Dexter loves Tracy '...*knowing her completely*. Specifically, he loves her, and indeed loves her unreservedly, knowing her flaws.'

But I don't think that this is quite fair to the positive light view. George's view of Tracy is not a slightly idealized view of Tracy, it isn't Tracy at all. In the case of Dexter, he consciously takes on board Tracy's flaws – her insistence on perfection in others, for example – and loves her anyway. This is because, I take it, that she is not *just* a perfectionist, *she* is much more. But if this is right, it means that there is room for overlooking flaws. One can love another aptly even when one does not see all of their flaws, as long as those flaws are not an element of the person's true self – that is, those flaws do not speak to their *core* set of values and commitments. Thus, we can judge some love as bad in virtue of the overlooking of very serious flaws in a person's character – being in love with a

[13] Susan Wolf 'Loving Attention: Lessons in Love from *The Philadelphia Story*,' in *Understanding Love: Philosophy, Film, and Fiction*, ed. Susan Wolf and Christopher Grau (Oxford University Press, 2014), 369–386.

mass murderer, for example. But when the person is fundamentally decent, love *can* overlook their flaws. This isn't to say that love *must* overlook defects of character. Indeed, Dexter's full appreciation of Tracy's character may render his love even better, more stable, less liable to disillusion.

On one interpretation of Murdoch, a moralized interpretation in which love is only apt in response to seeing the goodness beauty in others, love is what Kate Abramson and Adam Leite term 'reactive love'. For Abramson and Liete, it isn't the *only* kind of love, but is a very important kind of love:

> There is a variety of love that is, in paradigm or central cases, an affectionate attachment to another person, (a) appropriately felt as a non-self-interested response to particular kinds of morally laudable features of character expressed by the loved one in interaction with the lover (and others the lover loves), and (b) paradigmatically manifested in certain kinds of acts of goodwill and characteristic affective, desiderative and other motivational responses (including other-regarding concern and a desire to be with the beloved).[14]

Abramson and Leite note that love is disinterested – again, in the sense that one loves the other *for their own sake*. They also have another component that corresponds to Murdoch's second feature of unselfing, the seeing clearly of the other person's good qualities. Abramson and Leite also highlight the reactive nature of the emotion. It is in response to the beloved's goodness of character. It is an apt response if one sees the other clearly, that is, if the other person really possesses the qualities in question, they are *real*. Why is this 'reactive'? Because it is a response to quality of the will, the quality of the other person's character. It is quite right that utter delusion is not compatible with love in the sense that it renders the love inapt. If the love is *based on* a false belief, rather than merely tolerating it, the love is not apt.

This allows a middle way between two extremes. Love is a matter of one person seeing another clearly enough to understand and appreciate the beloved's true self. This isn't knowing everything there is to know about the beloved and is compatible with overlooking flaws that do not impact the self. Through empathy with the person one loves, one understands what they do and don't endorse. One can speak authoritatively about who they really are. Of course, this

[14] Kate Abramson and Adam Leite, 'Love as a Reactive Emotion,' *The Philosophical Quarterly*, 6 (245), 677.

process if not done correctly has its own pitfalls – we can deceive ourselves about others just as well as we can deceive ourselves about our own characters. But this is just part of the human condition that needs to be kept in line through maintaining our contact with reality.

The University of Texas at Austin
Julia.Driver@austin.utexas.edu

The Elusiveness of the Ethical: From Murdoch to Diamond

SABINA LOVIBOND

Abstract
Cora Diamond is a powerful witness to the originality of Iris Murdoch's writings on ethics, showing how Murdoch is at variance with contemporary orthodoxy not just in respect of particular doctrines (no 'ought' from an 'is', etc.), but in her questioning of mainstream assumptions as to what constitutes the subject-matter of moral philosophy. Diamond celebrates Murdoch as an ally in her campaign against the 'departmental' conception of morality – the idea that moral thought is just one branch of thought among others – and highlights Murdoch's enduring belief in the 'ubiquity of the moral quality inherent in consciousness'. In keeping with this belief, both philosophers affirm the value of general humanistic reflection on experience, an enterprise in which traditions of imaginative literature as well as of self-conscious theory can invite us to participate. While welcoming this vindication of the claims of ordinary (existentially embedded) moral intelligence, I will explore some difficulties flowing from the associated idea that 'morality' (in the guise of value-saturated human consciousness) is all-pervasive, and from the 'perpetually-moralist' account of our incentive to engage with fictional worlds.

1. Introduction

This discussion will be concerned with a certain tradition of dissent in twentieth-century (and subsequent) moral philosophy: a tradition, though, which I will treat as comprising just two main representatives.

Iris Murdoch and Cora Diamond, through their respective bodies of work – and I mean for present purposes only the philosophical work of Murdoch, not the fiction – command attention as highly original and distinctive personalities, each speaking in her own characteristic voice and generating a characteristic intellectual atmosphere. Their interests intersect to some extent; at the same time, each has a range of interests that remain largely outside the area of intersection. But a topic on which they are of one mind, and on which Diamond has laboured to bring out Murdoch's radicalism in relation to the academic mainstream, is the inadequacy of our customary ways of talking about 'morality', 'moral thinking', 'moral language' – and consequently 'moral philosophy', the branch of philosophy whose business it is to reflect on these things.

doi:10.1017/S1358246119000195

Among the most famous Murdochian themes is an insistence that morally significant events in human consciousness occur not only at the point where some choice is made or some principle adopted as a basis for action, but also in the outwardly uneventful passages between these points. The moral life, she says, 'is something that goes on *continually*'; the in-between element is indeed what is most important, issuing as it does (in a 'small, piecemeal' way) in habits of perception and attention – or of course *in*attention – which more or less determine in advance how we will respond to a real-life practical challenge. And this is not intended as a denial of our freedom, but simply as a suggestion that 'at crucial moments of choice most of the business of choosing is already over'.[1]

Many years later, in *Metaphysics as a Guide to Morals*, Murdoch still maintains 'the importance and omnipresence of a reflective experiential background to moral decision and action, and with this the omnipresence of value (an opposition between good and bad) in human activity';[2] she continues to hold that 'value, valuing, is not a specialised activity of the will, but an apprehension of the world, an aspect of cognition, which is everywhere'.[3] This is not to be understood as an expression of psychological optimism, but on the contrary as the announcement of an unending task. 'Certainly morality must be seen as "everywhere" but in a fallen and incomplete sense'; in fact, the '(daily, hourly, minutely) attempted purification of consciousness [is] the central and fundamental "arena" of morality'.[4] And while 'arena' has to be placed in inverted commas, since our efforts to correct what is bad in our habitual thought-patterns typically occur in private, we are not without resources to guide these efforts. Prominent, or perhaps foremost, among such resources is the realistic novel. In Murdoch's view, 'Novels ... exhibit the ubiquity of the moral quality inherent in consciousness';[5] they show us 'personal morality in a non-abstract manner as the stuff of consciousness',[6] or conversely, they support the idea of consciousness as 'the fundamental mode or form of moral being'.[7]

[1] *The Sovereignty of Good* (London: Routledge and Kegan Paul, 1970; hereafter 'SG'): all quotations in this paragraph are from 37 (emphasis added on 'continually').

[2] *Metaphysics as a Guide to Morals* (Harmondsworth: Penguin, 1993; hereafter 'MGM'), 259.

[3] Op. cit. note 2, 265.

[4] Op. cit. note 2, 293.

[5] Op. cit. note 2, 169.

[6] Op. cit. note 2.

[7] Op. cit. note 2, 171.

Cora Diamond correctly identifies the (variable) 'quality of consciousness' as a constant element in Murdoch's thought and a connecting link between its earlier and later phases.[8] She appeals to Murdoch as an ally in her campaign against the 'departmental' conception of morality – the 'idea that moral thought is a branch of thought, one branch among others',[9] and by extension that moral philosophy is one of a number of intellectually self-evident 'departments into which philosophy can be divided'.[10] This whole picture, she argues, is an artefact of educational or professional convenience; we would do well to be more critical of the practice of defining 'moral discourse' by the occurrence of a certain vocabulary, or by certain linguistic forms or patterns of rational order. Murdoch can help us address the philistinism of the 'moral discourse' approach through her conviction that 'consciousness is *always* morally colored',[11] and that 'moral thought, evaluative thought' is not just one among a family of cognitive activities but – precisely – something ubiquitous. To take this view seriously would mean suspending the assumption that it is just obvious (by reference to vocabulary or other surface phenomena) when something with 'moral' content is being expressed, and instead, attuning ourselves to the possible presence of such content in places where it is not explicitly signalled – an attunement that would rely on the exercise of some actual moral powers on our part, not merely on hazy memories of what we once heard in undergraduate lectures.

True, Murdoch holds fast to the view that 'Morality is and ought to be connected with the whole of our being'; that 'The moral life is not intermittent or specialised, it is not a peculiar separate area of our existence'.[12] In arriving at this view, however, and in affirming (or reaffirming[13]) that 'There are qualities of consciousness', she does

[8] '"We Are Perpetually Moralists": Iris Murdoch, Fact and Value', in Maria Antonaccio and William Schweiker (eds.), *Iris Murdoch and the Search for Human Goodness* (1996; hereafter 'WPM'), 79–109, at 95.

[9] 'Murdoch the Explorer', in *Philosophical Topics* 38 (2010) 51–85 (hereafter 'MTE'), at 54.

[10] Op. cit. note 9, 59. Compare also 53, where 'field of study' (borrowed from Murdoch) is mentioned as another term belonging to the objectionable idiom.

[11] Op. cit. note 8, WPM 106 (emphasis added).

[12] Op. cit. note 2, MGM 495.

[13] 'Reaffirming', since she has previously argued in SG op. cit. note 1, 84 that 'Our states of consciousness differ in quality, our fantasies and reveries are not trivial and unimportant, they are profoundly connected with our energies and our ability to choose and act'.

pause to concede that 'There are [also] "moral judgments", which may in some ways resemble judgments in law courts, or which take place at stated times and initiate clearly visible new courses of action or the embryos of new dispositions'.[14] And she acknowledges that the celebration of 'alert vivid experience',[15] the claim of the present moment on our attention, can appeal to aesthetic or hedonistic values as well as to those of a moral or spiritual kind: our conception of the attentive, undistracted consciousness can draw upon Walter Pater (in his famous lines from *The Renaissance* about burning with a 'hard, gem-like flame') as well as on Simone Weil. Murdoch simply notes that both ways of thinking are available and that we can 'switch' from one to the other – though her own interest is clearly in the Weilian direction of travel, the role of Pater being just to point to something precious in that momentary consciousness 'which philosophers tend to be embarrassed by, to neglect, or to analyse away'.[16]

2. Murdoch and Value

The concession that *there are* some (dateable) 'moral judgements' – and hence, presumably, something in the nature of a 'departmental' morality to which these judgements are indebted – looks like a helpful sign of willingness to remain in touch with ordinary, non-philosophical language. Certainly it would be difficult to emancipate oneself entirely from the familiar way of referring to 'moral' considerations: the kind of consideration invoked, for example, when one politician accuses another of an 'abdication of responsibility and morality',[17] or when a powerful corporation is described as a 'morality-free zone'.[18]Such remarks convey a criticism with a certain content, perhaps not fully determinate in the first instance, but nevertheless a criticism belonging to a determinate general area of concern.

Can it really be such a blunder to try to formulate some shared account, however rough, of what is meant by terms like 'moral' or 'morality' in so far as these are *less than* coextensive with the entire space of value? For example, if there is anything in particular that

[14] Op. cit. note 2, MGM 238.

[15] Op. cit. note 2,. 218.

[16] Op. cit. note 2,. 219.

[17] Jeremy Corbyn on Boris Johnson's attitude to Syria, *Guardian* 16 April 2018.

[18] Julian Knight MP, referring to Facebook: *Guardian* 27 April 2018.

can be identified as 'what moral life demands',[19] or if it is correct (or at least desirable) to think of artistic activity as subject to 'moral discipline',[20] shouldn't we be prepared to face the question: what kind of discipline is that? If morality 'pervades thought',[21] and yet also issues 'demands' (so that 'every single second has a moral tag',[22] and thus contributes to some eventual reckoning), where should we turn for clarification of *what is demanded*?

Murdoch would perhaps regard this question as symptomatic of the fixation of mainstream moral philosophy on issues of conflict-resolution in the public realm, which do typically call for the establishment and skilful interpretation of practical principles, and hence for a local form of epistemology. In opposition to this approach, or at any rate with a view to side-stepping it, she hopes to gain a hearing for the view of Weil that rather than straining over moral 'problems' we should be trying to achieve a quiet appreciation of 'the truths which are evident'[23] – to 'see reality clearly and justly',[24] where the obstacle to clear vision lies not in any great objective complication but in our own egoism and conceit.

Diamond agrees with Murdoch that to define the sphere of morality, or of moral philosophy, in terms of action and choice is a 'limited and limiting' specification.[25] She praises Murdoch's appreciation of the part played in our assessment of people – which can quite legitimately be called *moral* assessment – by the 'texture' of their being, as expressed in gesture or demeanour; or by the 'nature of their personal vision', revealed in modes of speech, or in what someone notices or fails to notice.[26] We can also observe that what Diamond wants to restore to a place of greater honour in our general picture of moral consciousness seems to have to do with *receptivity* (in contrast to 'rational agency'): her various reviews of the blind spots of analytical ethics touch on desiderata such as 'perceptiveness in regard to the currents of life'; a 'rejection of the spirit of knowingness'; a capacity for the 'acknowledgement of mystery' or for the experience of life

19 Op. cit. note 9, MTE 73.

20 Op. cit. note 9, 64, quoting Murdoch, SG op. cit. note 1 64.

21 Op. cit. note 9, MTE 52.

22 Op. cit. note 2, MGM 495.

23 *Simone Weil: An Anthology*, ed. Siân Miles (London: Penguin, 2005), 231.

24 Diamond (expounding Murdoch), MTE, op. cit. note 9 71.

25 'Having a Rough Story about What Moral Philosophy Is', in *The Realistic Spirit: Wittgenstein, Philosophy, and the Mind* (1991; hereafter 'RS'), 376.

26 Op. cit. note 25., 374.

as an 'extraordinary adventure'; or a response to individual life *qua* 'irreducibly particular'.[27] So we have at least this much of an indication of what might be regarded as belonging to the 'moral' side of life, over and above the usual hackneyed (and juridically orientated) examples. But Diamond holds nevertheless that 'no one knows what the subject [of moral philosophy] is';[28] that even a seemingly broad-brush account of that subject, such as the quasi-Aristotelian study of the good life proposed by Martha Nussbaum,[29] will struggle to qualify as consensual.

A conception of the 'moral life' that finds favour with all of Nussbaum, Murdoch and Diamond is that it is the life concerned with *values*. For each of these writers, the evaluative domain appears to be practically coextensive with the moral. Thus Nussbaum can say of Henry James that for him 'the artist's task is ... above all moral, "the expression, the literal squeezing out of value"':[30] here the words quoted from James are meant to support the preceding statement, with the implication that the business of squeezing out value is ('above all', anyway) a moral one. And in her view a novel like *The Golden Bowl* (of which more later) 'calls forth our "active sense of life", which is our moral faculty'[31] – again, apparently, an identity claim.

Murdoch, as we've seen, holds that 'value' or 'valuing' – and hence (though 'in a fallen and incomplete sense') morality – is 'everywhere', and she sometimes treats the two terms as interchangeable: thus '*Value, morality*, is eliminated by the structuralist picture if taken seriously'.[32] (This might admittedly be a compressed way of saying 'value, *and therefore* morality' – but compression is not in general a feature of Murdoch's late style.) Diamond, in the same vein, writes in approving exposition of Murdoch that 'thinking is always an

[27] Op. cit. note 8, WPM 93, 100; 'Martha Nussbaum and the Need for Novels', *Philosophical Investigations* 16:2 (1993) 128–53, at 139–40, 147, 152. The relevant notion of 'mystery' is illustrated by a passage from Wordsworth, *The Prelude*; 'extraordinary adventure' comes from G. K. Chesterton, who also contributes a view of the world as 'filled with the wonder of fairy tales'.

[28] Op. cit. note 25, RS 380.

[29] Notably in her *Love's Knowledge: Essays on Philosophy and Literature* (Oxford, 1990; hereafter 'LK').

[30] Op. cit. note 29, 163 (quoting James, *The Art of the Novel*).

[31] Op. cit. note 29, 162.Nussbaum has argued in detail for the recognition of this novel as a 'major or irreplaceable work of moral philosophy' (LK op. cit. note 29 138).

[32] Op. cit. note 2, MGM 190, emphasis added.

activity of ours as *moral* beings'; that 'Value, or moral value, is not the object of some *branch* of thought or discourse ... moral thought, evaluative thought, is not one member of the family [of cognitive practices] alongside the others'.[33]

3. Pluralism and monism

This treatment of 'value' and 'moral value', or 'morality', as functionally equivalent demands closer attention. On the face of it there are numerous *values* (plural) other than the moral variety. Most obviously (and traditionally), there are the values called into play by prudential and by hedonistic reasoning. But we also talk about aesthetic and artistic value, and about value of an intellectual, educational, economic or social kind; no doubt the list can be extended. Reflection on the distinct sub-species of value and their mutual relations constitutes (what was once, around a century ago) the well-defined discipline of 'axiological ethics', developed especially in Germany by philosophers such as Max Scheler and Nicolai Hartmann.[34] Of course it will be pointed out that some of these forms of value are affiliated to various 'hypothetical imperatives' over which philosophy has no special reason to linger. (Compare, for instance, 'nutritional value'.) But this does not dispose of the thought that what we value non-instrumentally, or 'for its own sake', extends beyond the moral. Aesthetic, artistic, intellectual and (hopefully) educational value are powerful examples.[35] To view any of these as a subdivision of the 'moral' looks worryingly reductive. Nor is value-pluralism discredited by Murdoch's (in itself persuasive) observation that 'Aesthetic insight connects with moral insight, respect for things connects with respect for persons'.[36] It is true that the destruction of ancient buildings, trees, animal life, and so forth often displays a morally reprehensible – not to say wicked – cast of mind. But it does not follow that the value of the things destroyed by such activity is itself *moral value*: these things have value in their own distinctive ways.

[33] Op. cit. note 8, WPM 82, 106.

[34] See J. N. Findlay, *Axiological Ethics* (London: Macmillan, 1970). Scheler, 1874–1928; Hartmann, 1882–1950.

[35] 'Hopefully', in that non-instrumental attitudes to education are not to be taken for granted. See Stefan Collini, *What Are Universities For?* (London: Penguin, 2012).

[36] Op. cit. note 2, MGM 495.

And as Diamond delicately but tellingly points out,[37] it is unclear that James's wish to produce an 'intelligent report' on social experience is really, as Nussbaum claims, such as to bring him 'into intimate connection with the Aristotelian enterprise'. The desire for an 'intelligent report', or indeed the aspiration to be someone 'on whom nothing is lost',[38] is naturally understood as an intellectual one: a wish or hope to become less stupid. And the stupidity for which a course of Henry James can serve as antidote may well be partly 'moral' in the familiar sense of issuing in bad behaviour towards others: from this point of view the treatment might consist in a remedy for our insensitivity or emotional blindness. But that can hardly be the whole story. To look no further afield than *The Golden Bowl*, the momentousness of the trap set for the Ververs (father and daughter) by devious old Europe is all about their failure – through no fault of their own, one may feel – to qualify as people 'on whom nothing is lost'. Some supremely important stuff is indeed lost on them at critical moments, with consequences for which they will spend the rest of their lives paying, though they will not be the only ones to pay. They suffer from not having a sufficiently developed sense, as Diamond puts it on James's behalf, of 'there being more to things than meets the eye';[39]and Diamond is probably also right about James's view of 'the characteristic danger of New England life, the danger of the Puritan spirit' – namely that 'one misses out on life through unconsciousness, unawareness, linked to moralism'.[40] Yes – 'moralism' in the sense of a lack of attunement to *values other than the moral*. And this without prejudice to the point on which Nussbaum lays particular stress, that Maggie Verver's response to her difficulties (once she fully understands them) is a *moral achievement*: one that bears witness to important qualities of character.

Returning to Murdoch, we might wonder if she would have any principled reason for objecting to this pluralist approach, which at first glance looks like a potentially helpful resource for her later philosophy. Certainly in *Metaphysics* the contrasting notion of 'monism' has negative – illiberal, anti-humanist – connotations; thus 'Structuralist (monist, idealist) thinking, by inflating coherence at

[37] 'Missing the Adventure: Reply to Martha Nussbaum', op. cit. note 25, RS 376.

[38] Op. cit. note 29, LK 148, quoting James's preface to *The Princess Casamassima*. Nussbaum refers to the attempt to become such a person as 'our highest and hardest task' – an 'ethical' task, as she explicitly describes it.

[39] Op. cit. note 25 315.

[40] Op. cit. note 25, 315.

the expense of correspondence, loses our ordinary everyday conception of truth',[41] and so becomes a hostile rather than a congenial tendency. However, the object under attack at this stage – namely the kind of social or linguistic holism which issues a challenge to 'ordinary everyday' evaluative notions – belongs to a quite different problematic from the one inhabited by 1960s Murdoch, who can say of herself (albeit confidingly rather than argumentatively): 'My own temperament inclines to monism'.[42] That (confiding) remark figures in an account of moral consciousness which can properly be called 'monistic' by virtue of its Platonist inspiration – that is, its orientation towards a single transcendent good. And though she deplores the totalizing ambitions of late twentieth-century critical theory (for example, the 'nightmarish schemata of deconstructionist thought'[43]), the mature Murdoch does not disown her earlier view that 'moral advance carries with it *intuitions of unity* which are increasingly less misleading'.[44] She continues to regard the conscientious mind as following a trajectory of which the ideal end-point is characterized by (impersonally) truthful vision; plurality of points of view, here as in Plato,[45] is a distraction rather than an asset, serving at best to furnish dialectical material which can help the understanding on its way; moral and intellectual progress is enabled by the Weilian principle of detachment or 'unselfing'. So the *purification* of consciousness – the moral project identified by Murdoch in *Metaphysics* as 'central and fundamental' – remains potentially at variance with the impulse of the story-teller or dramatist to explore a multiplicity of evaluative positions, not all of them compatible with morality in the 'departmental' sense. This is the problem with which Murdoch wrestles in *The Fire and the Sun*,[46] where she seeks to mediate between the moralism of Plato and the value we attach to (at any rate 'good' or 'great') literary art. Her stake in the success of such a mediation is due to the important didactic role which, as

41 Op. cit. note 2, MGM 267; compare also 227, 'Hegel's authoritative monism'; 235, 'the authoritarian aspiration to a unique systematic truth'.

42 Op. cit. note 1, SG 50. To supply some context for the confession: Murdoch has just stated that it is a 'great merit' of philosophy in the Oxford and Cambridge tradition, 'and one which I would not wish to lose sight of, that it attacks every form of spurious unity ... Perhaps it is a matter of temperament whether or not one is convinced that all is one'.

43 Op. cit. note 2, MGM 168.

44 Op. cit. note 1, SG 93 (emphasis added).

45 See for example *Republic* Bk X, 604e–605a and context.

46 *The Fire and the Sun: Why Plato Banished the Artists* (Oxford University Press, 1977).

we saw earlier, she assigns to the novelist – that role being to provide a concrete, though necessarily imaginary, demonstration of 'personal morality … as the stuff of consciousness',[47] and in doing so, to step forth for moral inspection by the reader.

4. A diversity of value

Without rushing to judgement on this claim, I want to see how it works in relation to some sample cases where an evaluative response to (fictional) experience is undeniably to the fore. My choice of texts has been guided by a sense of something puzzling in the denial of what might be regarded, a priori, as a truistic or commonsensical thought: the thought that *moral* considerations represent a *particular kind* of evaluative consideration, which may or may not speak to one at any given moment. My aim is to bring out a discontinuity between the 'morality is everywhere' view in (what we might call) its maximalist form, and on the other hand the more sharply focussed scepticism of Diamond about 'departmental' moral philosophy – her objection, for example, to the claim that 'moral discourse *unquestionably* has the surface form of a descriptive, property-attributing language'.[48] I will accordingly seek to direct attention – with some supporting literary evidence in the general spirit (I hope) of Murdoch and Diamond – to the internal diversity, the not exclusively 'moral' constitution, of the domain of value.

A. Anthony Powell, *Casanova's Chinese Restaurant* (1960) (Fontana 1980, 8–9)

From the vantage-point of a bombed-out street in Soho during the war, Powell's first-person narrator recalls a conversation with his friend Moreland on almost the same spot, back in the 1930s. The memory is prompted by hearing once again the voice of a woman, apparently a beggar or busker or just a local eccentric, singing 'Pale hands I loved beside the Shalimar' – an Edwardian drawing-room number, also known as the 'Kashmiri Love Song'. On the earlier occasion, the two young men had been speculating on the whereabouts of the Shalimar:

> '"A nightclub, do you think?" Moreland had said. "A bordel, perhaps? Certainly an establishment catering for exotic tastes –

47 Op. cit. note 2, MGM 169, 170. See also below, note 61 and context.

48 Op. cit. note 9, MTE 55, quoting Stephen Darwall, Allan Gibbard and Peter Railton, 'Toward *Fin de siècle* Ethics: Some Trends', *Philosophical. Review* 101:1 (1992), 115–89, at 119; emphasis added.

> and I expect not very healthy ones either. How I wish there were somewhere like that where we could spend the afternoon. That woman's singing has unsettled me. What nostalgia. It was really splendid. "Whom do you lead on Rapture's roadway far?" What a pertinent question'.

The tone here is playful, a bit silly; the speaker seems to be riffing on the theme of dullness and possible remedies for dullness. We cannot infer that Moreland has ever seriously thought about visiting a brothel – his use of the quaint word 'bordel' rather suggests otherwise – but equally, there is nothing to show that he has not. That question is none of our business; it is as remote from the narrative mood as the social reality of the sex trade, or indeed of the British Empire, relevant as these things are to the understanding of Moreland's words. What we can take from those words is that he is having an aesthetic moment of a certain (highly specific, concretely presented) kind.

I will assume that the passage just quoted, like those I will go on to discuss, can be accepted as a convincing depiction of a possible (small-scale) human situation. Now, how does this relate to the thesis that 'the moral life ... is something that goes on continually', or that 'all consciousness has a moral character'?[49]

The reply that suggests itself runs as follows: 'Certainly there are states of mind or consciousness – like those celebrated in the famous lines from Pater – in which the values that are salient for us, the ones that exert the most insistent claim, are not "moral" values in the departmental sense. However, this possibility is allowed for by the idea of morality as all-pervasive: the point is not that a "moral" attitude (in contrast, for example, to an aesthetic or a purely strategic one) is inescapable for us as socially situated individuals, but that however we see fit to conduct ourselves or to govern our mental life, the attitude we actually adopt will have *moral significance*: no morally neutral or "colourless" position is available; thus in the case of Moreland, we are being shown a *moral* snapshot of how things stood with him on a particular (fictional) afternoon, though of course we don't yet know how this snapshot bears upon his overall personality or life story'.

So far, then, we have before us an illustration of the idea that 'consciousness is always morally coloured', or that moral quality is 'ubiquitous' in it – not however in the 'departmental' way (since this would amount to the highly implausible claim that human beings are continually engaged in questioning their consciences, wondering

[49] Op. cit. note 9, MTE 52.

how they can become more virtuous, and so forth), but rather because the kind of value that is salient for someone at any given moment identifies them as a person with a certain 'moral' orientation, in the global sense that interests Murdoch and Diamond.

B. Colette, *Chéri* (1920) (trans. Roger Senhouse, Vintage, 2001), 95

> 'Thus, for a long time, she mused over her future, veering between alarm and resignation. Her nerves were relaxed, and she slept for a little. As she sat with one cheek pressed against a cushion, her dreams projected her into her fast-approaching old age. She saw day follow day with clockwork monotony, and herself beside Charlotte Peloux – their spirited rivalry helping the time to pass. In this way she would be spared, for many years, the degrading listlessness of women past their prime, who abandon first their stays, then their hair-dye, and who finally no longer bother about the quality of their underclothes. She had a foretaste of the sinful pleasures of the old – little else than a concealed aggressiveness, day-dreams of murder, and the keen recurrent hope for catastrophes that will spare only one living creature and one corner of the globe. Then she woke up …'

Léa, the heroine of this short novel, is a woman around the age of fifty coming to terms with the loss of 'Chéri', her lover of the past several years – a rich, spoilt, gloriously handsome creature half her own age, who is also the son of one of her oldest friends, though 'friendship' in this case is large enough to accommodate some pretty fierce feelings of hostility. Again a window is opened here upon a value-saturated state of consciousness, which can be all the more bracingly negative by virtue of its presentation as a dream (but a dream only just below the conscious level). Again, too, the passage shows us 'value' and (departmental) 'morality' parting company: Léa's sense of what lies ahead as she checks out of her sexually active existence is expressed in the language of disgust, but it is full of an implied contrast with all that has been joyful and thrilling – not to mention lucrative – in the life she has lived. So if this is an instance of 'personal morality as the stuff of consciousness', or of morality as something that 'pervades thought', the point must be that the contents of one's consciousness are such as to *situate* one morally, for better or worse; a weakness for the so-called 'sinful pleasures of old age' would fix some co-ordinates (maybe rather unusual, but who knows?) that someone might occupy within the total space of 'moral' possibility, construed in the non-departmental fashion.

Of course, once we recognize the inner life as a scene of moral activity, it will not be a matter of indifference to find oneself entertaining 'day-dreams of murder' or the 'keen recurrent hope for catastrophes'. We know that for Murdoch morality 'must be seen as "everywhere" but in a fallen and incomplete sense', and that our central moral task is the 'attempted *purification* of consciousness'.[50] Some work of 'purification', then, would seem to be indicated for Léa, if it is not too late; what such a person needs is a change of orientation within the total (non-departmental) moral space. Possibly that need could be met by reconnecting with the moral wisdom of Murdoch's iconic (uncorrupted) 'ordinary person'.[51] Or we might think of Léa as a victim of her own 'fat relentless ego',[52] someone whose vision has become clouded and who no longer has a just perception of her human surroundings. But really, when confronted by the unwavering coolness and dryness of Colette, this kind of commentary seems to bounce off without gaining much of a foothold. It is as if the question were being put: 'Morality, yes, we have known about that from our early years – we are familiar with its demands, at least the more obvious ones, and you should not infer that we hold them in any disrespect — but what *else* goes on in the mind? Aren't we allowed to acknowledge that as interestingly differentiated? In accepting that the *moral life* goes on continually, we are not yet consenting to pass over what is dubious or transgressive in that life. To say that the transgressive moments are not worthy objects of attention, or that we would be better off not "thinking on these things",[53] is a further and more contentious claim'.

C. Henry James, *The Golden Bowl* (1904) (Penguin, 1987), 553

In addition to its importance for Nussbaum, this novel supplies the haunting image of the pagoda, deployed by Murdoch in *Metaphysics*[54] to demonstrate the resources of an account of the inner life untrammelled by doctrinaire behaviourism. The mysterious, impenetrable structure represents Maggie Verver's sense that there is something about her husband's life, his relationship with her old friend Charlotte Stant (now married to Maggie's not very aged father), from which she, Maggie, is excluded – as indeed there

[50] Op. cit. note 2, MGM 293 (emphasis added).
[51] SG, op. cit. note 1 97.
[52] SG, op. cit. note 1 52.
[53] Compare Murdoch, MGM, op. cit. note 2 301 (quoting Paul, *Philippians* 4:8).
[54] Op. cit. note 2, MGM 170–1.

is, since the two are lovers, and had already been heading in that direction before the fateful marriages took place.

Later in the book – much later existentially, though it is just a few months by the fictional calendar – the tables have been turned and Maggie is no longer the ingénue but a deep practitioner of the 'conquest of appearances'.[55] By confronting her husband with the truth she has discovered, but then by acting in such a way as to prevent any public avowal or any clearing of the air with the other couple, she has succeeded in driving a wedge between the adulterers and tacitly communicating to her father that he may, with her blessing, remove himself and Charlotte permanently to the wasteland that is 'American City' ('the awful place over there').[56]

So complete is Maggie's eventual triumph – in respect of proprietorship, if not of spontaneous personal magic — that she can even allow herself the luxury of pity for her victim, who will now be mourning the loss of a relationship that was 'everything a relation could be, filled to the brim with the wine of consciousness'. Shouldn't her husband, in fact, be actively encouraged to honour Charlotte with some worthy gesture of farewell? In a certain weird mood of conscientiousness or compunction, Maggie feels ('at moments')

> 'the duty of speaking before separation should constitute its chasm, of pleading for some benefit that might be carried away into exile like the last saved object of price of the *émigré*, the jewel wrapped in a piece of old silk and negotiable some day in the market of misery'.[57]

This daring description shows us an instance not merely of the 'ubiquity' of value in consciousness, but also of the complex, nested (or perhaps fractured) mode of its manifestation. There is a high-flown lyricism of happiness (the wine, the jewel), but projected on to someone else, one's immediate rival for the relevant sexual object; projected, too, into the past, since what is being imagined is the other woman's ecstatic *memory*, not how things are for anyone at the (fictional) present time. But behind or beneath all this, as we have also been shown, is the (slow-burning) joy of victory in a power-struggle: the 'excitement', 'exaltation', or 'fascination of the

[55] Henry James, *The Golden* Bowl (Harmondsworth: Penguin, 1987; hereafter 'GB'), 486.

[56] Op. cit. note 55, GB 524: 'awful', that is, from Charlotte's (presumed) point of view. (She too is American, but a thorough-going expatriate.)

[57] Op. cit. note 55, GB 553.

monstrous' experienced by a hitherto dutiful daughter who is now, all of a sudden, having 'the time of her life'.[58] And Maggie's struggle has certainly involved the use of some unconventional weapons - 'duplicity', 'deceit', and 'merciless manipulation', to name but a few.[59]

'Value', in the sense of evaluative interest or significance, may well be all-pervasive in this scenario. But *moral* value? How might we set about accommodating the story of Maggie Verver's evolving consciousness to the 'theme of the cognitive as always moral'?[60] The idea would seem to be that Maggie's inner life reveals the 'ubiquity of the moral quality inherent in consciousness' not through any moral *correctness* disclosed to us as readers (except in so far as we may be gratified by the retaliation of an injured party), but rather in the guise of a strange, impressive and faintly sinister moral *phenomenon* – in effect, a rival pagoda constructed by Maggie herself as she emerges from her initial condition of ignorance.

5. Coda

My fictional source materials all present us, in their different ways, with characters who stand in a negligent, defiant, whimsical, or otherwise skewed relation to (departmental) 'morality'. However, according to the view we are considering, the characters in question experience states of mind which are none the less 'morally coloured' on that account — and none the less revealing, at least when suitably contextualized, of the moral qualities of their creator: as Murdoch puts it, 'The writer's own *morality*, displayed in the novel, is a major item'.[61]

An initial misgiving one might feel here is that while any literary utterance, fictional or otherwise, is apt to reveal something of the writer's general state of receptivity to value – their 'perceptiveness in regard to the currents of life' – it does not seem to be true of all fiction worth reading that a 'morality' in the sense of a *practical application* of that faculty is displayed in it, or that (if displayed) it constitutes a *major item*. Of course, a writer can present to us only the world that he or she can *see*, as Murdoch would put it. But not only may they decline to express themselves in a series of morally pointed vignettes, they may also be quite enigmatic about questions of ultimate

58 Op. cit. note 55, GB 473, 483, 487, 469.
59 Op. cit. note 55, GB 359, 543, 399.
60 Diamond, op. cit. note 8, WPM 82.
61 Op. cit. note 2, MGM 205 (emphasis in original).

importance – about their view of 'relations between the worthwhile and the practically demanded',[62] between (for example) the 'wine of consciousness' and that rather different medium through which one tracks the moral law. Just as our subjective 'valuational focus' can shift or wander[63] without necessarily calling for a decision on the objective lexical ordering of the relevant values (though it may *sometimes* do that), so the archive of fictional subjectivity offers us a world of opportunity to share in such wanderings imaginatively, with no obligation – Platonism aside – to commit ourselves to a final resting-place. In this respect a writer of fiction may be like Heraclitus's Delphic oracle, which 'neither declares nor conceals, but gives a sign';[64] the later Henry James would probably be a good example.

More seriously, however: don't we lose rather than gain insight if we insist on finding, or purporting to find, 'moral' consciousness everywhere, rather than in some places in contrast to others? True, it makes a difference whether, or to what extent, the suggested equivalence of 'value' and 'moral value' is construed *moralistically* – whether we take the proposition that 'consciousness is always morally coloured' to be *no more than* a reminder of the 'ubiquity of value', or whether we hear in it something more teleological. That is: something approximating to the view that unfamiliar value-attitudes (perhaps startling, or perhaps just comical) are to be treated as illustrative of some position or other on a scale of progress in the work of 'unselfing' or in the 'purification' of consciousness, a scale which – as it happens – can be displayed to us artistically as well as didactically. But if the latter kind of treatment is what is called for, the question arises: is this really a plausible account of the cultural significance of such offerings, or of our incentive to pay attention to them?

In evaluating such an account, it is hard to suppress the feeling that there is a difference between looking to imaginative literature as an aid to becoming *morally better* people, and as an aid to becoming people 'on whom nothing is lost'. The second of these approaches seems less instrumental, more disinterested: at any rate more willing to be content with an 'intelligent report' on human phenomena, more

[62] Findlay, op. cit. note 34, 4.

[63] Wording suggested by Findlay, op. cit. note 34, 74–5 (discussion of Hartmann).

[64] See G. S. Kirk and J. E. Raven, *The Presocratic Philosophers: A Critical History with a Selection of Texts* (Cambridge University Press, 1963), fragment 247.

accessible to scepticism with regard to any final imposition of order on the domain of value.

Of course, if we agree that an *intelligent* report must be one that *does justice* to the complexity of the world we encounter, we can hardly disown the idea of a certain 'moral' input to whatever local epistemological demands may happen to engage us, since the underlying demand will always be for a (potentially difficult) outward orientation, a commitment to getting things objectively right.[65] Also, to become more like a person 'on whom nothing is lost' would presumably be to gain additional resources for deliberation, and hence to become more skilful at it – a skill that might equip us to behave better in our day-to-day life (cf. §3 above). So the two approaches I have just distinguished can certainly be said to share some common concerns or reference points. But without the support of the distinctive moral psychology whereby clear vision requires, or proceeds in tandem with, the reduction of the ego to an extensionless point,[66] there appears to be no guarantee that the resources of our intelligent reporter will be placed at the service of (departmental) morality – the thing in respect of which there do, regrettably but all too obviously, exist 'morality-free zones'. Such a reporter might, as we've seen, interpret the realist imperative more as an injunction to avoid squeamishness than to think on 'whatsoever things are lovely'.[67]

And in fact there is a risk that by interpreting the 'ubiquity of value' thesis in a moralistic spirit, one may encourage some wrong ideas about what society at large stands to gain from the humanities. We can concede that there will be some connection between becoming, in a general way, less *humanly* stupid and becoming less *morally* stupid – but to overplay the directness of that connection is to court

[65] Thanks to David Garrard for helpful written commentary on this point.

[66] Compare Ludwig Wittgenstein, *Tractatus Logico-Philosophicus*, translated by D. F. Pears and B. F. McGuinness (London and Henley: Routledge and Kegan Paul, 1961), 5.64: 'Here it can be seen that solipsism, when its implications are carried out strictly, coincides with pure realism. The self of solipsism shrinks to a point without extension, and there remains the reality co-ordinated with it'. The *Tractatus* is an important influence on the moral philosophy of Diamond, though hardly on that of Murdoch. However, there does appear to be some affinity between the 'extensionless point' idea and Murdoch's 'unselfing' theme, an affinity which might repay study alongside the element of contingency - that is, the contingent or unstable aspect of the two philosophers' intellectual alliance - touched on in §6 below.

[67] See note 53 and accompanying text above.

(moral) disappointment. Just as humanistic education amounts to more than a training for citizenship,[68] so it is far from being coextensive with the business of training in virtue.

6. Conclusion

Let me now take stock and offer some hermeneutic suggestions about the 'morality is everywhere' view. That view appears to comprise some or all of the following elements:

(1) the idea of *valuing*, in the sense of value-discrimination, as all-pervasive;
(2) the refusal to recognize *moral value* as one kind of value among others, so that (on the basis of that refusal) 'value' and 'morality' can be treated as interchangeable;
(3) a conception of the moral – in some less than totalizing sense – as nevertheless *inescapable*, as when Murdoch refers to its 'indelible inherence in the secret mind'.[69]

Of these, (1) is probably the strongest in its own right, since it can draw upon powerful phenomenological considerations about the tendency to react *for or against* what is presented to consciousness at a given moment – sensations, emotional or cognitive stimuli, or possibilities for action, as the case may be. However, when (1) is conjoined with (2), we get a result that will be much more surprising to anyone inclined towards value-pluralism: that is, we now have to recognize value *in general* as implicitly 'moral' – so that the inventory of 'moral concepts' will include, for example, not only *truthfulness* (which is a traditional virtue of character), but also *truth* itself (an obvious bearer of value in that the distinction between truth and falsity is one to which, as thinkers and agents, we cannot be indifferent), and even *factual disagreement*, since this is an idea that – as Diamond puts it on Murdoch's behalf – 'plays a role in the moral vision of the nature and situation of human beings'.[70]

[68] In *Cultivating Humanity: A Classical Defense of Reform in Liberal Education* (Harvard, 1997: 35 for the idea just mentioned) Martha Nussbaum presents an account of the value of literary culture very different from the one suggested by *Love's Knowledge*, but similarly non-autonomous.

[69] Op. cit. note 2, MGM 259.

[70] Op. cit. note 9, MTE 75. Compare MGM op. cit. note 2 194; and for an earlier statement of Murdoch's unorthodox line on the relation between

What if we are minded to resist this imperialism of the 'moral'? To repeat: Murdoch herself leaves room for such resistance; she is aware of the possibility of a stand-off, with respect to the inner life, between aesthetic and moral ideals. She envisages the protest 'can we not rest sometimes!' – to which the eventual answer is that 'Every moment matters, there is no time off'; that 'every single second has a moral tag'.[71] The undertaking from which there is no time off is the purification of consciousness. And here we see the relevance of what I have identified as element (3) of the 'morality is everywhere' view: for Murdoch that undertaking is not just an elective project of the morally minded individual, but (again, as in Plato[72]) something *indelible* in the mind, namely a disposition to pursue the (objective) good as we – however inadequately – see it. To purify our consciousness is to progress towards a more adequate (or a less inadequate) grasp of the good. And in this connection Murdoch might well recommend that we accept from Plato a criterion of progress in terms of the 'intuition of unity'[73] – the growing conviction that what look like plural (and potentially conflicting) values are mere appearances, phenomena of the surface of things, not true guides to the underlying reality.

There is so much that is right in the insistence of Murdoch, and of Diamond, that our 'moral life' (in the sense of *morally significant* life) reaches beyond our deployment of some specified vocabulary or style of judgement, and into that qualitative or 'textural' domain addressed by humanistic fiction. Yet we might also wonder if the 'morality is everywhere' view owes something to a contingent encounter between two recognizably distinct intellectual influences: one received from Diamond in her capacity as a critic of 'departmental' moral philosophy (and also, at least in passing, of the restrictive 'Puritan spirit'); the other from Murdoch by virtue of the confessional or penitential atmosphere of much of her mature writing. And this encounter seems to threaten a certain cognitive dissonance. For the 'moralism' that comes into clear focus for Diamond when she

---

'moral' and 'factual' thinking, see 'Metaphysics and Ethics' (1957) in her *Existentialists and Mystics: Writings on Philosophy and Literature*, ed. Peter Conradi (Harmondsworth: Penguin, 1999), 59–75.

71 Op. cit. note 2, MGM 257, 484, 495.

72 *Republic* Bk VI, 505e.

73 Op. cit. note 72., Bk VII, 537c7: the mark of the *dialektikos* (the naturally philosophical or 'dialectical' person) is to be *sunoptikos* (disposed to see things as a unified whole). For 'intuitions of unity' see SG 93, discussed in §3 above.

enters into the thinking of Henry James (who sees this as a factor that may cause us to '[miss] out on life through unconsciousness') is also arguably present in Murdoch herself, not immediately through her idea of the 'omnipresence of *value* in human activity'[74] – since this (or so I have suggested) is compatible with a more pluralistic picture in which evaluative space is not exhausted by specifically moral forms of valuing – but instead, through her somewhat subjective preoccupation with the 'original sin' theme. ('We know very well what it is like to be obsessed by bad thoughts and feelings ... The ego is indeed "unbridled". Continuous control is required'.[75])

To be a person 'on whom nothing is lost'; to commit oneself to the 'daily, hourly, minutely attempted purification of consciousness': I persist in thinking that these are *different* ideals. Literary illumination is available to the adherents of each; they may draw upon a common body of material, and it may well be quite normal to feel the attractions of both. The ideals are not entirely discontinuous, nor are they starkly opposed. But they remain different for all that.[76]

Worcester College, Oxford
sabina-mary.lovibond@worc.ox.ac.uk

[74] Op. cit. note 2, 259 (emphasis added).
[75] Op. cit. note 2., 260.
[76] Thanks are due to the Honorary Director of the Royal Institute of Philosophy, Professor Anthony O'Hear, and to all who took part in discussion at the lecture at which this paper was given.

Iris Murdoch and Common Sense Or, What Is It Like To Be A Woman In Philosophy

HANNAH MARIJE ALTORF

> *On whether their originality had anything to do with their gender, I cannot make a final judgment, but I suspect that women are less prone to jump on to bandwagons than at least some of their male colleagues, and are also more reluctant to abandon common sense ...*[1]

Abstract

Philosophy is one of the least inclusive disciplines in the humanities and this situation is changing only very slowly. In this article I consider how one of the women of the Wartime Quartet, Iris Murdoch, can help to challenge this situation. Taking my cue from feminist and philosophical practices, I focus on Murdoch's experience of being a woman and a philosopher and on the role experience plays in her philosophical writing. I argue that her thinking is best characterised with the notion of common sense or *sensus communis*. This term recognises her understanding of philosophy as based in experience and as a shared effort 'to make sense of our life', as Mary Midgley puts it.

1. Introduction

One of the difficulties that women in philosophy face is not being taken seriously as an interlocutor. It is not just that, as in the well-known cartoon, their 'excellent suggestion' need to made by 'one of the men' before it enters the debate. It is also that their work may not be recognised as philosophy at all. As Kristie Dotson puts it:

> It is not unreasonable to expect, in a field that has been dominated by a rather monochromatic population, that the inclusion of diverse people will also introduce wider possibilities for philosophical engagement or, at the very least, demand greater

[1] Mary Warnock on Anscombe, Foot and Murdoch in *A Memoir: People and Places* (Duckbacks, 2002) 37.

doi:10.1017/S1358246119000201

> recognition for the existing diversity of methods available for philosophical engagement. Too often, people who voice skepticism about canonical questions and methods find they face a recurrent question: "How is your project 'philosophy'?"[2]

As Dotson explains, asking the question 'How is this philosophy?' indiscriminately is damaging because it risks the exclusion of diverse people and their thinking.[3]

The work of Iris Murdoch offers an illuminating case study of this phenomenon, because of the significant shift in its reception. The question how her work is philosophy is now much less prominent that it was at the beginning of this century. I was then a PhD student at the University of Glasgow, writing my thesis on Murdoch's understanding of imagination. Murdoch had died one year before I started my doctoral work. There was a growing interest in her life, but very few philosophers in the UK concerned themselves with her work. Most publications were by literary scholars and theologians or by philosophers from across the ocean.[4] This lack of interest in Murdoch's philosophical work confirmed what I was often told informally: philosophers in the United Kingdom

[2] Kirstie Dotson, 'Concrete Flowers: Contemplating the Profession of Philosophy'. *Hypatia* 26.2 (spring 2011), 403–409, 406. The cartoon I am referring to can be found here: https://punch.photoshelter.com/image/I0000eHEXGJ_wImQ.

[3] Dotson, 'Concrete Flowers', op. cit. note 2, 407. Dotson speaks of diverse people and her concern is with black women in particular. I do not want to suggest that the problems facing different women are identical, but the question of whether their work is philosophy is not limited to one group. As I will show, it has been asked of Iris Murdoch's work.

[4] The pioneering work of Maria Antonaccio must be mentioned here, both her monograph (*Picturing the Human: The Moral Thought of Iris Murdoch*, Oxford University Press, 2000) and the collection of essays, which she edited with William Schweiker and which included the work of such prominent thinkers as Charles Taylor, Martha Nussbaum and Cora Diamond amongst others (*Iris Murdoch and the Search for Human Goodness*, Chicago University Press, 1996). The most comprehensive study by a British thinker of her philosophical work which included *Metaphysics as a Guide to Morals* from around the same time is the chapter by Fergus Kerr (*Immortal Longings: Versions of Transcending Humanity*, S.P.C.K. Publishing, 1997). There have been various introductions and studies of her novels of course, but their focus is obviously not the philosophical writing.

seemed to think that Murdoch's philosophy was, as A.N. Wilson put it in his memoirs, '[not] really philosophy at all'.[5]

Since then much has changed. From 2002 onwards, there have been biennial Murdoch conferences, with an increasing number of philosophy papers. Even more recently, interest in Murdoch's work has been generated as part of the wider focus on the work of the wartime quartet: Elizabeth Anscombe, Philippa Foot, Mary Midgley and Murdoch. This recent development should be largely credited to the work of especially Rachael Wiseman and Clare Mac Cumhaill from *(In Parenthesis)*.[6] That this project has taken off so well is evidence of the talents of these philosophers, their creativity, their hard work and their openness to collaboration.

In this article I engage closely with some aspects of *(In Parenthesis)*. Specifically, I ask to what extent Murdoch can provide insight into the still marginal place of women in philosophy. My argument consists of three parts. In the first section I provide an outline of the project *(In Parenthesis)*. I consider different suggestions for making philosophy more inclusive and I also explore why diversity in philosophy is important. In the next section I look at Murdoch's experience of being a woman in philosophy and the reception of her work immediately after her death. In the last section, I consider to what extent her work offers an alternative philosophical method.

To engage closely with *(In Parenthesis)* seems to me the best way to commend this project, though I should add that my approach and some of my interests are also different from Wiseman and Mac Cumhaill. I am not an analytical philosopher and I do not classify

[5] A.N. Wilson, *Iris Murdoch as I Knew Her* (London: Hutchinson, 2003), 28. The rather defensive tone taken by consequent writings, arguing that Murdoch was indeed a serious philosopher, is further evidence to the initial disregard for her work. In the introduction to the 2012 collection of essays *Iris Murdoch, Philosopher* (which includes only two essays by philosophers working at British universities) Justin Broackes's writes: 'There are people who suspect now, I think, that Murdoch was either not quite a serious and substantial philosopher or not quite a professional, recognized by her fellows'. ((Oxford University Press) 6). See also my reflections on Murdoch as a serious philosopher: 'Iris Murdoch, or What It Means To Be A Serious Philosopher', *Daimoon: Revista Internacional de Filosofía* 60 (2013), 75–91.

[6] Of course, they are not the only ones working on the quartet. See here especially the work of Benjamin Lipscomb. For more information on (*In Parenthesis*), see: http://www.womeninparenthesis.co.uk/.

Murdoch as an analytical thinker either.[7] For one, her first book was on Jean-Paul Sartre and her last unfinished philosophical work on Martin Heidegger. For another, her writing is evidence of a very broad interest in thinkers and thoughts. As I hope to argue, philosophy needs this kind of diversity.

2. In Parenthesis and Women in Philosophy

(In Parenthesis) presents itself as first and foremost a *historical* project. It endeavours to rewrite the history of analytical philosophy to include Anscombe, Foot, Midgley and Murdoch as a school with its own method.[8] Yet, by studying the lives and works of these four philosophers Mac Cumhaill and Wiseman are also looking for insight into 'barriers to inclusion' and intend 'to discover unknown factors and ultimately new strategies for gender activism within philosophy'.[9]

(In Parenthesis) is then also a *feminist* project, if by feminism we mean any concerted effort to create equality between the genders. Of course, there are many feminisms, if only because it is not easy to decide what equality means. (To give a simple example with nevertheless significant consequences: to provide an equal number of toilets for men and women leaves women with a much longer waiting time than men.[10]) Yet, if *(In Parenthesis)* is a feminist project, it is remarkable how little it uses the word 'feminism'. It was not used in any of the descriptions of the 2018–2019 lectures series of the Royal Institute of Philosophy (and that includes mine). It is rarely used in its publications.

On the website of *(In Parenthesis)*, most hits for feminism are found in the wonderful lecture by Professor Pamela Sue Anderson,

[7] The distinction between analytical and continental philosophy and the notion of continent philosophy are not without their difficulties. See Simon Critchley, *Continental Philosophy: A Very Short Introduction* (Oxford University Press, 2001), 1–2 and throughout.

[8] Clare Mac Cumhaill and Rachael Wiseman, 'A Female School of Analytic Philosophy?: Anscombe, Foot, Midgley and Murdoch' [http://www.womeninparenthesis.co.uk/wp-content/uploads/2018/10/PENN-trip-blog-post-script-1.pdf]

[9] See 'About' [http://www.womeninparenthesis.co.uk/about/]. Those insights and strategies are unfortunately needed in a discipline that still has surprising few women in top positions and that has been shocked by some very public cases of sexual harassment.

[10] See for instance https://americanrestroom.org/potty-parity/.

entitled 'Silencing and Speaker Vulnerability'.[11] I should say the late Professor Anderson, who could tell us much about barriers against inclusivity and strategies for inclusion and who was a great inspiration and support for many young philosophers. To find the word feminism in the writing of Wiseman and Mac Cumhaill I had to go to the latest edition of *The Iris Murdoch Review*, where they explain their strategy as follows:

> To be defined as a school is to be recognised by one's community as serious interlocutors. This is a reminder about how we should approach the history of philosophy: if a set of voices are deemed by their peers to be irrelevant, uninteresting, unworthy, they may not be recognised by those peers as articulating a distinctive philosophical perspective, worthy of recognition as such. To recover those voices then, is to rewrite history – a feminist project, the social and political importance of which is plain.[12]

This quotation gives insight into *(In Parenthesis)*'s understanding of feminism. Firstly, it emphasises the importance of recognition as a serious interlocutor and secondly, it omits the the word 'philosophical' from its last line. Rewriting history has social and political importance, but not philosophical? I shall come back to both these points.

Even though the project is only a few years old, it has already provided a number of explanations for these four women's remarkable achievements. The first came in the exchange that was at the start of the project. In his column in *The Guardian* in November 2013 Jonathan Wolff had been musing about the exclusive nature of philosophy. He revisits his copy of Warnock's memoirs and asks: 'What was it that produced such a superb cohort of female philosophers, unmatched, I think, by anything we have seen since?'[13]

Midgley replied two days later: 'As a survivor from the wartime group, I can only say: sorry, but the reason was indeed that there were fewer men about then'. Men are not the problem as such, but

[11] Pamela Sue Anderson, 'Silencing and Speaker Vulnerability: Undoing an Oppressive Form of (Wilful) Ignorance'. [http://www.womeninparenthesis.co.uk/silencing-and-speaker-vulnerability-undoing-an-oppressive-form-of-wilful-ignorance/]

[12] Clare Mac Cumhaill and Rachael Wiseman, 'Anscombe, Foot, Midgley, Murdoch: A Philosophical School' (*The Iris Murdoch Review*, 2018, 39–49), 47.

[13] Jonathan Wolff, 'How can we end the male domination of philosophy?' (*The Guardian 26 November 2013* [https://www.theguardian.com/education/2013/nov/26/modern-philosophy-sexism-needs-more-women]. See also 'About' [https://www.womeninparenthesis.co.uk/about/.]

a certain style of doing philosophy is, as Midgley, tongue in cheek, suggests:

> It was clear that we were all more interested in understanding this deeply puzzling world than in putting each other down. That was how Elizabeth Anscombe, Philippa Foot, Iris Murdoch, Mary Warnock and I, in our various ways, all came to think out alternatives to the brash, unreal style of philosophising – based essentially on logical positivism – that was current at the time.[14]

An editor gave Midgley's reply the title 'The Golden Age of Female Philosophy'. This title is troubling for different reasons. Firstly, as Midgley points out in one of the interviews by *(In Parenthesis)*: 'Four of us don't make a Golden Age'.[15] Secondly, highlighting these women can make others even more invisible. Wolff's suggestion that he has not seen anything like this since seems to reinforce the difficulty that women and diverse people can face in being recognised as 'knowers', a difficulty mentioned by him in the same column and discussed at length by Anderson.[16]

This column and its responses, together with the memoirs by Mary Warnock (*People and Places*, 2000) and Midgley (*The Owl of Minerva*, 2005) have added to this first exchange to create an amalgam of explanations. Midgley points out that it mattered that there were fewer men around because of the war. Classes were smaller and the discussions less combative. This gave the women the space and time to find their voice. The women were also encouraged by their teacher, Donald MacKinnon. They were all middle class. They got together to discuss their shared despair at the moral philosophy of their time. (As Midgley puts it: 'We got quite indignant about that!'[17])

Some of these insights return in the website's enthusiastic suggestion to 'host a cocoa party' or start a reading group. One could think of

[14] Midgley, 'The Golden Age of Female Philosophy' (*The Guardian* 26 November 2013 [https://www.theguardian.com/world/2013/nov/28/golden-age-female-philosophy-mary-midgley.]

[15] See Midgley, 'Four of us don't make a golden age'. Video available at http://www.womeninparenthesis.co.uk/mary-midgley-16/.

[16] The adjective 'Female' in 'The Golden Age of Female Philosophy', op. cit. note 14, creates additional difficulties. Does it mean philosophy by women or philosophy practised in a female way? The difficulty becomes even more obvious when contrasting 'female philosophy' to 'male philosophy'.

[17] Midgley, 'We got quite indignant about that!'. [http://www.womeninparenthesis.co.uk/mary-midgley-15/].

others: a reevaluation of teaching at university, for instance, which – at least in Britain – has lost its prestige to research. A teacher like MacKinnon might not have been able to find or retain a position at a UK institution today.[18] The excellent report 'Women in Philosophy' by Jennifer Saul and Helen Beebee for SWIP/BPA (2011) should also be mentioned here and its recommendations for challenging implicit bias and stereotype threat and the inclusion of women in one's syllabi and conferences.[19]

Yet, what I find missing, is a more direct challenge to philosophy's method, goals or to the questions it asks. Thus, in the next section, I intend to heed to Dotson's call for 'alternative methods of philosophical investigation'.[20] I do so by by asking 'what is it like to be a woman in philosophy?' when it comes to Murdoch. This question is of course a direct reference to the website 'What is it like to be a woman in philosophy?'.[21] It asks about personal experience and partakes in feminist practice which takes personal experience seriously, that is telling stories and listening to voices that would otherwise go unheard. This practice is an important tool in challenging power relations. Yet, as Linda Martín Alcoff explains, women philosophers have been surprisingly reluctant to share their experiences.[22]

[18] Cp. Stefan Collini, 'Browne's Gamble': 'The devoted university teachers of a generation or more ago who were widely read and kept up with recent scholarship, but who were not themselves prolific publishers, have in many cases been hounded into early retirement, to be replaced (if replaced at all) by younger colleagues who see research publications as the route to promotion and esteem, and who try to limit their commitment to undergraduate teaching as far as they can.' (*London Review of Books*, vol 32.21 (4 November 2001), 23–25. [https://www.lrb.co.uk/v32/n21/stefan-collini/brownes-gamble]

[19] Helen Beebee and Jenny Saul, 'Women in Philosophy in the UK'. [http://www.swipuk.org/notices/2011-09-08/Women%20in%20Philosophy%20in%20the%20UK%20%28BPA-SWIPUK%20Report%29.pdf]

[20] Cp. Dotson, 'Concrete Flowers', op. cit. note 2, 408, 403 and also 'How Is This Paper Philosophy?', *Comparative Philosophy* 3.1 (2012), 3–29

[21] See https://beingawomaninphilosophy.wordpress.com. This website makes for depressing reading, when some of its greatest hits are 'failure to take women seriously' and 'sexual harassment'. The site is actually aware of the fact that it may discourage women from entering the profession.

[22] Linda Martín Alcoff, *Singing in the Fire: Stories of Women in Philosophy* (2003), 4–5. This collection is an important exception to the rule, containing the stories of twelve philosophers, all of whom are or have been employed by universities in the United States.

The reluctance to take experience seriously is also surprising when considering that in the field of philosophy there is an additional reason to take experience seriously. This is Socrates' famous phrase 'The unexamined life is not worth living' (*Apology* 38a). I mention this here for two reasons. First, all philosophy which is not a direct reflection on experience is a departure from this famous dictum. Secondly, for the last ten years or so, I have been inspired to think of alternative methods for doing philosophy as a participant and facilitator of Socratic dialogues in the Nelson-Heckmann-Specht tradition. Dialogues in this tradition are best described as *philosophical* investigations of *experience* undertaken *together*.[23] They offer a way of doing philosophy which is very different from much of what I have encountered in academic settings, because of the central role of experience and because the dialogue is a shared undertaking. Participants try to understand each other and come to a consensus (if possible). These dialogues allow participants to experience that combative forms of arguing are not necessarily the best means to wisdom. They can be detrimental to the philosophical investigation, especially but not exclusively when one discusses experience and thus makes oneself vulnerable.[24]

Before I turn to the next section, however, a brief reflection on the question of what it is to be a woman in philosophy. This may seem a trivial or elite pursuit, given the silencing of women in other situations that ask more urgently for voices to be heard. While this objection is not without its merit, it is also true that the exclusive nature of the discipline has resulted in an excluding understanding of who is

[23] For a fuller description of and reflection on this method, see Hannah Marije Altorf, 'Dialogue or Discussion: Reflections on a Socratic Method', *Arts and Humanities in Higher Education* 18.1 (2019), 60–75. In this article I comment too on the fact that the emphasis on experience is not always appreciated by the participants, especially philosophers.

[24] See also Helen Beebee, 'Women and Deviance in Philosophy', (Katrina Hutchinson and Fiona Jenkins (eds). *Women in Philosophy: What Needs to Change* (Oxford University Press, 63–73) and Marilyn Friedman (op. cit. 39–60). See especially 28: 'This constant responsiveness to objections and criticism, integrated into the very nature and presentation of philosophical work, may promote an atmosphere in which philosophers tend to avoid investing themselves too deeply in their philosophical positions lest they have to give those up at the next go-round. In this way, it is easy to regard philosophy as a game or contest rather than a genuine search for wisdom.'

and who is not capable of thought, which has had its repercussions beyond the discipline.[25]

More importantly, the objection implies that philosophy is a luxury and I do not think it should be seen as such. I am for that reason concerned about the number of philosophy departments that are in the process of closing or have closed at universities around the country. In the last few years, London alone has seen the closure of philosophy departments at London Metropolitan, Middlesex University, Greenwich University, Heythrop College (which has closed altogether) and St. Mary's University. This means that in London the opportunities for students with lower grades to study philosophy are dwindling fast. In the current British education system, students with lower grades are not necessarily academically less capable. They are often from a disadvantaged economic background. Philosophy thus runs the risk of becoming an elite subject again.

It is of interest to note some of the similarities in the closure of these programmes here. One is the fact that these universities combined European and analytical approaches to philosophy, were often near the top in terms of student satisfaction and offered modules that allow students to take philosophy outside the university. (For instance, Philosophy with Children at Greenwich University and Heythrop College, Socratic dialogue at St. Mary's University). Most significant is that the one degree that was saved was the MA in European Philosophy, which moved from Middlesex to Kingston. The deciding factor was the REF.

Here one cannot but be reminded of Mary Midgley's comments on the closure of philosophy in Newcastle in the 1980s. She writes in her latest work, *What is philosophy for?*:

> … it is surely the effort to examine our life as a whole, to make sense of it, to locate its big confusions and resolve its big conflicts, that has been the prime business of traditional philosophy. Only quite lately has a different pattern of philosophizing caught on – a pattern that is modelled closely on the physical sciences and is reverently called Research. [26]

The closure of those five philosophy departments confirms the judgment of research as the highest value. We are in a situation that is not that different from the one Mary Midgley describes. And yet, what if,

[25] Cp. Michèle le Doeuff, *Hipparchia's Choice: An Essay Concerning Women, Philosophy, Etc*. (Blackwell, 1991) 5–6.

[26] Mary Midgley, *What is Philosophy For?* (Bloomsbury 2018), 11.

philosophy is not a luxury, but, as Midgley would have it, a need for everyone?[27]

3. What is it like to be a woman in philosophy?

What is it like to be a woman in philosophy? When asked in interviews, Murdoch seemed reluctant to acknowledge any difference between being a man and being a woman in philosophy. Most famously, when asked in an interview with Sheila Hale in 1976 whether there was a contemporary woman she admired, she expressed her regard for Simone de Beauvoir, but also added: '... the subject bores me in a way. ...I have never felt picked out in an intellectual sense because I am a woman; these distinctions are not made at Oxford'.[28] Murdoch's words here are an obvious echo of the famous opening lines of De Beauvoir's *The Second Sex* ('For a long time I have hesitated to write a book on woman. The subject is irritating, especially to women'.[29]) Yet, unlike De Beauvoir, Murdoch avoids the subject or even warns against pursuing it.[30] What is it like to be a woman in philosophy? It is like being a man in philosophy.

These are curious claims, especially given the current debates about (the lack of) women in philosophy, which have not bypassed Oxford.[31] In March 2018 its Faculty of Philosophy decided to 'feminise' its reading lists and to introduce the target of 40% female authors. This decision was reported on various news sites, but – as

[27] Mary Midgley, 'Philosophical Plumbing'. *Utopias, Dolphins and Computers* (Routledge 1996), 1–14. See especially 14: 'it might well pay us to be less interested in what philosophy can do for our dignity, and more aware of the shocking malfunctions for which it is an essential remedy.'

[28] Sheila Hale, 'Interview from "Women Writers Now: Their Approach and Their Apprenticeship"'. (Gillian Dooley (Ed.), *From a Tiny Corner in the House of Fiction: Conversations with Iris Murdoch*. University of South Carolina Press, 2003, 30–32. The quotation is from 32).

[29] Simone de Beauvoir, *The Second Sex* (Vintage, 1997, 13). Murdoch probably read the French text. The phrase is similar in French.

[30] 'I am not interested in the "woman's world" or the assertion of a "female viewpoint". This is often rather an artificial idea and can in fact injure the promotion of rights. We want to join the human race, not invent a new separatism..." (Jack I. Biles, 'An Interview with Iris Murdoch, (Dooley (ed.) op. cit. note 28. 56–69. The quotation is from 61–62.)

[31] See https://www.dailymail.co.uk/news/article-5503059/Oxford-University-feminise-philosophy-reading-lists.html; cp. https://www.oxfordstudent.com/2018/03/27/philosophy-at-oxford-too-many-men/.

far as I have been able to determine – not on the website of Oxford University. On the news sites, the comments were largely critical. The following gives a good flavour:

> The reading list should include the best writers on the subject. If they are female or male should not matter.[32]

This comment is based on a number of suppositions. It assumes that it is only worthwhile to read the best writers and that it is clear who is better and who is worse and that this is not a matter of taste or tradition. Most importantly, it assumes that the reading lists now contain 'the best writers' and that some will need to go.

This last suggestion is in a way confirmed by the then chair of the philosophy faculty, Edward Harcourt, when he explains the rationale for this change: 'partly just because it's interesting, and partly to raise the profile and status of feminist philosophy at Oxford'.[33] There is no mention that there was anything wrong with the existing lists. It is, of course, interesting to include 40% women philosophers, as it interesting to, for instance, include one thinker from every century or to re-introduce some thinkers from the Medieval period, which seem to have disappeared from most departments. Yet, it would have been more honest and insightful to admit that any reading list can be improved and that philosophy is not as neutral as it is too often assumed to be.[34] It is significant that only the student newspaper invited experts in feminist philosophy to respond to the initiative. Both professors Mari Mikkola (Oxford) and Jennifer Saul (Sheffield) argue against an understanding of philosophy as 'value-free' or about 'timeless truths'.[35] This raises the question of what these values are, or whose.

I discuss this example here, because some of these assumptions seem to underlie Murdoch's replies in interviews. Most importantly, Murdoch assumes philosophy is gender neutral. This is a curious suggestion, given that in her writing Murdoch is keenly aware of 'would-be neutral philosophers [who] merely take sides

[32] Lucas Cahal, comment on https://www.telegraph.co.uk/education/2018/03/14/oxford-university-set-feminise-curriculum-requesting-inclusion/

[33] See https://www.dailymail.co.uk/news/article-5503059/Oxford-University-feminise-philosophy-reading-lists.html.

[34] Cp. Dotson, 'Concrete Flowers', op. cit. note 2, 407.

[35] *Cherwell*, the Oxford University student newspaper, 13 March 2018 [https://cherwell.org/2018/03/13/undergrad-paper-in-feminist-philosophy-to-be-introduced/.]

surreptitiously'.[36] That she does not extend this insight to gender could suggest a more general reluctance to consider gender in philosophy. It should also be noted that Murdoch's comments there are not the full story. Firstly, Murdoch's words in interviews are not a comprehensive account of her position. Murdoch gave more than 175 interviews between 1955 and 1996. These are at times illuminating and at other times baffling. Murdoch sometimes provides wonderful insight into her work and her life and at other times her words seem at odds with her writing practice.[37]

Secondly and more importantly, Murdoch was well aware of gender distinctions and discrimination. From Peter Conradi's bibliography we learn that on arrival in Oxford Murdoch was warned by the Dean of Somerville that 'women are still very much on probation in this University'.[38] Conradi also notes that she perceived herself 'as a mixture of the revolutionary Rosa Luxembourg, the philosopher Susan Stebbing and the feminist writer Simone De Beauvoir,' and was advised by MacKinnon never to repeat that to anyone.[39] The most immediate example comes from an interview with Sir Harold Hobson in 1962, which took place in the Ladies section of the Union Club. In this interview Murdoch points out the sexism and prejudice of the interviewer to which he subjects her in the actual conservation. He first suggests it is all a joke, but when pressed he is not so sure. (I used this example in an earlier article and am surprised how little it has been noted and discussed.[40])

It is clear that Murdoch experienced sexism, which should not come as a surprise. She was able to recognise and name it as such, but she did not discuss, let alone write about, her experience of being a woman and a philosopher. Perhaps MacKinnon's advice

[36] Iris Murdoch, *The Sovereignty of Good* (Vintage, 2001), 76.

[37] See Marije Altorf, *Iris Murdoch and the Art of Imagining* (Continuum, 2008) 2–6.

[38] Peter Conradi, *Iris Murdoch: A Life*. (HarperCollins*Publishers*, 2001) 82, quoting Fera Varnell, the Dean of Somerville. See also Marije Altorf, 'After Cursing the Library: Iris Murdoch and the (In)visibility of Women in Philosophy'. *Hypatia* 26–2 (2011), 384–402. In this article I offer a critical reading of the three biographies/memoirs that were published shortly after Murdoch's death in 1999 (the memoirs by her husband John Bayley, the biography by Peter Conradi and A.N. Wilson).

[39] Conradi op. cit., 256.

[40] See Marije Altorf, 'Reassessing Iris Murdoch in the Light of Feminist Philosophy: Michèle le Doeuff and the Philosophical Imaginary.' Anne Rowe (ed.), *Iris Murdoch: A Reassessment* (Palgrave Macmillan, 2007), 175–186.

stopped her from ever bringing it up again. There is, of course, no obligation to speak of one's experience, including one's experience of being a woman. The subject is 'boring' and 'irritating'. This was true in 1948, it was true in 1962 and, I would argue, is still true today. Any space that promises to take us out of that messiness has to be welcomed and philosophy still promises to be such a space.[41] Yet, it does not follow that Murdoch was not affected by being a woman. This is poignantly obvious when considering the first years after her death.

In the early 2000s Murdoch, philosopher and novelist, was even more famous for a third reason: for suffering from Alzheimer's disease at the end of her life and for having a lot of sex with different people when she was young. In those years people would mention the film first when I told them I was working on Iris Murdoch. This film, *Iris* (2001), is a moving portrait of someone who cares about a spouse with Alzheimer. Yet, even though there is ample talk about Murdoch's work and how wonderful it is, the film contains hardly any of her words or ideas. I counted one slightly adopted line from *Metaphysics as a Guide to Morals* and one quotation from the letter by Paul to the Philippians, with which Murdoch ends *Metaphysics as a Guide to Morals*.[42] What is it like to be a woman in philosophy? Is it to be remembered for someone other than your thoughts? Not to be given your own voice?

In addition to the difficulties noted above, Murdoch's oeuvre adds more complication. Murdoch was and probably is better known as a novelist. This creates the difficulty of her oeuvre. How do the two genres relate? Can we read the one without the other? Can we even make a distinction between the two? It may be possible that the novels allowed Murdoch a financial and intellectual independence, yet the growing distance to academic philosophy seems also to have troubled her. In interviews Murdoch was reluctant to call herself a philosopher.[43] She shares this reluctance with two other great thinkers from the twentieth century, De Beauvoir and Hannah Arendt, whose work – like Murdoch's – is not easy to pigeonhole.[44]

[41] Cp. Le Doeuff, op. cit. note 25, 9–10.

[42] On rereading *Metaphysics as a Guide to Morals* (Penguin, 1992) recently, I recognised a short quotation from 497 and of course the very last quote, 512.

[43] See the interview with M. Le Gros, quoted in Hilda Spear, *Iris Murdoch* (Palgrave, 2006), 9.

[44] Especially *Metaphysics as a Guide to Morals* (1992), her Gifford lectures from 1982, has puzzled readers even since it was first published. For a

What is it like to be a woman in philosophy? It is to be annoyed with that question, it is be deeply aware of gender distinctions and bored by it, it is to have your first name as the title of a film that has only one sentence from your own writing in it and it is to confuse future scholars with the nature of your oeuvre. In short, there is no easy answer to the question, but ignoring it may result in not seeing how some gender stereotypes have moved us away from Murdoch's work or to overlook its attempt at inclusivity. I discuss this last aspect in the next section.

4. Common sense - sensus communis

Murdoch may have denied the existence of gender distinctions in Oxford, but – like other members of the quartet – she was aware of the divergence between her philosophical thinking and that encountered in Oxford. In this section I argue that her work offers an alternative philosophical method, which I characterise as common sense, or *sensus communis*. I thus engage again more directly with the project of *(In Parenthesis)*, in particular their characterisation of the Quartet's attitude as 'uncommon sense realism'.

In almost all her writing Murdoch is concerned with not just arguments, but also the *form* which arguments take or should take.[45] The three essays in *The Sovereignty of Good* provide insightful examples. In the first, 'The Idea of Perfection', Murdoch proclaims that '[t]here is a two-way movement in philosophy, a movement towards the building of elaborate theories, and a move back again towards the consideration of simple and obvious facts.'[46] She announces that she will attempt a 'movement of return'. The second essay, 'On "God" and "Good"' begins with the provoking sentence: 'To do philosophy is to explore one's own temperament, and yet at the same time to attempt to discover the truth'.[47] The third essay, 'The Sovereignty of Good over Other

---

wonderful collection of illuminating articles in the work, see Nora Hämäläinen, Gillian Doolley (eds.), *Reading Iris Murdoch's* Metaphysics as a Guide to Morals (Palgrave Macmillan, 2019).

[45] This aspect was recently brought to my attention again in a lecture by Mark Hopwood, Pardubice 8 June 2019.

[46] Murdoch, *Sovereignty of Good,* op. cit. note 36, 1.

[47] Murdoch, op. cit. note 36, 47.

Concepts', takes issue with the disregard for metaphors held 'by many contemporary thinkers'.[48]

I am in particular interested in the return to simple and obvious facts, for this is a returning trope especially in Murdoch's earlier writing. Murdoch often distances herself from the dominant philosophical argumentation and takes the position of an outsider, siding with the ordinary, the 'simple' and 'obvious', with 'us,' 'when we are not philosophising'[49]. She also introduces outsiders to the philosophical debate: the virtuous peasants,'some quiet unpretentious worker, a schoolteacher, or a mother, or better still an aunt.'[50] She lets an argument be interrupted by 'people [who] may begin to protest and cry out and say that something has been taken from them.'[51]

This trope of the virtuous peasant has been criticised for being literary fiction more than an actual person and Murdoch has been accused of living in an ivory tower.[52] Murdoch seems aware of this criticism when she exclaims in *Metaphysics as a Guide to Morals*: 'I have known such aunts'.[53] While the criticism is not without foundation, I don't think it is sufficient reason to dismiss these references. The voices are disruptive to Murdoch's argument. Murdoch heeds to voices outside the academic debate, even when they are more like a cry and less like a fully fledged argument. These voices are thus proof of Murdoch's attempt to make philosophy more inclusive, even if it is not as inclusive as her critics might like.

This concern with the form of argument does not necessarily place Murdoch outside the tradition of philosophy. On the contrary, it can be understood in a long tradition of philosophers who marked a clear break with their predecessors (such as, for instance, René Descartes or A.J. Ayer). Yet, to do so would be to miss an opportunity to rethink the history and practices of philosophy. Alternative placing is suggested by the work of different feminist thinkers and most succinctly presented in the musings that conclude the first chapter of

[48] Murdoch, op. cit. note 36, 75.

[49] Murdoch 'Thinking and Language', *Existentialists and Mystics: Writings on Philosophy and Literature*. Edited and with a Preface by Peter Conradi. Foreword by George Steiner. (London: Chatto & Windus, 1997) 33–42. The quotation is from 33.

[50] Murdoch, *Metaphysics as a Guide to Morals*, op. cit. note 42, 429.

[51] Murdoch, *Sovereignty of Good*, op. cit. note 36, 13

[52] See Conradi, op. cit. note 38 244. Cp. too Lyndsey Stonebridge, *The Judicial Imagination: Writing after Nuremberg*. (Edinburgh University Press, 2011).

[53] Murdoch, *Metaphysics as a Guide to Morals*, op. cit. note 42, 429.

Virginia Woolf's *A Room of One's Own*. The narrator has talked of a visit to Oxbridge, where her thought is first interrupted when she is stopped from walking on the grass and next when she is barred from entering the library. She has had a copious lunch at a men's college and a more frugal dinner at a women's college and then on her way back to her room at the end of the day: 'I pondered ... what effect poverty has on the mind; and what effect wealth has on the mind; ... I thought how unpleasant it is to be locked out; and I thought how it is worse perhaps to be locked in'.[54] Woolf cautions that being an outsider is not an entirely undesirable condition, even if it is likely to be short on money. She thus makes us reflect on any attempt to move the outsider inside.

In their 'Women in the History of Philosophy' lecture at the University of Sheffield in 2017, Wiseman and Mac Cumhaill characterise the four women's stance as 'uncommon sense realism'. They explain this term as follows: 'The realistic spirit described involves a strong commitment to 'common sense', but not in the manner of linguistic philosophers like Hare and 'ordinary language' philosophers like Austin.' 'Uncommon sense' then, because of common sense's possible association with Hare and Austin. 'Uncommon sense' too, because of the realism of these women, taking a realistic attitude is 'an *uncommon* achievement.'[55]

I have wondered whether the term 'uncommon sense' has been inspired by the quotation at the start of my article. The quotation comes from Mary Warnock's memoirs and I have used it in an earlier text. Warnock reflects here on the exceptional generation who were her seniors by only a few years:

> On whether their originality had anything to do with gender, I cannot make a final judgment, but I suspect that women are less prone to jump on to bandwagons than at least some of their male colleagues and are also more reluctant to abandon common sense ...[56]

In an earlier article I attributed probably more significance to these lines than Warnock allows for. I related the quotation to the prominent trope of the outsider in Murdoch's writing and I argued that it was the literary tradition of Jane Austen, the Brontë sisters,

[54] Virginia Woolf, *A Room of One's Own* (Harcourt Brace Jovanovich, Publishers, 1957), 24.

[55] Mac Cumhaill and Wiseman, 'A Female School of Academic Philosophy?', op. cit. note 8.

[56] Warnock, *A Memoir: People and Places*, op. cit. note 1, 37.

Mrs Gaskill that allowed Murdoch to take her position of an outsider in academic philosophy.[57]

I agree that 'common sense' is a difficult term for the reasons Wiseman and Mac Cumhaill mention and perhaps even more so because in our everyday conversations it has the connotation of exclusion. People are admonished for not showing any common sense rather than appraised for showing any. One is told off for having no common sense when cutting oneself, rather than praised for exhibiting plenty of common sense when preparing a meal without the need for plasters. Yet, despite these concerns, I would want to plead for the use of the term 'common sense' – or perhaps the Latin *sensus communis* – to understand the achievements of these women and in particular of Murdoch. *Sensus communis* may challenge philosophical practice in a way that I am still exploring. What follows is a first indication of its promise.

Common sense has – as far as I know - two distinct histories in philosophy. The traditions are probably not as separate as I present them here, but I have found no cross reference. The one history is that of – roughly – Thomas Reid, G.E. Moore and others, who claim the certainty of self-evident truths. The assumption is that such truths are 'no sooner understood than they are believed'.[58] They form the foundation of philosophical reflection. The other tradition is that of Immanuel Kant and more recently, and for this article more importantly, Hannah Arendt. Common sense is here *sensus communis*.[59] Arendt understands this as the sixth sense and as a sense that we share. While historically Murdoch is associated more with Moore than Arendt, I shall use Arendt's rather than Moore's understanding here.[60]

[57] Altorf, 'After Cursing the Library', op. cit. note 38.

[58] Thomas Reid as quoted in Nichols, Ryan and Gidein Yaffe, 'Thomas Reid', Edward N. Zalta (ed.), *The Stanford Encyclopedia of Philosophy* (Winter 2016 Edition) [https://plato.stanford.edu/archives/win2016/entries/reid/].

[59] Arendt uses different terms for common sense ('common sense', *Gesunder Menschenverstand, le bon sense, sensus communis, Gemeinsinn*). See Marieke Borren, 'A Sense of the World: Hannah Arendt's Hermeneutic Phenomenology of Common Sense'. *International Journal of Philosophical Studies* 21(2) (2013), 22–255.

[60] There are, as far as I know, very few references to Arendt in Murdoch's writing. Nevertheless, there are important connections between the two thinkers. See Frances White 'Iris Murdoch and Hannah Arendt: Two Women in Dark Times'. M. F. Simone Roberts and Alison

Arendt understands common sense as a sense of what is in common. Common sense, she writes, '...assures us of the reality of the world and of ourselves'.[61] I know that the coffee in my cup is real, because my different senses confirm this (it looks like coffee, it smells like coffee, it tastes like coffee and as much as that is possible it feels and sounds like coffee). I also know it is real because it is common to myself and others (the moment of drinking coffee is often a social event at a particular time of the day. Or to put it differently, no one is behaving as if there is no cup on the table or as if I am about to drink poison, etc.). In *The Human Condition* Arendt writes: 'the presence of others, who see and hear what we see and hear assures us of the reality of the world and of ourselves.'[62]

Common sense reassures us of reality. The notion thus understood reminds of the experiences of women and diverse people in philosophy, who feel excluded and also disconnected when for instance the misogyny of a thinker is treated as a mere joke. In Arendt's work common sense plays an important part in her understanding of totalitarianism. Common sense is vulnerable and can leave us. We see innocent people being led away and yet we can't believe our eyes, especially when no one else seem to acknowledge the awful reality.

If common sense is thus understood, the question remains whether common sense is taken as either *a priori* or *a posteriori*. Do we hold whatever it is as common sense by virtue of our humanity or whether it is acquired during our lives and perhaps specific to the community we are part of? Both these understandings can lead to exclusivity, either when one is denied one's humanity or excluded from a community.[63] A way out of this problem is suggested by Marieke Borren, who emphasises the phenomenological nature of Arendt's writing: 'As a phenomenologist, [Arendt] rejects the idea of human nature altogether and instead adopts the perspective of human

---

Scott-Bauman (eds.), *Iris Murdoch and the Moral Imagination*. McFarland, (2010) 13–33.

[61] Hannah Arendt, *The Human Condition* (The University of Chicago Press, 1998), 50.

[62] Arendt op. cit., 50. The English language has at least two expressions for this experience of losing one's sense of reality, because one is longer certain that others see and hear what we see and hear: the elephant in the room and gaslighting.

[63] Borren, op. cit. note 58, 226–7. Borren argues that much of this debate is based around the question of whether Arendt's Kant-lectures are exegesis or present her own thinking and position.

conditions, which may or may not be realized, depending on other conditions and circumstances'.[64]

Common sense or *sensus communis* is then something to be valued. The remedy to any frightening loss of common sense, and thus of reality, is, for Arendt, to talk about what we share with friends and by talking make them more common.[65] This conversation does not mean all will agree, but only that something will become more common to all, that friendships are made stronger as well as our sense of reality. It seems to me that this characterises Murdoch's dialogical philosophy as well as the conversations Anscombe, Foot, Midgley and Murdoch had. Philosophy – as most intellectual endeavours – can be and has been an alienating activity. That Murdoch was able to redeem some of the outsiders perspectives for philosophy may well be thanks to these conversations.

If this understanding of philosophy as not abandoning common sense or *sensus communis* may not seem all that unusual, I would be glad. Of course, this kind of conversation is not alien to history of philosophy or to current philosophical practice. Yet, it may surprise those people who understand philosophy as a rigid pursuit of truth, as combat between adversaries, which may in its endeavour silence a diversity of voices.[66] What I hope to have shown is that this silence is not just to the detriment of those voices, but also to the philosophy developed. Why else would we be celebrating the voices of the wartime quartet, if not for their profound contributions?

5. Coda

What is it like to be a woman in philosophy? I hope to have shown that there is not a simple answer to this question, not in general and not in the case of Murdoch. In one interview Murdoch claimed that in Oxford there was no difference: to be a woman in philosophy is to be a man in philosophy. Yet, there is also ample evidence that she was keenly aware of gender discrimination and that she understood philosophy as not value free. Gender also affected her posthumous

[64] Borren, op. cit. note 58, 247.

[65] Hannah Arendt, 'Philosophy and Politics (*Social Research* 71.3 (2004), 427–454), 434–435: 'Friendship to a large extent, indeed, consists of this kind of talking about something that the friends have in common. By talking about what is between them, it becomes ever more common to them.'

[66] See Dotson, 'Concrete Flowers' op.cit. note 2, on the prominence of the adversarial method.

image for a while, when she was portrayed for the mind she lost rather than for the novels and works of philosophy that she wrote.

Being a woman in philosophy runs the risk of not being taken seriously as an interlocutor. When those who divert from the dominant discourse are asked once too often whether what they are doing is philosophy, it should not surprise that some of them decide to leave the profession. It is not obvious whose loss is greater, whether it is, as Woolf mused, better to be locked in or locked out, whether, as Dotson puts it, they have failed in philosophy or philosophy has failed them.

Philosophy is slowly becoming a more inclusive discipline, thanks to a growing number of proposals and recommendations. I have argued that to become truly inclusive philosophy needs to rethink its methods, goals and the questions it asks. Dotson is right to argue that philosophy needs a plurality of methods. Inspired by Murdoch and the wartime quartet I have characterised one alternative as 'not abandoning common sense'. This kind of philosophy is a shared investigation of experience. As a shared investigation it is markedly different from the adversarial method and its focus of experience allows us to confirm reality and recognise diversity.

There are good reasons for making philosophy more inclusive. Philosophy is a necessity in some ways and it should be open to diverse voices. The diverse voices, on the other hand, are needed for philosophy. Philosophy should not turn away from the world and from experience, for that should be instead its central concern. The practice of the wartime quartet gives us an inspiring example of what such philosophy may look like. It is a philosophy of people who do not abandon common sense, who have conversations about a world common to them and in those conversations the world becomes more common and more real and their friendships stronger.[67]

St. Mary's University
hm.altorf@stmarys.ac.uk

[67] I dedicate this article to Pamela Sue Anderson, whom I still miss very much. I like to thank audiences in Uppsala, London and Durham for their comments to earlier versions. Thanks also to my colleague Yasemin J. Erden for her careful feedback to an earlier version and for all those years in which we worked together to create and maintain a very good, pluralistic philosophy programme.

Philosophical Plumbing in the Twenty-First Century

LIZ MCKINNELL

Abstract
Mary Midgley famously compares philosophy to plumbing. In both cases we are dealing with complex systems that underlie the everyday life of a community, and in both cases we often fail to notice their existence until things start to smell a bit fishy. Philosophy, like plumbing, is performed by particular people at particular times, and it is liable to be done in a way that suits the needs of those people and those whom they serve. I employ Mary Midgley's philosophy and biography to explore the importance of a diversity of voices for academic philosophy, and for society as a whole.

1. Birth and Death

Mary Midgley died just a few weeks before the birth of my son. While she lived to a very good age, I was saddened that the two of them wouldn't occupy the world at the same time, with 99 years between them. I was grateful, however, that she had left us with a final book, *What is Philosophy For?*, which was written in tiny lucid chapters that could be read while I fed my baby. The closeness of these events led me to consider the nature of birth and death, and our vulnerability and interdependence as human animals. I hope that what follows will reflect some of that. I shall draw on some themes in Midgley's work, as well as some pertinent aspects of her life, to consider why it is important that women (and mothers in particular) should be able to work in philosophy, and briefly discuss what conditions are required for this to be practical.

2. Aristotle and Maggots

Bertrand Russell, with a characteristic twinkle in his eye, remarked that 'Aristotle maintained that women have fewer teeth than men; although he was twice married, it never occurred to him to verify this statement by examining his wives' mouths'.[1] Contrary to what

[1] Bertrand Russell, *The Impact of Science on Society* (New York: Columbia University Press, 1951), 9

doi:10.1017/S1358246119000183

Russell implies, Aristotle was, in general, a great believer in empirical observation as a way of discovering truths about the world. Of course, no empirical investigator works in isolation. In order to know things, we can go out and look, but this is not always possible. We also need to rely upon the observations of others. In contemporary science this usually takes the form of reading the results of experiments in trusted scientific journals. The matter of trust is very important here: which sources do we trust? Furthermore, to which do we even pay attention in the first place? Clearly this is at least as big a question in our time as it was in Aristotle's, where increasingly, different groups of people seem to occupy different worlds, and the question of who to trust becomes very significant. Here Aristotle cast his net wider than many of his contemporaries, taking seriously the observations of farmers and fishermen in order to discover things about the workings of the natural world.[2]

In addition to his mistaken beliefs about male and female dentistry, Aristotle maintained that maggots spontaneously generated from an admixture of water with putrifying matter. The mixture separated into sweet and putrified elements: the sweet elements became animals, such as maggots, and the putrified elements are the residue of the process and return to the earth.[3] Looking at the workings of any household compost bin can show us how Aristotle could easily have come to a conclusion along these lines. The fact that the eggs of flies and other insects are far too small to see in any detail with the naked eye makes it still more forgivable that Aristotle would have thought what he did, in a time before microscopes.

However, I like to imagine an alternative version of this story in which Aristotle arrived at the truth of the matter. In my version, just as Aristotle went out and spoke to the fishermen and farmers about the animals that they encountered, he spoke to those involved in food storage and preparation – women and slaves – about the practices that they used to complete their everyday tasks. He would, in this version, have been told that raw meat must be covered, especially in summer, and that if this was not done, maggots would be the unwanted guests at the dinner party. Perhaps Aristotle's interlocutors would have known that they were doing this to keep the flies out, or perhaps the fact that cloth was sometimes used as a covering, or that it was especially important to take these measures in the

[2] See, for example, Armand Marie Leroi, *The Lagoon: How Aristotle Invented Science*, (London: Bloomsbury, 2014)

[3] Aristotle, *Generation of Animals,* trans. A.L. Peck, (London : Heinemann, Cambridge, Mass. : Harvard U P, 1963), book I.

warmer drier months would have led Aristotle to realise that water coming into contact with the meat was not the sole cause of the problem.

While Russell thought that it should have occurred to Aristotle to open his wife's mouth and count her teeth, it didn't seem to occur to *Russell* that Aristotle could have ascertained the number of his wife's teeth by *asking* her. Aristotle might also, I speculate, have discovered revealing things about the natural world by paying heed to the observations of the women and slaves involved in food storage and preparation. However, in spite of his many great qualities, Aristotle did not rate the views of women very highly, regarding them as lacking in many of the rational capacities and potential that were possessed by (some) men. His views on slaves are somewhat more complicated, but he certainly thought that some people were naturally suited to being slaves, and that they were not the types with whom one could have a reasonable level of intelligent discourse.[4]

This little story is not designed to reject Aristotle in a wholesale way, or to ignore the fact that he thought in the same way as many of his contemporaries (we would not expect him to be a feminist) but rather to illustrate the dangers of ignoring or marginalising certain groups. By failing to take whole groups of people seriously, we are in danger of losing valuable insights that are particular to their ways of life, and in so doing, of falling into serious error.

3. Philosophical Plumbing

What I have said so far pertains to the natural sciences, but what of philosophy? A critic might maintain that rational thought has no gender, as well as no race, disability, age, sexuality, and so on. Surely, the critic might say, we are concerned with pure thought, with the connections between ideas, and not with the material circumstances or contingencies of everyday life. A philosopher, qua philosopher, has no particular identity in these senses. According to this model of thought, a philosopher's gender, and other aspects of her specific identity, is rather like a coat that she hangs up when she gets into the office in the morning, and puts on again once the day's philosophising is done.

Midgley can help us here. In her article 'Philosophical Plumbing', she argues that philosophy is not a mere set of timeless abstractions,

[4] See Catherine Rowett, *Dumb Beasts and Dead Philosophers*, (Oxford: Clarendon, 2007), 128–132.

but rather a practice that is rooted in practical concerns that arise in particular circumstances. Ideas crop up at specific times in history because they are needed to address concrete problems.[5] Philosophy, like plumbing, is a complex network that is vital to the life of any complex society, but which is rarely noticed until things start to go wrong. At that point, someone needs to take up the floorboards and have a bit of a tinker. Something that we might also draw from this is that if philosophy addresses practical concerns, it will be the kinds of practical concerns that are noticed by the types of people who do philosophy. Thus if philosophy is dominated by particular types of people, it will address the problems that affect those people, and deal with them in ways that are liable to suit those groups.

Some may be concerned that if we think that people will philosophise differently depending on their place in society, this will lead us to the conclusion that there is no such thing as truth, and that everything is relative to the individual. But the point is not that the truth will be different for different people, but that living in different ways can lead us to ask different questions, or to look at the same questions from different angles. It is rather like Midgley's metaphor of one aquarium with many windows, which she uses to emphasise the importance of conversations between different disciplines.[6] We can never have a top-down picture of everything, but by paying attention to a range of perspectives, we can get a more nuanced view. One such perspective is that of the new parent, and their attempts to see the world through the eyes of their child.

4. Babies and philosophy

In her first book, *Beast and Man*, Midgley says that 'We are not just rather like animals, we *are* animals'.[7] There is nothing that will make you consider your animal (and more specifically mammalian) nature more than having a small pink grunting pre-linguistic creature squirming at your breast and crying out for milk. Any small human baby is striking in his or her animality. At the same time, we look at our children, and recognise ourselves in them, both in specific

[5] Mary Midgley, 'Philosophical Plumbing', in *Utopias, Dolphins and Computers: Problems of Philosophical Plumbing*, (London: Routledge, 1996) 1–14.

[6] Mary Midgley, *Science and Poetry*, (London: Routledge, 2001) 141.

[7] Mary Midgley, *Beast and Man: The Roots of Human Nature*, (London: Methuen and co., 1980) xiii.

resemblances, in the connections we have with them, and the sociality that is present from the moment of their births. We are struck by this at the same time that we are struck by the baby's animality. This is a visceral feeling, rather than an intellectual exercise that puts the baby into a pre-determined category. This leads to a similarly visceral experience of our own animality. Of course, this reveals just as much about how we think about animals as it reveals about the way that we see the baby.

In Western culture at least, there is a deep-rooted historical tendency to see a sharp dividing line between what is rational, cultural, and freely chosen, and what is instinctive, natural, and entirely deterministic.[8] Humans are put in the first of these boxes, and animals in the second. Many of the experiences of new parents put a lot of this into doubt, as we see complex and seamless transitions between our choices and our instincts. The baby cries, and we find ourselves out of bed with the bedside lamp on before we are even properly awake. The baby himself seems in many ways like a creature of instinct: for example, a newborn baby, placed on his mother's torso, will crawl around moving his head from side to side until he finds the breast through sense of smell.

These natural instinctive behaviours are what often leads women and babies to be regarded as somewhat 'other', occupying the sphere of nature far more than cultural civilised man, who is therefore regarded as more properly free. This logic has traditionally been used as an attempt to justify the dominance of the masculine over the feminine, as well as the exploitation of the natural world: women and nature lack reason, and must therefore be dominated, and can be exploited for the ends of civilised man. Children too are considered to be a woman's responsibility, and women therefore serve as a kind of buffer that prevent men from getting too close for comfort to their animal beginnings: women thus sit halfway between civilisation and nature. The same logic is at play in the colonial notion of 'savage' races of people.

But if we see our natural animal responses as a threat to our freedom in this way, we might do well to interrogate the notion of freedom that is in play. If we see women and babies as entirely governed by our biological makeup, whether we talk in terms of evolution, genes, or hormones, we ought to come to the conclusion that *no* human being is truly free. In *Heart and Mind*, Mary Midgley discusses the idea of being free and being indeterminate. As is often the case, she uses a

[8] See Val Plumwood, *Feminism and the Mastery of Nature*, (London: Routledge, 1993).

striking metaphor to describe our intellectual inheritance. She talks about the various bits and pieces that we have lying around in our conceptual kitchen, which don't come to light until we give the place a proper spring clean.

> I want to take a look inside that elegant green jar at the end of the top shelf, marked Freedom.
>
> If we look in that jar on the communal shelf today, we shall find the extremely strange idea that to be free is to be indeterminate, that our having an innate constitution would destroy our freedom. Repeatedly of late, defenders of freedom have attacked scientists who were producing evidence that something in our emotional or intellectual capacities was inherited. ... They hold that these suggestions about our innate constitution simply have to be false – because, if they were true, they would make us slaves...
>
> ...I want to say that those who think they are defending freedom in this way have radically misunderstood it, and can only do it harm. The point is just this. Neither freedom nor equality demands that we should really be blank paper at birth, completely indeterminate beings. What this would be like is not easy to see, but it would certainly not be a state compatible with freedom. An indeterminate being cannot be a free one.
>
> To be free, you have to have an original constitution. Freedom is the chance to develop what you have it in you to be – your talents, your capacities, your natural feelings.[9]

Our freedom exists because we have particular constitutions, and is a product of our nature rather than a way of overcoming it. This is not to say that newborn babies come into the world free, in the sense that you and I are free, as freedom is a multivarious concept.

Take something as simple as the decision to get some rest. Although many of us suffer from insomnia from time to time, we generally know when we are tired, and will take steps to remedy it. This is not the case with tiny babies: any parent knows very well that even when the baby is utterly exhausted, it takes a great deal of work to get them to sleep. They need help from adults to do even this most basic of things. Part of the reason for this is that they do not know how they are feeling. It takes the help of those around them to gradually develop a sense of when they are tired, along with when they are

[9] Mary Midgley, *Heart and Mind: The Varieties of Moral Experience*, (London: Routledge, 1983), 39–40.

happy, sad, and so on. We instinctively mirror the facial expressions of our babies, and it is through this that they start to get a better sense of their own inner life.[10] It is only once this understanding develops to a certain extent that they can really be said to have freedom in certain senses of the word. If. For example, we understand freedom in terms of the ability to satisfy our desires, we might regard consciousness of our desires as a prerequisite. In another sense though, babies are incredibly free. If we follow Midgley in understanding freedom in terms of the chance to develop our capacities, talents, and feelings, we can witness babies developing these with a rapidity that adults could only dream of.

As babies develop, exercising their freedom and developing the capacity for new kinds of freedom, this happens *in virtue* of them being biological animals with certain natural characteristics, and not in spite of this. Significantly, it also happens in virtue of them being the type of animals who naturally exist in communities with other animals of the same species, who can reflect their personalities back to them to allow them to develop a sense of independent selfhood. Additionally, while babies may not be able to recognise their own desires, they are extremely good at having those desires satisfied by those who care for them. If we follow Midgley, as I believe we should, human freedom should not be set in opposition (as it so often has been) to our biology, our emotions, and our communal nature, but rather these things are vital building blocks for our freedom.

5. The ego and the world

Here we come to another aspect of philosophical thought that babies might lead us to rethink – the idea of the individual and their relationship with a community. A great deal of enlightenment thought takes the individual as the starting point for making discoveries about the world. We begin with the self at the centre, and work outwards towards things like the physical world, animals, and other minds.

In some respects babies turn this on its head. Right from birth, babies are intrigued by the world around them. My son, born by

[10] See Alison Gopnik, Andrew Meltzoff, and Patricia Kuhl, *How Babies Think*, (London: Orion Books, 1999) and Alison Gopnik, *The Philosophical Baby: What Children's Minds Tell Us about Truth, Love, and the Meaning of Life*, (London: The Bodley Head, 2009).

emergency caesarean section, emerged wide-eyed into the operating theatre, taking such an acute interest in this new bright and busy world that I suspected that he might be inspired to enter the medical profession when he grows up. However, now at the much more mature age of fifteen weeks, it will still be at least a year before he is able to recognise himself in the mirror.[11]

We often think of babies as self-centred, but this is because they simply don't have a clear sense of themselves as separate from the world that they are so busy exploring. This is part of why a baby's life seems to be full of high drama: when he has a tummy ache, the whole universe is infused with tummy ache – a tragedy by anyone's standards. It is only much later that babies begin to realise that other people are separate from themselves in any significant sense. Recent work in developmental psychology has shown this to be true in a variety of ways. For example, consider this experiment conducted by the psychologist Alison Gopnik and her colleagues:

> By the time babies are about one-and-a-half-years old, they start to understand the nature of these differences between people and to be fascinated by them. Again we can demonstrate this systematically. Alison [Gopnik] and one of her students, Betty Repacholi, showed babies two bowls of food, one full of delicious Goldfish crackers and one full of raw broccoli. All the babies, even in Berkeley, preferred the crackers. Then Betty tasted each bowl of food. She made a delighted face and said, "Yum" to one food and made a disgusted face and said, "Yuck" to the other. Then she put both bowls of food near the babies, held out her hand, and said, "Could you give me some?"
>
> When Betty indicated that she loved the crackers and hated the broccoli, the babies, of course, gave her the crackers. But what if she did the opposite and said that the broccoli was yummy and the crackers were yucky? This presented the babies with one of those cases where our attitude toward the object is different from theirs, where we want one thing and they want something else. Fourteen-month-olds, still with their innocent assumption that we all want the same thing, gives us the crackers. But the wiser ... eighteen-month-olds give us the broccoli, even though they themselves despise it. These tiny children, barely able to talk, have already learned an extremely important thing about

[11] Op. cit. note 10, and Charles Fernyhough, *The Baby in the Mirror: A Child's World from One to Three*, (London: Granta Books, 2009).

> people. They've learned that people have desires and that those desires may be different and may even conflict.[12]

This experiment tells us about the development of the knowledge that other people's desires may differ from our own. Other research has shown us that similar things are true about the knowledge that other people can perceive different objects, depending on their location in a room. Babies start out assuming that others can see exactly what they can see, and it is only later that they develop the idea that they can see things that are hidden from others.

This does not tell us that babies are unaware of the existence of other people, so much as it tells us that the babies are unaware that they have a separate self. Individuality is an end goal, rather than the starting point for enquiry. Relationships, with parents, wider family, and other people that babies encounter in their day to day lives, arrive almost from birth (and in some cases even beforehand). Individuality is a lot further down the line.

When G.E. Moore got from 'Here is one hand' to an external world, he had doubtless forgotten (as all of us do) that he, like my little boy, will once have spent weeks working hard, hopefully with the help of adoring adults, on discovering this thing that he now treats as a basic certainty.[13] He will also have forgotten that, if he is anything like my son, the eventual discovery that he had hands would once have prevented him from sleeping, as every time he started drifting off in his cot, his hands would fly up and catch his attention, and he would be gripped with the sheer amazement of it all, excited to put his new discovery to practical use by waving and grabbing at things. What he will have experienced as something more akin to basic certainty at that point in his life would have been the smell of mother's milk and the sound of his parents' voices. Only through further exploration, aided by the comfort and security that these things afforded, could he begin to make the investigations that would culminate in knowing about his handedness.

Moore, I suspect, would have responded that a baby could not be certain of anything, or even have desires or beliefs, in the sense that is relevant to his common sense philosophy. Without the rudiments of language, he might have maintained that the baby is unable to think propositionally, and therefore cannot believe or know things in the relevant ways. This may be true so far as it goes, but this neglects

[12] Alison Gopnik, Andrew Meltzoff, and Patricia Kuhl, How Babies Think, (London: Orion Books, 1999), 36–7.

[13] G.E. Moore, 'A Defence of Common Sense' in *G.E. Moore: Selected Writings,* ed. Thomas Baldwin, (London: Routledge, 1993).

the significant fact that the development of language is built on a foundation that is fundamentally embodied and interpersonal. My son began manipulating objects with a thumb and forefinger, and finding out that he can make different noises by moving his tongue around in his mouth, within an hour of each other. These discoveries are clearly connected, and both facilitated through play with a trusted adult. In this sense the knowledge of the parents, and/or other significant figures in one's life, can be understood as a more basic kind of knowledge than the knowledge of material objects, and even the knowledge of one's own body and mental states. We are interpersonal and social creatures before we can be anything else.

6. Attention

Many of these insights have only been formally demonstrated in developmental psychology in the last couple of decades. Before then, it was widely thought that babies barely thought or engaged with the world at all. They were simply thought to be crying blobs who weren't of much interest until they were a couple of years old. This belief was not held purely because of limitations in experimental techniques or technology, although videotape did play a role. It was more that, because it was assumed that nothing of interest happened at this stage, nobody thought that it was worth conducting the experiments in the first place. Babies were just not worth looking at.

Of course, the mothers of those babies have always thought that they were very much worth looking at, and indeed that they had capacities for thought that went well beyond what was maintained in traditional psychology, but this was written off as mere maternal sentimentality. However, this neglects the fact that those mothers had spent many hours of every day paying close attention to their child. What they noticed was borne out of the love that motivates them to pay this attention, but (as Midgley and her contemporary Iris Murdoch have observed) love and other emotions should not be pitted in opposition to rational enquiry and real discovery. This is what Gopnik and her colleagues have to say:

> As more women became scientists and more male scientists began to take care of young babies, and as videotape technology became available, we began to pay more real attention to babies. That itself made the "crying carrot" picture look a lot less likely. People who take care of young babies usually believe that babies can think, but it was easy, at first, for scientists to dismiss those

> intuitions (they were, after all, literally old wives' tales). It got a lot harder, though, when the scientist and the caregiver were the same person, and when you could back up your intuitions with videotaped proof. Old wives (and one old husband) are writing this book.[14]

The significant thing here is the notion of attention (something described so richly by Iris Murdoch) and where we think that attention should be directed. Science can allow us to discover truths about the world, but it does this differently depending on where and how it casts its gaze. This, in turn, is affected by other things that are going on in the life of the scientist, including their emotional life. This is a real case of what Murdoch calls 'a just and loving gaze directed upon an individual reality'.[15]

7. Conclusion

I have said that paying close attention to babies can help us see longstanding philosophical problems in a new light. I am not committed to the Platonic idea that babies have access to some form of knowledge that we have forgotten, and that they have all these profound philosophical questions sorted out. Rather it is a question of having a different angle on a problem. Things that might seem obvious to seasoned philosophers can be less so for babies, and their obvious starting points are quite different. Being able to spend time with small children as they grow and learn can therefore afford a different perspective on these problems. Rather than asking how we get from the Cartesian ego to the external world, we might instead puzzle over how we can explain how individual selfhood can emerge from the fog of common human experience. Rather than asking how we can convince the egoist of the merits of altruism, we might wonder how and whether self-interest can be set in opposition to the common good. Rather than thinking about free will in opposition to our biological and emotional nature, we might consider how biology and emotions might shape our projects and enable us to pursue them freely. The deepest and most longstanding problems of philosophy can be seen in a different light when you have spent

[14] Alison Gopnik, Andrew Meltzoff, and Patricia Kuhl, How Babies Think, (London: Orion Books, 1999), 144.

[15] Iris Murdoch, *The Sovereignty of Good*, (London: Routledge, 1970), 34.

many days and sleepless nights trying to help your child by understanding the way that they navigate the world.

This is why it matters that women are more easily able to pursue careers in academic philosophy while also raising families, and why men in philosophy are able to spend time paying close attention to their children. Of course, a child does not exist for the sake of being an object of philosophical contemplation, and these things matter for a good many other reasons too. My point is that it *does* matter from the point of view of philosophy as a discipline.

In our alternative history, Aristotle comes to understand the life cycle of maggots and flies by talking to the women and slaves who deal with food preparation. However, it is hard to see how this would have happened when their point of view was already disregarded, and their concerns seen as trivial. Perhaps a better alternative history would enable those who deal with food to gain the same recognition in philosophy as Aristotle and his contemporaries, and (just as importantly) for Aristotle to do his share of work in the kitchen.

So what, practically speaking, is to be done? The current typical career trajectory in academia is unsuited to people who are keen to have children, especially if they are women. The years in which we can have babies are typically spent on our PhDs, and then on a series of insecure contracts that offer no financial security, and move us around the country (or around the world) making it difficult to form supportive communities and putting strain on relationships.

Babies turn many of our philosophical questions on their heads. Midgley turned the structure of an academic career on its head, with respect to babies. There is, at present, a lot of social and financial pressure to establish oneself as an academic and gain some stability before having children. This is difficult, when the typical female new PhD graduate will have a decade or so left to have children naturally, and potentially (at least if she has Midgley's good health) another six decades in which she can write good philosophical work.

Mary Midgley started publishing in earnest in her late fifties after taking early retirement once her boys had grown up. When Tony Benn announced his retirement from the House of Commons at the age of 74, he said that he did so in order to devote more time to politics. Similarly, Midgley might be said to have left academia to devote more time to philosophy. However, the current climate in academic philosophy makes a career of this shape very difficult to achieve, and pretty much impossible for anyone who doesn't have an alternative source of financial support, as well as help with childcare and domestic chores. Serious effort is required in order to rethink the academic career structure so that young scholars are able to have families without fear of losing a roof over their heads, and without the constant pressure to publish world-leading articles at times when their priorities in life are very different.

More broadly, it is vital that anyone in academic philosophy has sufficient time to pay attention to the details of life outside of academia. Many early career academics find every waking moment taken up with their work, partly because the insecure job climate means that their responsibilities change year on year and need to be relearned from scratch. This can lead to a very cloistered environment in which people rarely read outside their fields, rarely socialise with people who do other jobs, and barely have time to notice the many details of everyday life that provide the impetus to do philosophical work in the first place.

This absence of free time, in academia as elsewhere, impacts on the possibility of having good open dialogue in the public sphere. We are all encouraged to rush home from our long hours at work, and spend the little time left on the basics of home life, before rushing back to work the following day. This robs us of the capacity to *notice* things about the things that matter in our own lives, and also of the capacity to listen and engage with a range of experiences. In principle, many scholars may believe that it is a good idea to listen to a broader range of voices, and to gain the wider range of insights that this would provide, but a working climate that militates against this is liable to make us blinkered, as well as contributing to the present mental health crisis that beleaguers university life.

Durham University
lizmckinnellphilosophy@gmail.com

Relationality in the Thought of Mary Midgley

GREGORY S. MCELWAIN

Abstract
For over 40 years, Mary Midgley has been celebrated for the sensibility with which she approached some of the most challenging and pressing issues in philosophy. Her expansive corpus addresses such diverse topics as human nature, morality, animals and the environment, gender, science, and religion. While there are many threads that tie together this impressive plurality of topics, the thread of relationality unites much of Midgley's thought on human nature and morality. This paper explores Midgley's pursuit of a relational notion of the self and our connections to others, including animals and the natural world.

1. Introduction

One of the more central themes in Mary Midgley's work is her emphasis on integrated notions of human nature and the self. These notions can become disintegrated or fragmented when central elements of our lives – reason and emotion, mind and body, self and others, human and animal – are isolated and divided against each other as warring alternatives. Throughout her career, Midgley endeavoured to reintegrate these and other aspects of human nature and the self as complementary, rather than oppositional. She long argued for the practicality of philosophy, showing that the ways in which we think of ourselves and the world around us greatly impact how we live. She argued, in particular, that our visions of human nature and the self – how we imagine ourselves and our place in the world – shape our moral principles, attitudes, and actions. For this reason, these visions should be scrutinized regularly and refined.

One significant component of these visions is how we picture human sociality and relationality. In this paper, I will focus on this relatively underexplored aspect of Midgley's work.[1] Relationality involves our intrinsic connections to others, human and nonhuman alike. Throughout her work, Midgley makes the case that this central element of human life should feature more prominently in

[1] This paper is adapted from portions of Gregory S. McElwain, *Mary Midgley: An Introduction* (London: Bloomsbury Academic, 2019).

doi:10.1017/S1358246119000225

our imaginative visions of the world. In what follows, I will first focus on Midgley's critique of individualistic visions – primarily atomistic ones – that fragment our notions of human nature and the self by unrealistically emphasizing the isolated individual (or ego) over more relational or holistic visions of ourselves and our place in the world. From there, I will trace the more constructive elements of Midgley's relational account, which ultimately run throughout her influential approach to animals and the natural world.

2. Critique of individualism

Midgley's emphasis on the relational aspects of the self emerges from her critique of atomistic individualism, which unrealistically isolates individuals and threatens to fragment our understandings of the self, society, and our place in nature. Social atomism, in brief, is the idea that people are distinct individuals. Like atoms or billiard balls, people are envisioned as discrete, self-contained units. Society, in this sense, is nothing more than the aggregate of individual units. Within this atomistic framework, which is often assumed within a contract framework, people are originally separate and isolated individuals.

Thomas Hobbes is perhaps the most vivid and influential proponent of this approach. Hobbes claimed that, in the state of nature, we are originally atomistic and egoistic – that is, inherently solitary and motivated primarily, if not entirely, by self-interest and self-preservation. These assumptions underlie his influential formulation of the social contract, in which he argued that it is in our best interest to strike a collective bargain with each other in order to escape the ruthless and destructive state of nature. Otherwise, there is little stopping us, in the 'war of all against all', from pursuing our own individual interests to the destruction of others. Life, if our egoist natures were to prevail, would be 'solitary, poor, nasty, brutish, and short'.[2] Thus, we contract with each other in order to live – rather than merely survive – in a lawful society. Here, under the power and protection of the sovereign, we then give up some of our more dangerous freedoms – for instance, the freedom to kill and steal – to live in a lawful world that is, in the end, more conducive to other freedoms and, ultimately, self-preservation. Thus, Hobbes's vision offers an account of why originally solitary and egoistic individuals are able

[2] Thomas Hobbes, *Leviathan: With Selected Variants from the Latin Edition of 1668*, ed. E. M. Curley (Indianapolis, IN: Hackett, 1994), 76.

to come together and live in society: the contract is, ultimately, a bargain of calculated self-interest in which we are much better off than the cutthroat alternative.

Hobbes's vision, and others that followed, involved real efforts to allot more significance, protection, and self-determination to individuals in the face of tyrannical and oppressive social and political forces. Midgley does not question or disregard these significant contributions to individual autonomy and political reform. Her concern is with the wider impacts of such visions, which have remained influential over time and variously emerged in aspects of Social Darwinism, sociobiology, and free market idealism (these were significant targets of Midgley's criticism in her early writings). She argues that an emphasis on atomistic egoism, the social contract, and correlated notions of individual freedom, though often politically useful, are not necessarily representative of or conducive to the types of lives that people want (and perhaps need) to live. They can, perhaps even more significantly, distort our moral visions by obscuring our connection with each other and the natural world.

2.1 Atomist and egoist visions

Midgley argues that atomist and egoist visions of the world tend to paint a somewhat bleak and isolationist view of others. These vivid dramas misconstrue our social landscape, portraying the illusion that we are much less connected and interdependent than we are (and always have been) as social animals. We are depicted, first and foremost, as selfish, disconnected individuals struggling for limited resources. In this competitive climate, we need a strong, self-interested reason to come together and live peaceably with each other (i.e., the contract for self-preservation). Rather than recognizing our intrinsic social natures and bonds – which are prior to, as opposed to consequences of, the contract – and the wider communities of significance to which we belong, atomistic visions chop the world up into separate agents and entities. Other people become *externals* – things out there that may be more or less useful but not really necessary. Relationships, in turn, appear provisional and instrumental, things we do not necessarily seek out and need, but things we use and easily dissolve.

Midgley argues that this vision of the world and its offshoots are unrealistic and undesirable. Hobbes's theory relies too heavily on the assumptions that we are inherently isolated and egoistic. Midgley points out that, while these may be *aspects* of our nature, this is not the *whole* picture. Hobbes's vision, in other words, exaggerates and hyperbolizes these aspects of our nature to the exclusion of much that makes our species. 'Far from being originally solitary', Midgley writes, 'the earliest human beings were heirs to a long, complex tradition of group life, deep social affection and interdependence, a tradition which dates from many ages before their emergence as a separate species and their famous rise in intelligence'.[3] To even exist as a social species today – with the hindsight of a Darwinian worldview unavailable to Hobbes – we required much in our evolutionary development besides isolation, competition, and selfishness. The requirement for social connection and dependence is intrinsic to our species and much less calculated and intellectual than it may at first appear. Midgley explores our social development in a Darwinian context:

> Early theorists as well as Hobbes often gave this strictly intellectual explanation of human sociability. Assuming that people had once been solitary, they asked: how, then, did they ever get together? They too thought this must have been due to intelligent planning, assuming that, as somebody once put it, language had been invented by a congress of hitherto speechless elders who had agreed to assemble and determine the rules of grammar. But this does not sound very plausible. If, however, you look at the issue zoologically instead, as Darwin did, these difficulties vanish. It becomes clear that the human species did not arise as an isolated miracle but as just one in a wide spectrum of other social creatures. The inborn sociability that these creatures all share actually provides the only possible context in which language could ever have developed. Speech only makes sense as a device for creatures who were already intensely sociable, creatures interested in each other who already communicated eagerly, but who needed to do it better. And, suitably enough, our immediate neighbours on that spectrum are indeed the great apes, who, like other primates, are well known for their rich variety of social interaction. It would have been an extraordinary evolutionary step if, in this situation, our species had reverted to the simpler, ego-bound emotional constitution that suits a crocodile. This, however, has important consequences. It means that the intellect of which we are so proud is not really our prime mover. It is not the inventor of our social nature. Instead, it is a later, benign outgrowth and

[3] Mary Midgley, *The Ethical Primate: Humans, Freedom and Morality* (London: Routledge, 1994), 119.

instrument of that nature. Before we are thinkers, we are lovers and haters, creatures deeply aware of those around us and fully integrated into their life. As soon as we start to think, our thoughts draw their force from those rich flows of natural feeling.[4]

This original connectivity and dependence, moreover, goes much further in contextualizing motives and behaviours that span beyond self-interest, including altruism, care, friendship, and so on. In fact, as Midgley notes, 'selfish' itself is one among many human traits, which indicates a lack, rather than the rule:

If this bizarre story [*of overriding selfishness*] *had been true, the notion of selfishness could never have arisen. Had regard for others really been impossible, there could have been no word for failing to have it. And it needs to be stressed that the word "selfish" in its normal use is essentially a negative word. It means a shortage of this normal regard for others. Calling somebody selfish simply does not mean that they are prudent or successfully self-preserving. It merely says that they are exceptional – and faulty – in having too little care for anybody else.*[5]

We have many traits and needs, some of which, such as solitude, are more self-contained. But many or most of our deepest and overarching needs require other people: bonds, love, attention, help, companionship, sex, and so on. Without these, the very self that egoist visions emphasize risks being fragmented and disintegrated from the social landscape that makes individuals possible.

2.2 Relational visions

Midgley maps an alternative social landscape to the egoistic atomist picture. Her approach highlights our natural relationality and sociality, emphasizing the interdependence of the self and others. We are parts of networks of relationships and dependencies that mold and shape us throughout our lives, making any vision of intrinsic isolation largely unrealistic. However active or passive we are in this dynamic process – for instance, we are completely dependent on others as young children – we are almost certainly never, really, as originally free or self-determined as egoistic atomism would lead us to

[4] Mary Midgley, *The Solitary Self: Darwin and the Selfish Gene* (Durham: Acumen, 2010), 130–131.

[5] Mary Midgley, *Evolution as a Religion: Strange Hopes and Stranger Fears* (London: Routledge, [1985] 2002), 136–7.

believe.[6] We do, of course, have freedom and agency in the world. Yet, the paths we wish to forge are never in isolation or without a wider map or landscape of relationships and dependencies, many of which are unnoticed or overshadowed in visions of individual choice and freedom (she points out the extent to which male freedom has historically relied on the support of 'non-automous females'[7]). Much like LEGO blocks, people are here imagined as separating with ease. Midgley resists this plastic vision, arguing that we cannot snap so easily in and out of each other's lives. We are, rather, intrinsically 'members one of another'.[8] With this context in mind, she writes, 'It may even become possible for our species to admit that it is not really a supernatural variety of Lego, but some kind of an animal. This ought to make it easier to admit also that we are not self-contained and self-sufficient, either as a species or as individuals, but live naturally in deep mutual dependence'.[9]

Midgley argues that the history of Western philosophy displays much of this strange negligence toward meaningful relationships.[10] Bonds and dependencies are regularly portrayed as weaknesses rather than strengths, as dangers that may bring pain and sorrow (thus, the Stoic advice not to become too attached to others and their well-being). Midgley faces the other direction, suggesting that our visions of the self should integrate our need for others and emphasize 'all the riches around us, the great stores of *otherness* in which we need to live'. She continues: 'Of course, our dependencies are dangerous, but who wants to live safely like a billiard ball or a doll that never leaves its package?'[11] She argues that there are realistic ways

[6] Midgley sees connections between notions of the radically free agent and Hobbesian atomism. These notions – which often grow out of the vivid visions of heroic individualism in Nietzsche and Sartre – imagine the self to be radically shaped and determined by the active will. This agent forges its way in the world, independent of the connections and dependences of the outside world.

[7] Mary Midgley, *The Myths We Live By* (London: Routledge, [2004] 2011), 132. This coincides with her critique of traditional individualist conceptions of the self as largely masculinist (see McElwain, *Mary Midgley*, 107–20).

[8] Mary Midgley, 'Philosophical Plumbing', in *The Impulse to Philosophise: Royal Institute of Philosophy Supplement 33*, ed. Phillips Griffiths (Cambridge: Cambridge University Press, 1992), 145, italics mine.

[9] Op. cit. note 8, 146–47.

[10] Midgley, *The Solitary Self* op. cit. note 4, 64–65.

[11] Op. cit note 4, 64.

of balancing this picture of individuality and sociality, and that philosophers too often have followed their visions far away from the reality of our social nature and needs. 'I am suggesting', she challenges, 'that this extreme individualism is itself just a local and limited point of view, like other cultural world-pictures ... it is one of the many partial visions that we must use in our attempt to forge a workable worldview'.[12]

Thus, Midgley implores us to reimagine our place and connectivity in the world. Rather than envisioning ourselves as isolated atoms or billiard balls bouncing off each other, we can picture ourselves in any number of interconnected and holistic ways. We might, for instance, think of ourselves as dancers: 'Our life', she writes, 'is not a collection of solo performances but an immensely intricate large-scale dance in which solos take their place among figures performed by groups of the most varying sizes'.[13] Our places and roles in this dance may shift and change, but our unique expressions as soloists are cultivated *within* the larger dance itself. The dance and the dancer need and complete each other. And, in the more holistic sense, this dance is embedded in a larger whole still, composed of many other entities and collectives, from our local communities to the global ecological networks of which we are part. If we abstract individuals away from this setting, we again lack the total picture through which we can envision the integrated or 'whole' self:

> This "whole person" of whom we have been talking is not, then, a solitary, self-sufficient unit. It belongs essentially within a larger whole, indeed within an interlocking pattern formed by a great range of such wholes. These wider systems are not an alien interference with its identity. They are its home, its native climate, the soil from which it grows, the atmosphere which it needs in order to breathe. Their unimaginable richness is what makes up the meaning of our lives. The self's wholeness is not, then, the wholeness of a billiard ball but that of an organism, a transient, struggling creature which has, of course, its own distinct shape but which still belongs in its own context and background.[14]

In this context, though we value our freedom and individual pursuits, they are embedded within these inescapable connections to the wider whole. This does not, to be sure, mean that we are subsumed to

[12] Op. cit. note 4, 125.
[13] Op. cit. note 4, 140.
[14] Mary Midgley, *Science and Poetry* (London: Routledge, [2001] 2006), 20.

society or other collectives. Rather, it means our visions should negotiate the interplay of collectives and individuals and resist 'compressing individuals into a homogenous mass and isolating them completely; between lumping and splitting'.[15]

3. Animals and the natural world

This general overview of Midgley's relational (and holistic) emphasis helps in understanding other aspects of her work, particularly her influential animal and environmental thought. Our many connections and interdependencies simply do not stop at the species or even sentience barrier. Rather, our dynamic embeddedness in the world involves relations and networks that stretch far beyond the human realm, reminding us of our animality in context. Midgley's refrain is that we should take this wider natural context more seriously in scrutinizing our moral visions.

3.1 The mixed community

Midgley's philosophy grows out of the statement that 'we are not just rather like animals; we *are* animals'.[16] Her thought locates humans alongside other animals in the natural world and takes the reality and implications of this picture seriously. This is apparent in Midgley's emphasis on human-animal relations. In focusing on our innate sociality, she draws attention to the fact that relationality is not exclusive to our own species. Animals are significant members of our 'mixed communities', locally (in our homes and neighborhoods) and globally (in our ecosystems and on our planet). All of these connections and communities matter, from the particular and local to the general and global. However, localized human-animal communities – typically the 'domestic' settings with which we are most familiar – are especially unique. These communities are manifestations of the wider human impulse to connect to the world around them. 'All human communities have involved animals', she observes, and it is 'one of the special powers and graces of our

[15] Mary Midgley, *Can't We Make Moral Judgements?* (London: Bloomsbury, [1989] 2017), 111.

[16] Mary Midgley, *Beast and Man: The Roots of Human Nature*, revised ed. (London: Routledge, [1979] 2002), xxxiii.

species not to ignore others, but to draw in, domesticate and live with a great variety of other creatures'.[17] Such domestication was achieved largely because many animals (dogs, horses, pigs, etc.) share a number of social and emotive characteristics with us. They were, in turn, able to form bonds, understand social signals, learn to obey particular persons, and so on. These shared traits and behaviours made possible the historical development of complex human-animal communities that have taken innumerable shapes and forms over time and space.

Though animals may not be equivalent to 'persons' in these communities – a term Midgley argues is too loaded with legal baggage – as members of our mixed community, they are certainly fellow *subjects*, not objects or things. That is, the simplistic Kantian antithesis of 'persons *versus* things' is unhelpful here and obscures our recognition of animal subjectivity and relationality.[18] We have long recognized the subjectivity of animals – indeed, animal cruelty paradoxically underscores this fact.[19] Yet, we need not dwell on the negative. Genuine interspecies love and care are pervasive, from intense bonds of companionship – many of which are held to be as important as human bonds – to altruistic acts toward animals (rescuing injured animals, animal welfare charities). Instances of cruelty do arise, but these are unfortunate episodes in a long history of coexistence and community. In fact, animals are typically seen as significant elements of human life. They are featured prominently in our imagination, identity, and social worlds. It is hard to even imagine life without animals, be they companion animals, songbirds and squirrels, or characters in books and films. In this mixed-species context, in which our very language is reflective of our history and coexistence with other animals, most of us are imprinted by interspecies sociality from a

[17] Mary Midgley, *Animals and Why They Matter* (Athens, GA: University of Georgia Press, 1983), 111 and 112.

[18] Mary Midgley, *Utopias, Dolphins and Computers: Problems of Philosophical Plumbing* (London: Routledge, 1996), 111–12.

[19] Midgley, *Animals and Why They Matter,* op. cit. note 17, 114. Cruelty involves a belief that something is a subject capable of suffering. Dogs are kicked and horses are beaten not because they are things (like machines and stuffed animals), but because they are beings that feel and experience pain in a significant way. In other words, belief in animal sentience is essential 'for exploiting them successfully'. In fact, Midgley points out, 'exploitation *requires* sympathy' (114 and 116). Abuse and cruelty to animals is an outcome of our ability to understand and relate to the 'inner' as well as the 'outer' states of other animals, coupled with the tendency to devalue or disregard these states.

young age. We crave animal contact from our youth, and it is a foundational element of our early lives along with song, dance, and play.[20] Bonds with animals work alongside our bonds with people as part of a 'full human life'.[21] They are, in other words, significant parts of our intrinsic relationality with the world. Human and animal worlds intermix and overlap in powerful ways, especially in our youth, which shapes and influences how we view life from the beginning:

> The species-barrier, imposing though it may look, is rather like one of those tall wire fences whose impressiveness is confined to their upper reaches. To an adult in formal dress, engaged in his official statesmanly interactions, the fence is an insuperable barrier. Down below, where it is full of holes, it presents no obstacle at all. The young of Homo sapiens, like those of the other species present, scurry through it all the time. Since all human beings start life as children, this has the quite important consequence that hardly any of us, at heart, sees the social world as an exclusively human one.[22]

This childlike wonder and curiosity motivates us, throughout our lives, toward 'otherness' in the world, human and nonhuman alike. That is, we are drawn to and capable of appreciating the world and its many inhabitants in affective and moving ways. In this intra- and interspecies community, bonds with animals and the nonhuman world complement and enrich our connection with humans. By caring more, we widen our horizons.

Thus, Midgley argues that our community with animals – and the sympathy, compassion, and care therein – is a significant aspect of our existence and must feature more prominently in our moral visions. Yet, these features can be easily overlooked in approaches to animal ethics that favor sweeping moral principles. Principles that promote equal consideration of the interests of sentient beings or respect for subjects-of-a-life make sense in devising compelling and consistent reasons to treat animals better in accordance with our general notions of moral worth.[23] Here, animals are shown forcefully to meet at least some of our prevailing standards for moral consideration

[20] Op. cit. note 17, 118.
[21] Op. cit. note 17, 119.
[22] Op. cit. note 17, 118.
[23] These positions are presented influentially, respectively, by Peter Singer (*Animal Liberation*, 2nd ed. [New York: New York Review of Books, (1976) 1990]), and Tom Regan (*The Case for Animal Rights* [Berkeley, CA: University of California Press, 1983]).

(possessing certain capacities, for instance). In charting a more pluralistic moral map, Midgley argues that this account is incomplete without the relational element: 'If we ask what powers can give a higher claim, bringing some creatures nearer to the degree of consideration which is due to humans, what is most relevant seems to be sensibility, social and emotional complexity of the kind which is expressed by the forming of deep, subtle and lasting relationships'.[24]

3.2 Our connection to nature

These threads of relationality and community extend beyond humans and animals and continue further still to the whole of nature, or to what Midgley often refers to as 'the biosphere'. She envisions our connections to each other and the natural world in terms of 'wholeness and separateness'.[25] As we have already seen, we do indeed exist as individuals, but we are also deeply entangled with wider, overlapping collectives of varying types and intensities: families, communities, cultures, ecosystems, and so on. Utilizing another vivid image, this time a tree, she writes of the 'variety of asymmetrical relations found within a whole. Leaves relate not only to other leaves, but to fruit, twigs, branches, and the whole tree. People appear not only as individuals, but as members of their groups, families, tribes, species, ecosystems and biosphere, and have moral relations, as parts, to these various wholes'.[26] She reminds us:

> Of course, human beings are distinct individuals. But they are also tiny, integral parts of this planet – framed by it, owing everything to it, and adapted to a certain place among its creatures. Each can indeed change its life, but does not organically invent it. Each receives life in a family (as a petal does in a flower), in a country (as the flower does on the tree), and in the biosphere (as the tree does in the forest). Our environment gives us nearly everything we have.[27]

Our environments are not alien entities or mere aggregates of competitors, but the vibrant contexts of the self, a self which 'unavoidably looks for its fulfilment to horizons far beyond its private

[24] Mary Midgley, *Utopias, Dolphins and Computers*, op. cit. note 18, 116.
[25] Mary Midgley, *The Ethical Primate*, op. cit. note 3, 102–3.
[26] Mary Midgley, *Evolution as a Religion*, op. cit. note 5, 178.
[27] Op. cit. note 5, 170.

destiny'.[28] This more relational and holistic way of thinking may not always be forefront in our visions. Yet, she believes it is essential to replace atomistic visions with more holistic and connective ones if we wish to alter our treatment of the nonhuman world. This, again, is because our visions are 'crucial for our moral attitude. When this larger imaginative vision changes, the light in which we see all our various concerns is altered. Priorities shift, carrying a corresponding change in duties'.[29]

People can and often do look to this wider horizon. As parts of the wider community of life, the fates of other beings need not be a matter of indifference to us. In fact, we often feel and express this connection to the greater whole. Midgley expands:

> You feel akin to the whole thing. And that, I think, is probably a central point. We rejoice in the whole of nature and being part of it, as something to which we belong. It follows that if some important part of it is threatened, then we take alarm, as if for ourselves, so to speak, but presumably in proportion. Nature is a whole of which we are quite a small part. ... If we hear news of the destruction of a forest, the point is it is not something totally alien to us. It's not something to throw away like last month's newspapers. It concerns us. It's how we identify ourselves, isn't it? What we feel ourselves to be. People, surely, mostly, have thought of themselves as a small part of something much larger.[30]

Given this relational and holistic emphasis, Midgley gravitates toward more ecosystemic ways of envisioning nature. These approaches, which focus on the interconnection and interdependence of organisms, positive feedback mechanisms, and local and global patterns of natural systems, tend to go much farther than atomistic and mechanistic approaches in capturing the dynamism and vitality of the natural world and its entangled constituents.[31] And,

[28] *Midgley, Science and Poetry*, op. cit. note 14, 20.

[29] Mary Midgley, *Utopias, Dolphins and Computers*, op. cit. note 18, 124.

[30] Mary Midgley, Interview by Gregory S. McElwain, March 6, 2011, in Newcastle Upon Tyne, UK.

[31] Donald Worster examines the extent to which organicist visions of nature influence ethics in *Nature's Economy: A History of Ecological Ideas (Studies in Environment and History)*, 2nd ed. (Cambridge: Cambridge University Press, [1977] 1994). See also C. J. Glacken, *Traces on the Rhodian Shore: Nature and Culture in Western Thought from Ancient Times to the End of the Eighteenth Century* (Berkeley: University of California Press, 1967).

significantly, rather than treating wholes and collectives as mere aggregates of individuals, holistic and ecosystemic approaches recognize that 'wholes and parts are equally real', and that each is unintelligible without the other.[32]

One such vision that integrates ecosystemic thinking on the largest scale is the notion of Gaia. Originally advanced by James Lovelock, Gaia is a scientific vision that sees 'Earth and the life on it as an active, self-maintaining whole'.[33] Gaian theory, which draws its name from the ancient Greek earth goddess, maintains that this great whole is constituted by the totality of systems and their organic and inorganic parts, all of which are connected to all others through complex webs of interactions and dependencies. From local interactions between organisms and their environments to global weather patterns and currents (such as the massive flows of Saharan dust to the Amazon basin and the Amazon's 'Rivers in the Sky'), the earth can seem like a vibrant, active organism. Life, in this picture, is not simply 'a loose, chance jumble of competing entities but an interdependent system, a symbiotic whole that keeps itself going by a constant interchange of benefits between its parts'.[34]

Midgley employs the concept of Gaia as a *metaphor* for understanding the interconnections of the earth as a whole. She argues that Gaian thinking, as something of a readymade holistic vision, is one way among many – including atomistic and mechanistic models – of picturing the world. And, given the global climate crisis, she suggests that this type of vision might help us in understanding our role and impact on the earth. That is, the whole system, in these approaches, is vulnerable. This vulnerability does not mean that the system can be destroyed, but rather that it can, in its current state, be damaged or altered in response to stimuli (i.e., human intervention and harm). And, on a more ominous note, will carry on in whatever state, with or without *us*. Thinking in these more global, interdependent terms is a direct counter to the hubristic view that humans – and, furthermore, individuals – are at the center of the cosmos.

32 Mary Midgley, *Science and Poetry*, op. cit. note 14, 258. Emphasis removed.

33 Mary Midgley, 'Introduction: The Not-So-Simple Earth,' in *Earthy Realism: The Meaning of Gaia*, ed. Mary Midgley (Exeter: Imprint Academic, 2007), 3. See James Lovelock, *Gaia: A New Look at Life on Earth*, 3rd ed. (Oxford: Oxford University Press, [1979] 2000).

34 Mary Midgley, 'Visions, Secular and Sacred', *The Hastings Center Report* 25, no. 5 (1995), 26.

Holistic thinking, in this way, might help us out of some of our more abstractionist and exploitative visions. 'I regard [Gaia]', Midgley reiterates, 'as a *myth* about the earth, and a good myth, that the Greeks and many others have had of the earth as a parental relation to us. This means that we *owe* it a great deal. … It's not just something that we have been given to work with'.[35] This relational view of the earth, she emphasizes, is 'pretty important because people really do need this sort of inclusive place within which everything takes place. We really do need the unity'.[36] There are, of course, a number of ways to conceive of this wholeness and connectivity, but, regardless of the exact language or metaphors used, Midgley argues that these holistic concepts better capture the collectives or wholes in which we live, as well as our interdependence with them. Nature is not our 'static background', but the whole of which we are part. Seeing ourselves as part of this larger community is not fantasy, but a reasonable understanding of the earth's systems and inhabitants.

4. Conclusion

Given the length and scope of this paper, I cannot offer an exhaustive account of Midgley's relational account of human nature and the self. My goal has been to provide an overview of her critique and construction in such a way that makes apparent the unity of her expansive work without forcing it into one simple narrative. The relational (and holistic) element is, again, one of many unifying threads in her thought. Yet, it is an influential thread that grows out of her resistance to visions that unrealistically fragment notions of human nature, the self, and our place in the world. As such, she emphasizes our intrinsically relational nature as social animals as a sort of antidote to these imbalanced visions. This approach, consequently, has the added benefit of encouraging us to re-envision, re-think, or maybe even discover significant features of our moral landscape. Midgley's animal and environmental thought, with its relational and holistic overtones, does just this by encouraging us to revise our visions in ways that more fully account for what matters in the world.

The College of Idaho
gmcelwain@collegeofidaho.edu

[35] Mary Midgley, Interview by Gregory S. McElwain, May 26, 2015, in Newcastle Upon Tyne, UK.

[36] Mary Midgley, Interview by Gregory S. McElwain, October 23, 2017, in Newcastle Upon Tyne, UK.

‘Removing the Barriers’: Mary Midgley on Concern for Animals

DAVID E. COOPER

Abstract
This paper focuses on Mary Midgley’s influential discussions, over more than thirty years, of the relationship between human beings and animals, in particular on her concern to ‘remove the barriers’ that stand in the way of proper understanding and treatment of animals. These barriers, she demonstrates, have been erected by animal science, epistemology and mainstream moral philosophy alike. In each case, she argues, our attitudes to animals are warped by approaches that are at once excessively abstract, over-theoretical and guilty of a collective hubris on the part of humankind. In keeping with Midgley’s own position, it is argued in this paper that, to remove these barriers, what is required is not yet another theory of how and why animals matter, but attention to actual engagements with animals and to the moral failings or vices that distort people’s relationships with them.

1. Introduction

‘We are animals’.[1,2] ‘No human has ever been anything but an animal’.[3] These two remarks are, respectively, from the beginning of Mary Midgley first book, *Beast and Man*, published in 1978, and the start of the last paper she wrote on animals thirty-four years later. They serve as bookends, as it were, to the many writings in-between that indicate Midgley’s abiding interest in the relationship between human beings and non-human animals. These writings

[1] References are to the following writings of Mary Midgley: *Beast and Man: The Roots of Human Nature* (BM) (London: Methuen, 1980); *Animals and Why They Matter* (AWM) (London: Penguin, 1983); ‘Persons and Non-Persons’ (PN), in P. Singer (ed.), *In Defence of Animals* (Oxford: Blackwell, 1985), 52–63; ‘Should We Let Them Go?’ (SW), in F. Dolins (ed.), *Attitudes to Animals: Views in Animal Welfare* (Cambridge: Cambridge University Press, 1999), 152–63; ‘Why Farm Animals Matter’ (WF), in M. Dawkins and R. Bonney (eds.), *The Future of Animals Farming: Renewing the Ancient Contract* (Oxford: Blackwell, 2008), 21–32; ‘On Being an Anthrozoon: How Unique Are We?’ (OBA), *Minding Nature* 5 (2012), 1–16.

[2] Op. cit. note 1, BM, xiii.

[3] Op. cit. note 1, OBA, 1.

doi:10.1017/S1358246119000213

ranged widely over a great variety of topics. These range from such general philosophical questions as 'Why do animals matter?' and 'Are animals persons?' to specific issues of animal welfare – those raised by factory farming, for example, or by the confinement of animals in zoos.

Midgley's attention to questions surrounding animals was not incidental to, or hived off from, her wider philosophical concerns. Indeed, it will become apparent in this paper, I hope, that her criticisms of various distorted views about animals are of a piece both with her powerful rejection of scientism and other 'myths we live by', and with her repeated lament for the atrophy in the modern world of wonder and a sense of cosmic humility.

The clarity and forcefulness of Midgley's writings on animals have ensured their considerable influence, both in the world of animal welfare and upon many philosophers, myself included, whose thinking about animals has been decisively shaped by these writings. The environmental philosopher, J. Baird Callicott, for example, refers to Midgley's 'marvellous insight' into the ways humans and animals form 'communities' together, and to the promise this insight offers for a rapprochement between the typically individualistic aims of 'animal liberation' and the more holistic ones of environmental ethics.[4]

Despite such testimonies to Midgley's influence, however, she has not been cited and discussed in the professional literature of animal ethics with anything approaching the frequency of some other contemporary philosophers, such as Peter Singer and Tom Regan. The reason for this, as I intend to demonstrate, is that she critically distances herself from the mainstream or orthodox approaches adopted by such authors.

I shall be focusing on two themes that are central in Midgley's writings on animals, each of them belonging to her abiding ambition to 'remove the barriers' that, as she sees it, have been 'erected against concern for animals'.[5] The first theme is an epistemological one, relating to the understanding of animal lives. It consists of a critique of behaviourism, 'ritual scepticism' and other refusals to accept that many animals indubitably enjoy a rich subjective life that we are able at least partly to understand. The second theme is an ethical one, and takes the form of a rejection of what deserve to be called 'mainstream' approaches in animal ethics, including utilitarianism and moral theories in which the central notions are rights, justice and equality.

[4] J. Baird Callicott, 'Animal liberation and environmental ethics: back together again', *Between the Species* 4 (1988), 163–9.

[5] Op. cit. note 1, AWM, 144.

I speak of there being two themes in Midgley's writings, but it is important, I shall argue, to recognise how closely connected they are for her. Both behaviourism and its relatives and mainstream moral theories are made possible and encouraged by similar mind-sets, and it is these that must be exposed and rejected if progress is to be made in our understanding and treatment of animals.

2. Are human beings animals?

Before turning to these two themes, however, I want to respond to the worry some people might have that, in highlighting these themes, I am ignoring what they might regard as the paramount claim that Midgley makes in her writings on animals. This is the claim, encountered in the two remarks of hers with which I began, that human beings *are* – or are not 'anything but' – animals. In responding to this worry, I am, in effect, registering one of the very few points on which I disagree with Midgley.

In my judgement, the question of whether humans are animals is best left aside. Coolly regarded the question is a dull one. In one obvious sense, human beings are indeed a kind of animal. They ingest food, they metabolise, they move themselves around, and so on. They have the kinds of properties, that is, that biologists identify when distinguishing animals from vegetables. But, in an equally obvious sense, human beings are not animals. This is the familiar sense, as it is defined in the OED, of being 'a brute or beast, as distinguished from man'. Clearly, too, it is this second sense that is operative in many, perhaps most, ordinary conversational contexts. If I tell you that there are some animals in my neighbours' garden, then you'll immediately judge that I was not speaking literally – but jokingly, perhaps insultingly – when you realise I am referring to the neighbours' children.

'Humans are (just) animals!' is, in effect, a slogan, and the only question is whether it is a good one. It is surely wrong to suppose, as many champions of it do, that by endorsing the slogan one indicates that our differences from animals are vastly outweighed by our similarities to them. Peter Hacker begins his book, *Human Nature*, with the words 'Human beings are animals ...', but immediately adds the qualification '... with a distinctive range of abilities'.[6] His book then focuses on just these distinctive abilities, including

[6] Peter Hacker *Human Nature: The Categorial Framework* (Oxford: Wiley-Blackwell, 2010), 1.

cognitive and linguistic ones, and argues that the differences between us and any other animals are, in fact, much greater than many scientists and philosophers imagine.

It is a mistake, too, to suppose, as its champions usually do, that the slogan must register and inspire a tender moral concern for animals in a way that the counter slogan, the denial that humans are animals, cannot. Social Darwinists thought that, as just one species of animal among others, humankind was engaged in a red in tooth and claw struggle for survival and supremacy with other species. Nothing tender-hearted here. Conversely, The Buddha and St Francis of Assisi emphatically denied that human beings are just a kind of animal, but are rightly esteemed for their compassion for animals.

Probably, we are better off without any slogans and counter slogans here. But if someone is wedded to the claim that human beings are (just) animals, then he or she should not be blinded to the salient and deep differences that exist between people and (other) animals. An important reason for being alert to these differences is that some uniquely human capacities need to be emphasised in any proper appraisal of our treatment of animals – the capacities, for example, for hubris, wilful ignorance, hardness of heart, vanity, self-deception, and the recreational enjoyment of killing other creatures.

To be sure, these are not distinctive aspects of humankind that Mary Midgley pastes over. On the contrary, as we shall see, she constantly reminds us of them. But this, it seems to me, is despite, and not because of, her insistence that humans are nothing but animals. So let's return, with slogans set aside, to what I identified as the main themes in her writings on animals.

3. Animals and epistemology

When I sketched those two themes earlier, I indicated that, for Midgley, they are closely related. Each of her critical targets – epistemological and ethical – exhibits, in her view, the same general defects. They are both, for a start, overly theoretical and abstract, the products of a failure of attention to the actual engagements people have with animals in real life. Second, they are both guilty of hubris, of an unwarranted elevation of humankind over other species. Midgley was well aware of the connection between her two themes. It is through engaging with animals that we can 'grasp more fully how their lives work', and doing so also and 'inevitably gives us a sense of fellowship with them' – an acquaintance that is not only incompatible with hubris but inspires further engagement with animals and hence deeper understanding of them.[7]

Let's begin with the epistemological theme – with, that is, Midgley's criticisms of the behaviourist or sceptical 'idea that the subjective feelings [and mental life, more generally] of animals are ... quite hidden from us, cannot concern us and may not even exist'.[8] In two ways, she argues, this idea betrays a surfeit of theorising and a corresponding deficit of common sense realism. First, the idea typically relies on loading ordinary concepts – including those of understanding, belief, hope, and concept itself – with theoretical baggage that they do not carry in everyday talk and practice. Midgley singles out for special criticism the insistence that no creature can count as believing or hoping for anything unless it can give linguistic expression to the belief or hope.[9] From this insistence, together with a suitably demanding notion of what counts as language, it follows that animals cannot believe or hope – or at any rate, that we can have no good reason to think they do.

Midgley's response to this idea is blunt. 'Neither with dog nor human do we need words to reveal to us what expressive and interpretative capacities far older and far deeper than words make clear immediately'.[10] Put differently, the abilities of humans and animals alike both to express and to recognise beliefs, hopes and many other ingredients of mental life predate and are presupposed by the use of a psychological vocabulary. More generally, she argues that the application of everyday mental concepts is determined not by theoretical accounts of, say, understanding or emotion, but in and through practices of engagement with people or animals.

Second, Midgley argues that the scepticism of behaviourists and their cousins towards the mental life of animals is a 'ritual scepticism' – an 'artificial', 'hollow' and 'unreal' one to which no more than lip-service can be paid.[11] It is not a stance that people who actually engage with animals – vets, trainers and the like – can genuinely adopt. She points out that even ethologists and biologists, like Nikolaas Tinbergen, who seem to feel obliged to proclaim a ritual scepticism in the prefaces to their books soon put it aside when they get down to recording their experiences of and with animals.

7 Op. cit. note 1, AWM 14.
8 Op. cit. note 1, AWM 115.
9 Op. cit. note 1, AWM 57.
10 Op. cit. note 1, AWM 59.
11 Op. cit. note 1, SW 157–9.

This scepticism, Midgley continues, is not only incompatible with what people who live with animals surely know, for example that cutting off the tail of a puppy hurts it. It is incompatible as well with any skilful intercourse with animals. A sceptical mahout who decided that it was a matter of mere speculation whether his elephant could really be angry, suspicious, pleased or excited would soon either be out of a job or dead.[12] Attributing subjectivity to animals – seeing their behaviour as, for instance, manifesting emotions and understanding – is a precondition of intelligent practical dealings with them. Proclamations of scepticism are possible only for detached observers for whom the movements, gestures, cries and faces of animals – or, indeed, of men and women – are 'data' from which it is problematic to infer to the presence of emotions, moods, beliefs and so on. By contrast, for the vet, the pet owner, the dog trainer – for people, that is, whose lives are spent in the company of animals – the thought that there is anything problematic here is an idle one.

Midgley has another, and morally-charged, criticism of behaviourism and its cousins. In her judgement, they betray a kind of collective hubris on the part of humankind. They both feed and feed *on* a sense of a human uniqueness and separation from the rest of life on earth that places us far above the animals. This is a sense that, for some people, may in itself be gratifying, serving to boost their self-image. But it serves as well to help 'establish that we have a right to exploit other creatures'[13], and to encourage a perception of them as 'things' or 'products' for human use.[14]

There are, of course, striking examples from the history of religion of the elevation of human beings over all other creatures. They alone are made in the image of God, we hear, or are the very purpose of His creation, or are uniquely capable of liberation from the cycle of rebirth – and so on. But Midgley's focus is on a more modern form of hubris. Science, as she sees it, has inherited the hubris of religion, to the degree indeed that, as she notes with some irony, such champions of the sciences as Auguste Comte and Julian Huxley actually commandeer the term 'religious' to express the unbounded enthusiasm they want to arouse in us for the scientific enterprise.

For Midgley, this 'anthropolatry' or human 'self-worship' – this faith in the humankind as the culmination of evolution and masters of the universe who, as J.D. Bernal anticipated, will turn the stars into 'efficient heat-machines' – represents an 'absurd over-estimate

[12] Op. cit. note 1, AWM 115.

[13] Op. cit. note 1, OBA 10.

[14] Op. cit. note 1, WF 12.

of human separateness and superiority'.[15] It is an exaggeration that behaviourism and its allies exploit and reinforce. For how better to relegate the beasts than to insist that, even if they are possessed of some feelings and intelligence, their mental or subjective life is meagre and impoverished? This is a relegation that serves, in turn, to justify what would otherwise seem to be cruel treatment of animals.

It is no accident, Midgley argues, that it is in technologically and scientifically informed practices involving animals – animal experimentation, genetic engineering of farm animals, and so on – that we most frequently encounter the many 'distancing devices' that people employ to disguise, perhaps from themselves, the reality and import of these practices. It is much easier, she implies, to run a battery farm or work in an animal research laboratory if you think of a chicken as 'a very efficient converting machine' or of a rat as 'a standardised biological research tool'[16]. And, as Michel de Montaigne for one would agree, it is only a vainglorious, hubristic species that could describe other creatures in these terms.

4. Animals and ethics

The second main theme I identified in Mary Midgley's writings on animals is her rejection of what she and I call the 'mainstream' approach in modern animal ethics. The following, I suggest, is a recognisable sketch of the dominant, mainstream approach in animal ethics that is shared by various well-subscribed theories – utilitarian and rights-based ones included:-

> 'How animals should be treated and regarded depends on their possession of 'moral status' or 'moral considerability'. For them to possess this, animals must have features that are identical or relevantly similar to those in virtue of which we human beings have moral status or considerability. They must, for example, be sentient and capable of pleasure and pain, or be at least relatively autonomous 'subjects of a life', or be parties to an implicit social contract – and so on. Failure of moral regard for animals if they really have such features, as many of them surely do, is a violation of principles of equality, justice and indeed reason. The failure would constitute a form of discrimination, manifesting a

[15] Op. cit. note 1, OBA 10, 12.
[16] Op. cit. note 1, AWM 80.

'speciesist' attitude comparable to racist or ageist ones that ignore the moral status of certain human beings.'

The central idea here is often explained and supported with the help of the image of an 'expanding moral circle'. Moral regard, the story goes, begins at home, as it were – with one's family and friends. But people are compelled by logic to extend this regard to any other beings who are relevantly similar to family and friends. And gradually it has been extended. Historically, it may have taken a long time for the circle to expand so as to include all human beings and not just one's fellow tribesmen, say, or people of the same race as oneself. And it may yet take a long time for animals to be brought securely within the circumference of the circle. The circle's expansion is, in effect, a history of the power of reason: for it marks the gradual appreciation that it is irrational to regard this or that irrelevant difference between different groups of people, or between human beings and other creatures, as a ground for withholding moral regard.

Midgley is not, of course, 'against' moral theory if, by this, is simply meant philosophical reflection on moral concepts, or on 'the rules and principles, standards and ideals, that emerge' in our efforts to 'guide ourselves through the jungle of the human condition'.[17] But there is a kind of moral theorising that takes the form of producing 'highly abstract theories' and 'sweeping generalisations', and this, she thinks, 'gives philosophy a bad name, and rightly so'.[18] For Midgley, crucially, mainstream moral theories in animal ethics of the kind sketched earlier are of precisely this kind.

Bluntly put, the abstractions of mainstream theories betray a lack of realism and a failure of proper attention to the contexts, facts and details of our complex relationships with animals. (Her charge, here, is parallel, of course, to her epistemological complaint against behaviourism and related attitudes.) This lack of realism is perfectly illustrated, for Midgley, by the image of the expanding moral circle that I described above, an image constantly invoked by mainstream animal ethicists. Far from regard for animals being a very late and still emerging episode in the history of moral development, all societies have always been, to a greater or lesser degree, 'mixed' or 'multi-species' ones in which at least some – often, very many – animals have been regarded as fellow members of human communities to which duties of care and decency of treatment are owed.

[17] Op. cit. note 1, BM 169.
[18] Op. cit. note 1, SW 161-2.

Indeed, the further we go back – to, say, various totemic or nomadic societies – the greater tend to be the moral links and 'fellowship' between beast and man. In many of these societies, moreover, some animals were the subjects of a significantly greater moral regard than were some human beings. Duties might be owed, for example, to a tribe's totemic animal, such as a bear or eagle, that are not owed to people from a different tribe. The idea that the story of morality can be represented by 'concentric circles' that gradually grow outwards to include neighbours, women, slaves, foreigners and, eventually, animals, is a historical nonsense.[19]

This unrealistic image is encouraged by the tendency of mainstream theorists to wrench moral concepts like respect, dignity, rights and person from the actual contexts in which they obtain their sense and force and to turn them, instead, into abstractions. (The parallel with a similar tendency on the part of behaviourists, ritual sceptics and the like is again obvious.) The idea, for example, that all mammals – mammals as such – are in effect persons, possessed of dignity and rights, and thereby deserving of respect, would be unintelligible to hunter-gatherer peoples whose respect for, say, bears owes to their particular relationship to these animals. The idea would be equally alien to tribespeople who count as persons only those animals with whom they share a communal life, or to farmers whose dogs, horses and oxen have a dignity that is earned and manifested through the uncomplaining work they do, or indeed to pet owners whose pets have rights that other animals do not precisely through being their pets, creatures for whom they care and share their home with.[20]

Wrenched out of their real life contexts, moreover, talk of animal rights, dignity and the like is hollow, its implications for the treatment of animals entirely opaque. For example, 'the word *right* ... cannot be salvaged for any clear, unambiguous use' once abstracted from concrete relationships between animals and people in actual societies.[21] The respect the hunter-gatherer has for the bears that share his environment is one that makes a difference to how he will act

[19] Op. cit. note 1, AWM 110-1. On the shortcomings of the expanding circle image, see James Serpell, *In the Company of Animals: A Study of Human-Animal Relationships* (Oxford: Blackwell, 1986), and Gregory S. McElwain, 'The Mixed Community', in I.J. Kidd and L. McKinnell (eds.), *Science and Self: Animals, Evolution, and Ethics: Essays in Honour of Mary Midgley* (Abingdon: Routledge, 2016), 41–51.

[20] See op. cit. note 1, SW 160 on dignity, and AWM on pets.

[21] Op. cit. note 1, AWM 63.

towards bears – honouring it in death, perhaps. But a respect that people are urged to have for *all* animals, despite there being a connection with only a tiny number of them, is idle. Are we supposed to honour every animal who dies?

The claim, central to mainstream animal ethics, that it is discriminatory and hence irrational *not* to extend moral regard to all creatures that are relevantly similar or equal to ourselves itself suffers from its excessive abstractness. 'The notion of equality', notes Midgley, 'is a tool for rectifying injustices within a group', whose members count as equals, and 'not for widening that group'.[22] It is useless, therefore, to invoke the notion in support of treating certain animals as we treat human beings in the absence of a practical consensus that they are the equals of the latter.

More generally, the question of what counts as a 'relevant' similarity between humans and animals, or between some animals and others, cannot be separated from what, in practice, people *do* regard as relevant. The hunter-gatherer who extends to wolves the regard he has long had for bears isn't noticing some hitherto unnoticed similarity – in intelligence, say, or the capacity to feel pain – between wolves and bears. Rather, he is bringing wolves into the same sphere of practices and attitudes already occupied by bears. Wolves, one might say, now have a place, similar to that of bears, in the hunter-gatherer's form of life.

Invocation of allegedly relevant similarities is liable, too, to be idle in any attempt to modify people's ways of treating and regarding animals. There is little point in insisting that sentience, say, is a relevant similarity between beast and man to people who just don't see that, say, a mouse's susceptibility to pain has any significance – like the scientist, mentioned by Midgley, who, on being asked whether sentient animals should 'count at all' morally, replied no, 'why should they?'.[23] People whose forms of life have no place for moral concern for certain animals – mice, chickens, moles, snakes, or whatever – will greet the information that they have intelligence and feeling with a 'So what?', a shrug of the shoulders.

Midgley notes another reason why appeals to some very general similarity, like 'sensibility' and 'complexity of life', between people and animals are liable to be idle and leave the implications for practice obscure. The locust's sensibility and complexity are presumably less than the dog's, but there are a lot more locusts than dogs. With her tongue at least half in her cheek, she asks if the locust's 'joint

22 Op. cit. note 1, AWM 67.
23 Op. cit. note 1, AWM 10.

sensibility [should] outweigh that of a dog, or even the small human settlement' the insects are 'about to overwhelm'.[24] Instead of worrying about these and other unprofitable questions that mainstream moral theorising helps to generate, the focus should be on our practical relationships with animals and 'within the limits of what we can know and can try to do'.[25]

5. Hubris

There's a second kind of charge, a moral one, against mainstream theories that may be found in Midgley's writings, even if it is never made entirely explicit.The charge is parallel to the second criticism she made of behaviourism and related epistemological positions. Mainstream moral theories, she implies, reflect and encourage the collective hubris of humankind.

This may sound a strange, even perverse charge to bring against moral theorists who, typically, are 'on the side' of the animals, who genuinely want to extend the compass of moral concern so as to include animals and, like Midgley, to 'remove barriers'. The trouble, as Midgley sees it, with their approach is that, by focusing on the extension of rights and respect to animals – on, in effect, combatting irrational discrimination – issues of justice now 'monopolise attention'. What lies outside the sphere of justice therefore gets 'neglected'. Virtues like 'mercy and compassion', for example, 'begin to seem like mere matters of taste', desirable no doubt but, in comparison with attention to rights and justice, not central or entirely 'serious' components of a commitment to an enlightened morality.[26]

If mercy and compassion are marginalised or neglected by mainstream theorists, so too are the vices 'opposite to these virtues', such as harshness and cruelty.[27] And it is at this point that the charge of hubris enters in. The effect of the mainstream approach is to paint an unwarrantedly rosy picture of humankind. For, on this approach, the wrongfulness of our treatment of animals is a failure of information or of reason and consistency. It is due either to ignorance, a failure to note and recognise the relevant similarities between animals and ourselves, or to a failure to realise that these similarities entail the extension of moral regard to animals.

[24] Op. cit. note 1, SW 159.
[25] Op. cit. note 1, SW 159.
[26] Op. cit. note 1, AWM 50-1.
[27] Op. cit. note 1, AWM 50.

Now this is a picture that unduly flatters human beings. Entirely left out of this picture, Midgley remarks, are human 'greed, meanness, envy, cowardice, sloth, ingratitude' and the rest of our vices, including 'in most people's opinion, one of the worst vices ... cruelty'.[28] When all that gets 'lit up' by a moral theory are matters of injustice and discrimination, the impressively and depressingly large number of the remainder of our failings and vices remain out of sight and out of mind. And this, of course, suits us very nicely. Who wouldn't prefer to own up to deficiencies of knowledge or consistency than to admit to the catalogue of vices on Midgley's list? Instead of concentrating on confronting, for example, our meanness, vanity and brutality we can instead focus, more agreeably, on brushing up our logic. In this kind of self-exculpation of humankind, there is hubris and vanity. To the extent that mainstream ethics contributes to this self-exculpation, it is guilty of 'boosterishness', of helping to inflate our undeservedly high opinion of ourselves.[29]

6. Coda

With mainstream moral theorising in animal ethics rejected, what does Midgley want to replace it by? So entrenched in contemporary moral philosophy is the conviction that it can only proceed by way of constructing theories that, unsurprisingly, several commentators insist that Mary Midgley must herself be trying to replace mainstream theories by one of her own. Callicott, for instance, concedes that she does not 'elaborate a positive moral theory', but adds that she would surely 'if pressed ... sketch a Humean ethical theory ... grounded in feelings, not reason'.[30] Another writer claims that, despite her apparent denials, Midgley does have a theory of the 'moral status' of animals, albeit one that is 'grounded in *relationships* with people' rather than in intrinsic features of the animals themselves.[31]

It is true that Midgley that devotes considerable attention to the emotions that different people feel for different animals, and also to

[28] Op. cit. note 1, AWM 50.

[29] On 'boosterishness', see Alain de Botton's remarks in *Do Humankind's Best Days Lie Ahead?: Munk Debate* (London: OneWorld, 2015), 13.

[30] Op. cit. note 4, 165–6.

[31] David DeGrazia, *Animal Rights: A Very Short Introduction* (Oxford: Oxford University Press, 2002), 29.

the duties of care that come with certain relationships with animals, such as owning pets or raising them for meat. But it is a mistake, in my judgement, to construe any of this as indicating adherence to some moral theory. For Midgley, no theory is needed if by a theory is meant something that purports to give a general ground for why we should treat animals in some ways and not others. For her – as for the Buddha and (*pace* Callicott) David Hume – moral concern for animals is not *grounded* in anything. In particular, it is not grounded, as it is for mainstream theories, in an alleged moral status that animals possess. To be sure, a good person feels compassion and sympathy for animals that are suffering. But this feeling is not a *premise* from which to draw moral conclusions about how animals are to be treated. Again, good pet owners will properly care for their dogs and cats. But they do not do so because they think that animals as such are 'subjects of a life', beings that enjoy 'dignity', or anything else that, on the mainstream approach, is supposed to confer moral status on animals.

No syllogisms are required in order to judge how, in most cases, we should act towards an animal. 'Confronted with a flotilla of ducklings', writes Midgley, most people will just 'see' that things matter to animals and recognise without further ado that 'the way in which we treat these creatures matters' as well.[32] More generally, many of us simply 'see what we ought to be doing' in relation to animals and that there are many things we do to them that are 'glaringly and unmistakeably wrong'.[33] Some people, of course, do not see this, but in their case, no amount of insistence on the moral status of animals is going to be effective. Like the scientist quoted earlier, they just don't get that animals can matter.

The best way, for Midgley, of coming to 'see what we ought to be doing' to and for animals – to seeing that much of what we do is 'unmistakeably wrong' – is to recognise that all too often our behaviour manifests vices and human failings. Indeed, for her, what makes such treatment wrong is precisely that it does exemplify cruelty, greed, indifference and a depressingly large number of other failings. What is wrong with our treatment of animals is, one might say, *us*. Some of the most powerful passages in her writings on animals are those where Midgley draws attention to our refusal to admit to, or even discern, the vices that our treatment of animals betrays. To the list of vices I cited earlier, one could add those that serve to blind us to our failings, including themselves. They include self-deceit, bad

[32] Op. cit. note 1, WF 21.
[33] Op. cit. note 1, SW 159.

faith, mindlessness, and the kind of ritual 'objectivity' displayed by animal experimenters and others who pretend to doubt the reality of animal suffering.[34] In this last example, we begin to see how Midgley's denunciation of so many of our practices towards animals is integrated into her wider critique of a civilisation in which science dictates the boundaries of knowledge and economic, technological imperatives determine what is worth doing and what is allowable in the process of doing it.

Mary Midgley was too generous a person to second Mark Twain's verdict that, 'of all the creatures that were made, man is the most detestable'.[35] But she would, I am confident, endorse Montaigne's judgement that man is 'the most blighted and frail of all creatures', and the one 'most given to [a] pride' that prevents him from appreciating this.[36] In this collective hubris she recognised what is, perhaps, the greatest of the barriers to be removed in the endeavour to promote concern for animals.

Durham University
d.e.cooper@durham.ac.uk

[34] See David E. Cooper, *Animals and Misanthropy* (London: Routledge, 2018) on the vices and failings reflected in our treatment of animals.

[35] *What is Man? And Other Philosophical Writings* (Berkeley CA: University of California Press, 1973).

[36] *The Complete Essays* (London: Penguin, 1991), 505.

Evolution as a Religion: Mary Midgley's Hopes and Fears

ANTHONY O'HEAR

Abstract
This paper considers Mary Midgley's views on evolution, especially as developed in her book *Evolution as a Religion*. In this she continues the critical campaign she waged against Dawkins' notion of the selfish gene, but broadens her attack out to encompass many other thinkers (whom she calls the 'Omega' men), who are predicting dramatic and revolutionary futures for humanity, based supposedly on what evolutionary science tells us. Midgley argues that no such conclusions are scientifically warranted – hence evolution as a religion. Her own attempts to absolve Darwin himself from this sort of scientism, and to remove from him any taint of social Darwinism are criticised, particularly by reference to *The Descent of Man*. Something is then said about Midgley's own alternative view of nature and humanity, a more holistic view, which itself has religious overtones.

1. Introduction

Mary Midgley's own book on evolution is called *Evolution as a Religion: Strange Hopes and Stranger Fears*[1], and it was published in 1985, in the aftermath of her now famous run-in with Richard Dawkins on the 'selfish' gene back in 1979, which, it is worth remarking here, took place in the pages of *Philosophy*.[2] The locus of Midgley's attack was Dawkins' *The Selfish Gene*, published by Oxford University Press in 1976, before becoming a best selling paperback.[3]

Midgley later admitted to being intemperate in her original foray into 'gene juggling'. But, intemperately expressed or not, her point about talk about selfish genes involving a host of category mistakes is surely destructive of Dawkins' position, undermining the basic stance of his book. All to the good, one might think, given that the

[1] Mary Midgley, *Evolution as a Religion: Strange Hopes and Stranger Fears*, London: Methuen, 1985. Hereafter *ER*.

[2] Mary Midgley, 'Gene-Juggling', *Philosophy*, **54**, 1979, 439–58; Richard Dawkins, 'In defence of selfish genes', *Philosophy*, **56**, 1981, 556–73; Mary Midgley, 'Selfish genes and Social Darwinism', *Philosophy*, **58**, 1983, 365–77.

[3] Richard Dawkins, *The Selfish Gene*, Oxford University Press, 1976; paperback edition, London: Granada, 1978, and many subsequent editions.

doi:10.1017/S135824611900016X

Dawkins' view involves damaging misconceptions about human agency (we are 'prisoners' of our genes' or 'machines created by genes'), about life itself (a form of unbridled competition directed by unconscious strings of cellular matter – genes or DNA, and often single genes – actually manipulating our conscious thoughts and motivations for their own ends), and about human society and morality (in which we are born selfish, and in which genuine altruism morphs into so-called 'reciprocal altruism', a euphemism for Hobbesian prudential bargaining). While Midgley may have been intemperate in 1979, Dawkins and his views, including his later views on religion and on memes (ideological analogues of genes, which apparently colonise living human minds in much the same way that genes (abstract entities, as far as I can see) colonise living tissue), have gone from strength to strength in the public consciousness and in influence. Maybe Midgley in 1979 was not intemperate enough, because what she did then did little to stem the apparently unstoppable Dawkins surge; or more likely, maybe she did not get the support she should have received from her philosophical and academic colleagues, no doubt unwilling to back her – a then little known philosophy lecturer from Newcastle – against an eminent and fashionable Oxford scientist.

Evolution as a Religion does take up the earlier opposition to Dawkins, but it has a much larger agenda, as is suggested in the title. It attempts to analyse and criticise the way that the theory of evolution has, for many of its admirers, taken on a quasi-religious dimension. It has, for example, been used to develop a faith in the emergence of a kind of superman – Omega man – and his world, under the direction of scientists of the future who will bring this result about by genetic engineering and the development of artificial intelligence. Such figures as the biologist William Day, the geneticist J.H.Muller and the Marxist physicist J.D. Bernal are given as examples of this type of thinking, in Bernal's case leading to a new world in which scientists would 'emerge as a new species and leave humanity behind'. It cannot, of course, be said that tendencies of this sort have in any way declined since 1985; almost every day we hear yet another claim about a singularity, shortly to be upon us, in which artificial intelligence will supersede natural intelligence, or yet more extravagant claims about the potential genetic engineering has to rewrite human nature.

If anything, the critique offered by *Evolution as a Religion* is more relevant now than it was when it appeared. It is interesting to note that in her recent book *What is Philosophy For?*[4], Midgley spends a

[4] Mary Midgley, *What is Philosophy For?*, London: Bloomsbury, 2018.

good deal of space challenging the efforts of such luminaries as Ray Kurzweil and Martin (Lord) Rees to depict a future in which we will be dominated and manipulated by super-advanced or hyper computers, in Rees's case apparently even merging with them, in a future in which we will not be able to switch the machines off or challenge their awesome powers of intelligence.

All this, according to Midgley is at best a fable, though a fable still flourishing even more in 2018 than it was in the last century, at least among the semi-educated. Lord Rees is making much the same points even in 2018, in *On the Future*, a book clearly directed at the general reader which appeared in the same month as this paper was first given as a talk, and in his *Brief Answers to The Big Questions*, also out in late 2018 (and note the apparently innocent 'the' in the title), Stephen Hawking had similar things to say about a race of 'self-designing beings' morphing into hopefully benevolent immortal digital surrogates of us humans.[5] According to Midgley, fables of this sort, with their focus on AI – artificial machine generated 'intelligence' – misunderstand the multifarious nature of human intelligence, and rely on completely improbable and untestable predictions, and about which their proponents seem strangely complacent that were their fables true, they would be making themselves redundant. Apart from the point about human intelligence being highly protean, varied and context-specific, Midgley also points out that many aspects of human experience – intelligence of a practical sort – are involved in intelligent decision making, aspects which have in no serious way been or probably could be replicated in AI. She also makes the very Midgleyesque observation that unlike science fiction writers delving into such imaginary futures, Kurzweil, Rees and company woefully underdescribe the situations they are envisaging, or their implications for life and practice. And she might also have mentioned Karl Popper's master-argument about the impossibility of predicting the course of technological development, because if we could predict it with any degree of precision we would be able to do it now.[6] (And who, even ten years ago, could have predicted the current extraordinary proliferation of uses and abuses of the internet?)

[5] Martin Rees, *On the Future*, Princeton University Press, 2018; Stephen Hawking, *Brief Answers to The Big Questions,* London: John Murray, 2018.

[6] See Karl Popper, *The Poverty of Historicism*, London: Routledge and Kegan Paul, 1961 edition, vi-vii.

2. The Omega Men

In her initial criticism of the extravagance of evolutionary and AI utopians, what she calls the omega men, Midgley is anxious to dissociate Darwin himself entirely from any taint or influence. She tells us that Darwin detested the very name 'evolution' and denied that his theory carried with it any 'innate tendency to progressive development'.[7] Her book is indeed dedicated to 'The Memory of Charles Darwin Who Did Not Say These Things', and much of her own animus in the book is against the way that, in her opinion, Darwin's theory has been co-opted by thinkers such as Spencer and Galton into a full-blooded apologia for the merits of unbridled competition.

At this point we need to be careful. Darwin did not say some (many) of the things Midgley is objecting to, but when we come to the matters to do with what has come to be known as Social Darwinism and the concept of evolution itself, things are somewhat less clear. Part of the problem here is that Darwin himself is ambivalent on the progressive significance of his theory, and different commentators stress different aspects here. Thus, in line with Stephen Jay Gould, Midgley herself emphasises the modest interpretation of 'evolution', or rather, as Darwin preferred, 'descent with modification'. She points out that he thought that the idea of a linear, progressive evolution was vacuous; evolution was by no means uni-directional, but rather more like the development of a 'humble' bush, 'a rich radiation of varying forms, in which human qualities cannot, any more than others, determine a general direction for the whole'.[8] Midgley takes this Darwinian picture to stand in strong contrast to what she calls 'melodramas' like the Social Darwinist or Spencerian one, which became so influential in the years following the publication of *The Origin of Species* and, in various mutant forms, on into our own day, as Midgley's book illustrates.

One can indeed reinforce Midgley's general point here. In *Origin* Darwin appears reluctant to use the term 'evolution', preferring the more neutral 'descent with modification', and formally speaking he is correct to do so.[9] For what the theory of natural selection says is that in the struggle for existence better equipped competitors will outbreed and replace less well equipped ones. This replacement.strategy does not

[7] *ER* op. cit. note 1, 34.

[8] *ER* op. cit. note 1, 6.

[9] Charles Darwin, *The Origin of Species*, cited here in the Penguin, 1982 edition, edited by J.W. Burrow (Harmondsworth: Penguin, 1982).

require progress in any sense other than that of surviving better and reproducing more. As Darwin himself points out, this is actually consistent with losing capacities and even organs which are costly, but which provide no selective advantage. (Flightlessness in birds unthreatened by rodents; loss of sight in cave dwelling creatures.) The basic point is that in the absence of certain types of threat, it will actually be disadvantageous to develop along particular lines, costly in terms of the need for nutrition or in disproportionally heavy limbs or organs, for example, even if from some other point of view (ours, perhaps) those lines might seem superior. But that is not the point of view of Darwin or implicit in his theory.

Or so it might seem, so long as we stick to the main text of *Origin* and overlook its last three paragraphs. The third last paragraph is short, and enigmatic: 'In the distant future I see open fields for far more important researchers. Psychology will be based on a new foundation, that of the necessary acquirement of each mental power and capacity by gradation. *Light will be thrown on the origin of man and his history*' (my italics).[10] Objectionable as Day, Muller, Bernal and their associates – the Omega men – might be, in the light of Darwin's talk of a distant future and of the necessary acquirement of each mental power and capacity it would be unfair to accuse them of being wholly un-Darwinian.

Social Darwinism we will return to, but for now I will just note the italicised sentence, about light being thrown on man and his history. Man, as a species, is not mentioned in *Origin* before this point, but he is clearly lurking in the background, or perhaps rather more than that – as emerged in the ensuing controversies. Everyone knew that what evolution (or descent with modification) meant would have huge implications for our thinking about ourselves, implications spelled out, as we will see in *The Descent of Man*, to which I regret that Midgley paid scant attention in *Evolution as a Religion*.[11]

To return to *Origin*, the penultimate paragraph concludes 'And as natural selection works solely by and for the good of each being, all corporeal and mental endowments will tend to progress towards perfection', which is hardly a modest claim about a humble bush branching out in indefinite and random directions. And in case we were still thinking that Darwin's view encompasses a modest agnosticism regarding perfection, I will simply quote *Origin*'s concluding two sentences: 'Thus, from the war of nature, from famine and death,

[10] Op. cit. note 9, 458–60.

[11] Charles Darwin, *The Descent of Man*, 2nd edition, London: John Murray, 1898.

the most exalted object which we are capable of conceiving, namely the production of the higher (note) animals, directly follows. There is a grandeur in the view of life, with its several powers, having been originally breathed into a few forms or into one; and that, whilst this planet has gone cycling on according to the fixed law of gravity, that from so simple a beginning endless forms most beautiful and most wonderful have been, and are being, evolved'. Apart from the point that all these wonderful results follow from a ceaseless war of nature (competition), it is significant that the very last word in the book is 'evolved'. Whatever Darwin's own linguistic and theoretical austerity in the body of his text, there can be no doubt that he saw himself as propounding not just a theory of *evolution*, but also one charged with progressivist implications, which he himself took to follow from the theory. Indeed Darwin's own position here is, as we have just seen, at the very least a mild version of the Escalator view which Midgley attacks in her book, that is the view that she dubs the 'irresistible escalator', the notion that evolution is set on a road that leads to inevitable and continuous improvement. That this road encompasses us humans too is made clear by Darwin himself when he wrote in a letter to Lyell on April 27th 1860 that he hoped that there would come a time when, through generations of moral and intellectual training, human beings would come to look at the thought of his time, including his own and Lyell's presumably, as that of 'mere barbarians'.[12] I can't go into epistemological implications of this thought here, save to remark that to his credit Darwin was clearly anticipating the pessimistic meta-induction of contemporary philosophy of science by a century and a half.

Do we in fact detect a slight ambivalence on this point in Midgley herself? While wanting to dissociate Darwin from the futurism of the omega men, in *What is Philosophy For?* Midgley is keen to emphasise that Darwinian thought involves co-operation between and within species and also within whole organisms, as part of evolutionary development, so it is not simply a matter of selfish genes competing ruthlessly at an atomistic level. But, over and above that, following biologists such as Simon Conway Morris, she argues that there is convergence in evolution, with drifts within different species to such capacities as increased awareness and towards what Conway Morris refers to as islands of 'biological habitability', the classic case being the separate development of the eye in a number of different species. Against austere descent with modification, we can, then,

[12] Charles Darwin (ed, Francis Darwin and A.C. Seward), *More Letters of Charles Darwin*, London: John Murray, 1903, Vol II, 30.

see in evolutionary development a directedness of sorts, providing we do not interpret this as a progress to a single over-arching goal. We can on occasion ask which 'way of living is life aiming at here?' We can speak of increased awareness as being important and valuable for living creatures, and so highly probable in evolutionary development, though whether this value is instrumental or intrinsic (as some might see it) Midgley does not say.

Darwinian qualifications and even concessions to a degree of directnedness in evolution do not, of course, imply that Darwin would have had any truck with the futuristic people Midgley singles out. Darwin does not say anything specific enough on the broad picture of progressive evolutionary development, and unlike the authors Midgley singles out for attack in her book, he may well have been suitably cautious about predicting in any detail the future course of evolutionary development. But, despite the impression given by Midgley, Darwin does say quite a lot, in some detail, on the immediate social consequences of his view, and what he says is not nearly as far from what she dubs 'Social Darwinism' as she might like. Thus, for example, Midgley describes the view that 'life has been scientifically proved to be essentially competitive... an individualistic law showing such things as co-operation, love and altruism to be unreal' as nonsense, at the same time as dissociating Darwin from the idea that evolution is a steady process of improvement to a single point, which, she says did not convince Darwin at all.[13]

Actually, the last point aside (about a single point of direction), Darwin did acknowledge considerable difficulty, as he wrestled with the implications of his theory for social policy: wrestled – he certainly did not take the view that life was essentially competitive to be nonsense. The third chapter of *Origin* is actually entitled 'Struggle for Existence', and in it he tells us that every organic being is striving to the utmost to increase in numbers, that each lives by a struggle at some period of its life and that heavy destruction inevitably falls on either young or old during each generation, or at current intervals. And he rounds off this bleak picture with a strange and unsettling image: 'the face of nature may be compared to a yielding surface, with ten thousand sharp wedges packed close together and driven by incessant blows, sometimes one wedge being struck, and then another with greater force'.[14] It is noteworthy that in his own pre-publication notebook the phrase 'by incessant blows' is followed by talk of the blows being accompanied by 'a

[13] *ER* op. cit. note 1, 6.
[14] Op. cit. note 9, 119.

forcing out of others'. Maybe Darwin felt that this thought was too brutal for the general public, but it is certainly consistent with the general drift of Chapter 3, and indeed of *Origin* as a whole. Nor in *Origin* did he reject all or any form of the progressive interpretation, as we have seen.

3. Darwin's Progressivism

Moving away from nature as a whole, what he did think – alarmingly perhaps to us to-day – was that there were tendencies in his own society which, if unchecked, would impede progress, and these tendencies were precisely the ones of love, cooperation, compassion and altruism which characterised contemporary Christian morality, that espoused by Bishop Sam Wilberforce, the supposed loser in the Oxford Union debate. It is interesting that T.H.Huxley, Darwin's 'bulldog' in the debate, rejected what came to be known as Social Darwinism, arguing that in civilised society, altruistic virtues came into play, replacing the unbridled competition of the 'survival of the fittest'. The problem is how to make this no doubt admirable view consistent with Darwin's own theory, a point which ultimately led Alfred Russel Wallace to postulate divine intervention in the formation of human nature, making humanity discontinuous from the animals to which evolution and natural selection applied.

The first uncomfortable aspect of Darwin's thinking about human nature is its unqualified progressivism, which is something actually present in his thinking ever since his encounter with Tierra del Fuegians on the Beagle voyage as early as 1832. He wrote in his diary for December 17th of that year that the difference between savage and civilised man was greater than that between wild and domesticated animals, 'inasmuch as in man there is a greater power of improvement'. By the time he came to write *The Descent of Man* in 1871, this view had hardened: 'They possessed hardly any arts, and like wild animals lived on what they could catch; they had no government, and were merciless to everyone not of their tribe'. Darwin goes on to aver that he would rather be descended from a monkey or a baboon who manifested traits of loyalty and self-sacrifice as from a 'savage who delights to torture his enemies, offers up bloody sacrifices, practices infanticide without remorse, treats his wives like slaves, knows no decency and is haunted by the grossest superstitions'.[15] Darwin also (unfortunately) spends a whole chapter in

[15] Op. cit. note 11, Vol II, 440.

Descent to explaining how inferior races have been supplanted by superior ones, and even at the present day 'civilised nations are everywhere supplanting barbarous' ones.[16] He explains this as being due to the working out through natural selection of the effects of better intellectual and moral faculties and sensibilities (though quite how moral sensibilities are supposed to help is unclear, given that their development may well lead to decadence and decline, as we will see). And he also points out that human development is not from a basic level, from which some races declined, but is rather an ascent from lower forms of humanity, which are progressively supplanted by higher forms.

A significant aspect of Darwin's view of human development is that, like some of the thinkers Midgley attacks, it is an escalator view (though without their extravagance), as we have already seen. Darwin hopes that our successors, 500 years further up the escalator, will be inclined to treat our science like we treat that of the medievals, or even like the superstitions of the Tierra del Fuegians, but what we need to look at now is Darwin's social doctrine. We have seen that he sees mankind on an escalator of progress, but he is worried that we could slip off this escalator if we do not take sufficient care to follow the logic of natural selection. That his Victorian contemporaries might not be taking sufficient care worries him. In *Descent* he notices a tendency for the unfit, the inferior 'in body and mind', and even the abject poor to breed. If mankind is to advance, we must uncover the laws of inheritance, and then legislate against marriages among the biologically inferior. We must not encourage the poor to marry, because abject poverty 'tends to its own increase by leading to recklessness in marriage'. To counterbalance this, we have to encourage the prudent and the able to rear the largest number of offspring. 'Man, like every other animal, has no doubt advanced to his present high condition through a struggle for existence consequent on his rapid multiplication; if it is to advance further, it is to be feared that he must remain subject to a severe struggle.' Above all we must ensure that the struggle for existence is not softened in its severity by well-intentioned laws and customs – there must continue to be 'open competition for all men': 'otherwise (mankind) would sink into indolence, and the more gifted men would not be more successful in the battle of life than the less gifted'.[17]

[16] Op. cit. note 11, Vol I, 197.

[17] All the quotations in this paragraph are from Darwin's 'General Summary' at the end of *Descent*, op. cit. note 11, Vol II, 438–40.

Mary Midgely inveighs against what she calls the 'egoistic myth of universal cut-throat competition'[18], and against 'an unrealistic acceptance of competitiveness as central to human nature'. Indeed much of her animus against the omega men, and indeed against social contract theorists such as Hobbes is against their advocacy of individualism and free-market competiveness. No doubt there are all sorts of objections to such views, which do in fact allow for a degree of co-operation where that enhances mutual survival. Once again much more could be said here, but in the light of the passages from *Descent* we have just been looking at, that a stress on the necessity for competition is in tension with Darwinian biology is not one of them.

There is, indeed, some conflict in Darwin himself personally at this point. We have seen him referring to human moral improvement, and he is conscious that the improvement he values here, involving a mutual sympathy that encompasses the weak, the poor and the inferior, may itself militate against improvements in other areas. 'It is surprising', he remarks, 'how soon a want of care leads to the degeneration of a domestic race; but excepting in the case of man, hardly anyone is so ignorant as to allow his worse animals to breed'.[19] For humanitarian reasons we have to bear 'the undoubtedly bad effects of the weak surviving and propagating their kind'. But what we must do, if our own race is not to decline, is to ensure that 'the weaker and inferior members of society do not marry as freely as the sound'.[20] We must also allow in our society for institutions and structures which allow the most able to succeed best and rear the largest number of children. At the same time, however, we must allow our moral qualities to advance further, though in this case, not through natural selection, but through the effects of habit, reasoning powers, instruction and religion, etc., working on what he calls our social instincts.

While we – and Midgley – might like an emphasis on social instincts as a counter to pure individualism, what is not immediately clear is how that emphasis can be squared with the competitive spirit required by natural selection. Darwin does try in *Descent*: 'it must not be forgotten that although a high standard of morality gives but a slight or no advantage to each individual man and his children over the other men of the same tribe, yet then an increase in the number of well-endowed men and an advancement in the standard of

[18] *ER* op. cit. note 1, 68.
[19] Op. cit. note 11, Vol I, 206.
[20] Op. cit. note 11, 206.

morality will certainly give an immense advantage to one tribe over another. A tribe including many members who, from possessing in a high degree the spirit of patriotism, fidelity, obedience, courage, and sympathy, were always ready to aid one another and to sacrifice themselves for the common good, would be victorious over most other tribes; and this would be natural selection'.[21]

These are noble sentiments, but hardly enough to show that in a tribe whose members were always ready to sacrifice themselves for the common good would avoid the decline into indolence Darwin fears in the absence of a strong competitive spirit. There would also be a danger of free-riding, a constant problem in welfare states, where too many people simply live off what is provided for them by others. And, historically, how true is it that tribes of the sort Darwin describes have actually been victorious over 'most other tribes'? Might history not favour other tribes, more steely, more militaristic, better armed, more aggressive? (Ask the Jews, who are now vilified for being no longer prepared to endure in a moral way.) Even if there are examples of successful tribes operating as Darwin describes, he would still have to show that it was precisely their moral traits that enable(d) them to prevail in the cauldron of natural selection. There is inevitably a degree of wishful thinking in Darwin's position here.

Of that Mary Midgley cannot be accused. She does not attempt to justify her communitarianism on its success in getting a society to flourish under the constraints of natural selection. Her starting point is quite different, emphasising the reliance of both human beings and other animals on wider and deeper wholes in which they live and move and have their being. 'Social psychologists have drawn attention to the complex dependence of human individuals on their background. Ethologists have shown from animal parallels how deep the function of this is likely to be'.[22] And from this perspective she rejects egoism, social contract theory and unbridled capitalism, and any interpretation of evolution which might seem to support any of this. What we are primarily up against is 'a chaotic mob of dollar-snatching cormorants, doing damage of an order undreamed of in previous ages'.[23] Unfortunately with the rise of scientific materialism, Enlightenment rationalism and individualism, economic and philosophical, we have lost a grip on much of the traditional, often religious, morality which might once have been a bulwark

[21] Op. cit. note 11, Vol I, 203.
[22] *ER* op. cit. note 1, 143.
[23] *ER* op. cit. note 1, 144.

against all of this. According to Midgley, perhaps echoing trends in the thinking of Elizabeth Anscombe (about the conceptual mess current moral philosophy languishes in) and anticipating that of Philippa Foot (about something called natural goodness inherent in human nature, and prefigured in the natural world, allowing us to rise above the constrictions of utilitarian and Kantian ethical frameworks), what we need to do is to get beyond the standard philosophical talk of rights, justice and individualism – and the scientific reductionism which often supports such thinking – and attempt to build, or re-build a system which replaces destructiveness, moral and ecological, with a sense of multiple duties we owe, not just to each other but to the natural world in which we live. We are to see ourselves as playing 'a tiny part in a vast, irreplaceable and fragile whole'.[24]

4. Midgley and Evolution

This might seem to bring us back to an evolutionary perspective, and true enough it does. But it is not the perspective of the evolution of Darwin and his followers, which emphasises competition and struggle. The Darwinian picture, as commonly interpreted is also one in which life is presented as a random and meaningless occurrence on one tiny and insignificant planet in a universe which is fundamentally hostile to life and to feeling. For all the purple prose of the end of *Origin*, as early as 1856 Darwin was writing to Hooker of the 'clumsy, wasteful, blundering, low and horribly cruel works of nature'. In *Origin* he famously writes of the waste, profligacy and cruelty in nature, bees being killed by their own stings, drones being produced for the performance of just one act, then to be slaughtered, ichneumonidae feeding in the bodies of live caterpillars: 'the wonder indeed is, on the theory of natural selection, that more cases of the want of absolute perfection have not been observed'.[25] In 1865, in a letter to Joseph Dalton Hooker, there is an even more downbeat reflection on the certainty of the extinction of all life: 'To think of millions of years, with every continent swarming with good and enlightened men, all ending in this, and with probably no fresh start until this our planetary system has been again converted into a red hot gas. *Sic transit gloria mundi* with a vengeance'.[26]

[24] *ER* op. cit. note 1, 160.
[25] Op. cit. note 9, 445.
[26] Darwin, *More Letters of Charles Darwin,* Vol I, 260–1.

Were the up-beat reflections about a grandeur in this view of life put in to hearten his audience to the bleakness of the message, which is surely there beneath the surface at least, or were they an attempt to boost his own morale and that of his family?

However we might interpret Darwin's own attitude to these matters, his followers have shown no ambiguity. Typical, and effectively criticised by Midgley, is Jacques Monod in the best-selling *Chance and Necessity* (from 1972), in the evolutionary popular science stakes a noted precursor to Dawkins. In a melodramatic effort to establish the rigour of his scientific atheism and the absolute meaninglessness of life and existence in a universe which cares nothing for us, Monod writes that 'the universe was not pregnant with life, nor the biosphere with man'.[27] We human beings are here by chance, in a universe which is not responsive to us at all, and within which our existence has no significance. Mankind 'must realize that, like a gypsy, he lives on the boundaries of an alien world; a world deaf to his music, and as indifferent to his hopes as it is to his suffering or his crimes'.[28]

Without entering into debates about fine tuning and the anthropic principle, one could point out that, given that life has emerged, there must be a sense in which the universe was pregnant with life, and indeed the biosphere with man. Life and ourselves could not have come from nowhere. Our existence must in some rudimentary way have been present in the universe before we existed. Equally Monod is silent on the way that this alien world seems to have allowed for the appearance of gypsies (us) who are able to perceive it and find value in it. Midgley takes Monod to task for overplaying the chance aspects of evolution and denying that evolution is continuous with, and at home in, the surrounding world (a position which he calls animism).[29]

What Midgley is urging against her evolutionary opponents is a view of nature and of life itself which could be called 'holistic'. The tendency of reductive physicalism and of those interpretations of evolution which Midgley rejects is to see the world in terms of individuals (atoms, genes) all individually the source of their activity and also of the activity of the larger beings which they compose (biological organisms in the evolutionary case). Against this, as we have seen, Midgley will urge a far more holistic picture, in which individuals are rooted in nature and a wider society, and in which genes function

[27] Jacques Monod, *Chance and Necessity*, London: Collins, 1972, 137.
[28] Op. cit. note 27, 160.
[29] *ER* op. cit. note 1, 78.

in complexes, without their activity being predetermined in isolation. To use a more modern term, one of her targets will be genocentrism; it isn't the genes running the show, but the whole organism in which genes are component parts whose operation is partly moulded top-down by the organism itself. And of course Midgley will also look at biological organisms in their natural environment, as part of that environment, affecting and being affected by it. Furthermore Midgley rails (especially in *What is Philosophy For?*) against the tendency of contemporary philosophers and scientists to see the problems of life and consciousness as being to show how brute matter could come alive or 'mere meat' (the brain) come to be aware. The cells and matter of our bodies are alive, and our brains are not mere meat, but organised in such a way as to live, as to think.

One of the points which Midgley makes about Monod and the scientific atheists is that their dramatically bleak view is not actually required by science. Questions about the ultimate meaning of reality are not scientific ones; 'a hunger for meaning is central to our lives... To keep this wider impulse out of factual investigations is not just emotionally difficult. It is conceptually impossible'.[30] We have to connect things up into world-pictures, and the task is to choose between good and bad world-pictures. Obviously the type of evolutionary thinking and the associated individualism she has been criticising is for her a bad world-picture for the reasons she has given.

So what does she propose, beyond the type of holistic thinking we have been examining already? She tells us that she is not religious in a formal or dogmatic sense. 'However, I am struck by the strong intellectual need there is to have some view of the cosmos as a whole. It does seem to me that the project of entirely depersonalizing this view may not be a possible one. Possibly for human beings, the only alternative to thinking of the universe as, in some vast and remote way, purposive and benign, is to think of it as purposive and radically malignant. It may simply not be within our capacity – except of course by just avoiding thought – to think of it as having no sort of purpose or direction whatever. And since the notion that it is radically malignant is a crazy one, benignity seems to me the only usable option'.[31]

Earlier she had written warmly of William James' view of a religious view being one directed to the world as a whole, 'about which there is something solemn, serious and tender' (in James' words).

[30] *ER* op. cit. note 1, 134.
[31] *ER* op. cit. note 1, 136.

It must also be an attitude of enthusiastic rather than grudging acceptance, resting on a belief that there is an unseen order, involving absolute surrender to that larger power.[32] This, according to James and Midgley, intellectual fashion has been against for more than two centuries. I think that Midgley's view here, like James's, would be that there is enough in human life and experience to support such a view even against the tough minded critics who would dismiss it. It would certainly be wrong simply to dismiss it.

5. Conclusion

Cosmic benignity, a sense of a power solemn, serious and tender. Not very Darwinian, one might think, and certainly not scientistic. The significance of Midgley's book is not the detail of her interpretation of Darwin himself, but the masterly way she has analysed and shredded of set of popular beliefs, which their proponents like to present as scientific, but which are not actually demanded by science, which are not actually scientific, and, in their totalising tendency, share many of the characteristics of the traditional religious views they have replaced in popular culture. This is what Midgley calls 'evolution as a religion', and she gives us plenty of reasons for questioning it and its overweening pretensions. She is against evolution as a religion, but in her crusade against the neo-Darwinians and the sociobiologists, she is encouraging us to entertain a religious view of her own.

University of Buckingham
anthony.ohear@buckingham.ac.uk

[32] *ER* op. cit. note 1, 112.

Index of Names

Index of Names